GREAT

SHORT

BOOKS

A Year of Reading—Briefly

Kenneth C. Davis

SCRIBNER

New York London Toronto Sydney New Delhi

Scribner

An Imprint of Simon & Schuster, Inc.

1230 Avenue of the Americas

New York, NY 10020

First Scribner hardcover edition November 2022

SCRIBNER and design are registered trademarks of The Gale Group, Inc., used under license by Simon & Schuster, Inc., the publisher of this work.

For information about special discounts for bulk purchases, please contact Simon & Schuster Special Sales at 1-866-506-1949 or business@simonandschuster.com.

The Simon & Schuster Speakers Bureau can bring authors to your live event. For more information, or to book an event, contact the Simon & Schuster Speakers Bureau at 1-866-248-3049 or visit our website at www.simonspeakers.com.

Interior design by Kyle Kabel

Manufactured in China

1   3   5   7   9   10   8   6   4   2

Library of Congress Cataloging-in-Publication Data has been applied for.

ISBN 978-1-9821-8003-4

ISBN 978-1-9821-8007-2 (ebook)

For my family
Joann
Jenny and Colin
Kit and Archer

In these tales will be found a variety of love adventures, bitter as well as pleasing, and other exciting incidents, which took place in both ancient and modern times.

—Boccaccio, *The Decameron*

There should therefore be a time in adult life devoted to revisiting the most important books of our youth.

—Italo Calvino, "Why Read the Classics?"

17. Omit needless words.

—William Strunk Jr. and E. B. White,
The Elements of Style

Contents

Notes of a Common Reader

Time. We all wish we had more of it. To do errands. To hit the gym or take a long walk. To bake bread or whip up that recipe we clipped last year. And, maybe, to simply read. The intrusion of the screen—first the big ones in our living rooms, then those sitting on our desks, and finally, the little ones many of us carry around—has made it more challenging to make space for the simple joy of getting lost in a book.

"In our society, where it is hard to find time to do anything properly, even once, the leisure—which is part of the pleasure—of reading is one of our culture-casualties," writes novelist Jeanette Winterson. "For us, books have turned into fast food, to be consumed in the gaps between one bout of relentless living and the next."

And then a pandemic made it even more challenging. For many of us, reading anything besides the deluge of news—catastrophically bad, between Covid-19 and the toxic political atmosphere—became increasingly difficult, particularly for those who felt compelled to "doom scroll."

The pandemic changed the way we all think, feel, and behave. Sleep became harder. Our normal patterns of working and socializing were demolished by "languishing," a term coined by sociologist Corey Keyes, and what psychologist Adam Grant called "Zoom fatigue." We all stressed about finances, jobs, our children's education, and the basic right to pursue happiness. These demands hit hard at our attention spans, which meant less time and motivation for reading, even though many experts advised this was the right prescription for what ailed us.

During the first months of the Covid outbreak in early 2020, and then as a bitterly contested presidential election tested the very soul of American democracy, I rediscovered the balm of reading fiction. Not as an *escape* from the constant press of dreadful news, but as an *antidote*. Fiction can provide insight, instruction, and inspiration, even as it takes our minds from the anxiety of the moment.

An expansive universe, fiction includes mystery, historical fiction, science fiction, fantasy, thriller, romance. For those who seek a complete education, reading fiction occupies a central pillar of our "Cultural Literacy." For many people, that still means commencing with the classics, the so-called Great Books or Western Canon. You know those literary heavyweights we were all supposed to read and even reread: *Anna Karenina*, *Bleak House*, *Pride and Prejudice*, *Middlemarch*, and *Moby-Dick*. Not to mention all seven volumes of Proust's *In Search of Lost Time*.

Of course, some of those literary sacred cows have been supplanted by a new generation of modern classics, an alternative canon that is more inclusive of overlooked women writers as well as people of color and gay writers.

But let's get real. Even when we're not in lockdown mode, many of us simply lack the energy, inclination, or patience to get through some of those illustrious but weighty tomes, in spite of our very best intentions. Whether you were inclined to read the old or new classics, I am reminded of Mark Twain's definition of "classic": "A book which people praise and don't read."

Then I found a simple solution: short novels.

During an earlier plague, the Italian writer Boccaccio understood this basic truth: short is beautiful. As the Black Death struck Florence in 1348, Boccaccio began writing a series of stories he completed in 1353. Boccaccio's *Decameron* is a collection of one hundred brief tales, each called a novella. In this masterpiece, ten characters—seven women and three men—each tell a story every day for ten days as they seek refuge from the plague in a villa near Florence. A combination of parables, adventures, and love stories, some quite bawdy and many skewering the Church and the priesthood, Boccaccio's work was composed in the vernacular Italian. It remains a foundational text in Western literature.

Early in the pandemic, I began reading one tale a day from the *Decameron*. And I realized that Boccaccio was on to something. There is a liberating quality about brief tales told in the midst of a pandemic. From Boccaccio, I moved on to short novels.

At first, my reading was dictated by the books on my shelves, as the library and bookstores were also in lockdown and the very valuable and pleasurable act of browsing was out of the question. When my local branch of the New York Public Library reopened, it was one of the most liberating moments in the pandemic. I read as the books I had requested became available for "grab and go." Praise the library! I soon had a stack of thirty books—the library's max checkouts allowed. Then my local bookstore, Three Lives & Company, reopened for five customers at a time—another moment of jubilee.

In celebration of this tradition of plague-bound short narratives, welcome to *Great Short Books: A Year of Reading—Briefly*. Based on my reading experience over a year in lockdown, and considerable research into the world of literature, this survey offers a curated book lover's guide to some of the greatest short fiction from around the world and published in English.

Why short books?

A short novel is like a great first date. It can be extremely pleasant, even exciting, and memorable. Ideally, you leave wanting more. It can lead to greater possibilities. But there is no long-term commitment.

Short novels can often be read in one to several sittings. With careful rationing, they can be easily enjoyed at the rate of one book per week. And that is why I have chosen fifty-eight books: one for each week in the year plus six bonus books, the literary equivalent of the proverbial "baker's dozen." That still means getting through fewer than five books per month. It is highly reasonable to suggest that most readers could easily navigate all of the titles in *Great Short Books* in a year's time. Thus, a year of great reading—briefly.

Here you will find fifty-eight entries, each featuring a single work, listed in alphabetical order by title, along with the author and original year of publication.* In addition, I have noted the publisher, publication year, and the page length of the edition I read. Several of my selections are works in the public domain and available from various publishers; others are more recently reissued editions. I also sought out the most current and authoritative English versions of translated works. This basic information is followed by the novel's opening passages and a brief overview of the plot and action—NO SPOILERS! I once accidentally revealed the fate of Captain Ahab of *Moby-Dick* to my daughter. I have never lived down the ignominy of this grievous error.

Next comes a life of the author in which I offer a sense of how the author's times and circumstances are reflected in the work. It is impossible to encounter such writers as Alberto Moravia, Natalia Ginzburg, or Albert Camus among others without recognizing their confrontations with fascism and Nazis.

I would add that researching these biographies has often been a study in profound unhappiness. Mental illness, alcoholism, broken marriages, and struggles with sexual identity plagued many of these writers. Did they write because they were troubled? Or were they troubled because they were writers? Or were they just troubled people who happened to be writers? Questions, perhaps, for another book.

---

* There is one exception. Michael Cunningham's *The Hours* was placed after *Mrs. Dalloway*, as this Pulitzer Prize–winning novel was inspired by and modeled on Virginia Woolf's masterpiece.

"Why You Should Read It," brief observations that include critics' appraisals alongside my own reflections, follows. Finally, "What to Read Next" offers suggestions for exploring some of the author's other works.

By now you may be asking: Why doesn't such a guide to short novels already exist?

For me, the answer is simple. Short novels are literature's equivalent to stand-up comedian Rodney Dangerfield's signature line: they "get no respect."

Certainly, when set against short stories they do not. Esteemed magazines such as the *New Yorker* continue an honored tradition of publishing short stories, which are often the writer's stepping-stone to producing longer work. And many novelists have published prize-winning story collections, including Ernest Hemingway, Katherine Anne Porter, and others in this guide. At the other extreme are those long novels and multivolume sagas that attract the attention of critics, reviewers, and many readers.

Short novels, on the other hand, have been shortchanged. They occupy the place of the neglected middle child of the literary world. It is as if length determines merit. Short-listed—no pun intended—for the prestigious Man Booker Prize in 2007, Ian McEwan's *On Chesil Beach* provoked controversy because it was deemed too short—sniffed at as a mere novella. So, a degree of critical prejudice—call it literary sizeism—exists against short fiction.

This raises the first question: What is short? Number of pages? Word count? Weight?

As I define them, short novels encompass fiction of about one hundred to two hundred pages in length, again an arbitrary measure that does not account for type size. But much shorter than that gets into the territory of the long short story. Much longer than two hundred pages, in my book, no longer qualifies as a short novel. Again, this is an arbitrary yardstick and I left some room for fudging, so you will find some notable exceptions. A handful of shorter novellas—Richard Wright's *Big Boy Leaves Home* measures fifty highly charged pages and *No One Writes to the Colonel* by Gabriel García Márquez weighs in at a magical sixty-four—and slightly longer books are represented, such as *A Portrait of the Artist as a Young Man*. Allowance was also made for Agatha Christie. Anyone who sells billions of books merits special consideration.

Brevity is chief among the short novel's virtues. So, size matters—at least in this book. And while it should go without saying, I will say it: brevity does not mean lack of artistry. Great Short Books pack timeless themes and powerful stories into profound but highly compressed narratives. As novelist Ian McEwan told a literary festival audience in 2012, "the novella is the supreme literary form. . . . The prose is better, more condensed, more rigorous."

Short can be masterful. Short can be rewarding. Evidence of that fact is the inclusion of several Pulitzer-winning books and eleven Nobel Prize winners in this collection. The short work of such Nobel laureates as Thomas Mann, Ernest Hemingway, Nadine Gordimer, Doris Lessing, Toni Morrison, and Kazuo Ishiguro offers ample evidence of why these literary virtuosos won their accolades.

So why these books? Definition set, how did I make these selections?

Like many lists, this one reflects my prejudices, preferences, and passions. The most difficult part of creating this guide was culling down an extensive list of short fiction, including the recommendations I sought from friends, librarians, publishing colleagues, and others. There will be considerable debate over my choices—especially the books and writers omitted. I anticipate howls of, "How could you leave out _____! [fill in the blank]."

I set out to reflect a broad diversity of writers and voices. This is not just about "dead white guys," although they are well represented. My first rule was to include an equal number of male and female novelists, based upon how they themselves chose to identify. Next, I chose a mix of books that might be deemed established classics alongside more recent works. For me, that meant revisiting some familiar works.

"The classics are books that exert a peculiar influence, both when they refuse to be eradicated from the mind and when they conceal themselves in the folds of memory, camouflaging themselves as the collective or individual unconscious," wrote Italian novelist and essayist Italo Calvino. "There should therefore be a time in adult life devoted to revisiting the most important books of our youth."

But I also set out very deliberately to encounter writers for the first time. These include several novelists whose work might be less familiar to many American readers. My own attempt to learn Italian is reflected in the choice of several Italian novelists whose work was recommended by my professors.

I hope, Gentle Reader, that you too will venture out of your literary comfort zone, stretching to experience unfamiliar or challenging writers. Many of these selections plumb the most consequential literary themes, from coming of age and coming out, despair, marriage and its discontents, to confronting racism, totalitarianism, and fundamental questions of meaning. Did I mention sex?

I wanted to make certain that this collection included "Must Reads"—books by writers everyone should experience at least once. I also focused, first unintentionally and then more deliberately, on works that reflect the current atmosphere of politics and society. A novel is a measure of the times in which it is written.

The relevance of these books to our time is clear in such works as *Animal Farm*. After I witnessed the January 6 Capitol insurrection and recently published *Strongman*, a nonfiction book about the rise of dictators and the threats they pose to democracy, the dangers of authoritarianism were very fresh in my mind. Several selections also explore the act of writing, including *The Ghost Writer* by Philip Roth, Joyce's *A Portrait of the Artist as a Young Man*, and Clarice Lispector's *The Hour of the Star*.

This guide also represents a form of lifelong learning: having enrolled in a local community college several years ago to learn Italian, I strongly believe that the process of ongoing education is critical, especially as we age. Reading fiction is just one more way to achieve that. In the end, the lifelong learner may find a richer, deeper sense of fulfillment in life, especially in a moment when it feels in such short supply.

When the pandemic's intrusion meant a shift to remote learning, I must confess I dropped out. Without classes to attend and missing the personal connections with professors and fellow students, my daily reading became even more important. This book is meant to convey some of what I have gleaned in my year of reading briefly. There are few pleasures greater than sharing the experience of a beloved book.

This guide is not a lecture or dissertation. It is a conversation— a friendly exchange among book lovers. I do not consider myself a literary scholar or a book critic. I view myself as what Virginia Woolf once described as "the Common Reader" who "differs from the critic and scholar."

"He is worse educated, and nature has not gifted him so generously," wrote Woolf. "He reads for his own pleasure rather than to impart knowledge or correct the opinions of others. Above all, he is guided by the instinct to create for himself, out of whatever odds and ends he can come by, some kind of whole—a portrait of a man, a sketch of an age, a theory of the art of writing."

For most of my life, I have been that "Common Reader." I suspect that a great many people would place themselves in that category. Whatever genre or style they might prefer, they read for their "own pleasure," as Woolf put it. I take exception to the notion that any reading constitutes a "guilty pleasure."

While many readers might know me for works of history, my life has largely been about books. Yes, I wrote *Don't Know Much About History*, which gave rise to a series of books and audios on geography, the Civil War, the Bible, and mythology, among other subjects.

More recently, I have written about people enslaved by presidents, the 1918 influenza pandemic, and the rise of dictators and the fall of democracy.

But as a child, my world was shaped by trips to the majestic, temple-like Mount Vernon Public Library, an Andrew Carnegie jewel, just outside New York City. My mother took me there weekly—until I could get there by myself—and those visits were rituals as significant to me as going to church on Sunday.

I remember the day I graduated from the street-level Children's Room to the Adult Room. That entailed a climb up a grand staircase into a reverential world of books. These visits were supplemented by the weekly arrival of the Bookmobile: if you couldn't get to the library, the library came to you in the form of a large, bus-like vehicle. You climbed aboard, and it was lined with books, floor to ceiling. At the rear exit, a librarian awaited with an inky red stamp that filled in the due date.

As a kid I might have loved playing soldier, basketball, and football, but I also loved to read. Along the way, I had influential guides. There were the librarians and teachers who made recommendations and got me started on Dos Passos, Upton Sinclair, and Steinbeck. There was the lady in the church choir who handed me a copy of *Dubliners* when I was about fourteen. It would take me some time to appreciate James Joyce, and I have often wondered why that woman gave me that book at that moment.

Halfway through college with an uncertain path as an English major, I dropped out of school to start my professional life in the book business by packing and checking out orders at a book wholesaler in Westchester County. From there, I moved to work in a small independent bookstore in Manhattan. But I still had no clue that I could, or would, become a writer. In that shop, I met a woman who read my college writing. She told me I was wasting my time selling books, I should be writing them. And yes, I did marry her. (She hates it when I tell that story, but it is true.)

My future wife also started me on my career as a freelance writer, reviewing books for the trade journal *Publishers Weekly* for the majestic sum of ten dollars a book—more if it was unusually long. It was a valuable apprenticeship in writing. One of the bonuses was being among the first readers of such memorable works as *Midnight's Children*, *Waiting for the Barbarians*, *The Color Purple*, and *The Executioner's Song*. After a period of reviewing books, I moved on to writing feature stories and later to interviewing writers. As a young journalist, I had the thrill of interviewing and writing about Norman Mailer and Gay Talese, among others.

From there, I wrote my first book—a book about books. In 1984, I published *Two-Bit Culture: The Paperbacking of America*, a history of mass-market paperback publishing. In addition to charting the rise of the paperback business, the book examined how these inexpensive paperbacks, all priced in the beginning at twenty-five cents, or "two bits," democratized reading in America. In writing it, I also got confirmation of the central importance of literacy and access to books as essential to the free exchange of ideas in our culture.

It is more important than ever to foster reading. As a small boy forbidden to learn his ABCs, the great American abolitionist Frederick Douglass understood why enslaved people were not permitted to learn to read. It was one way the white man kept the Black man in chains. There is a reason that dictators order the burning of books and seek to silence writers, from Voltaire to Solzhenitsyn and in our own time. Reading fiction can provide "that glimpse of truth for which . . . [we] have forgotten to ask," as Joseph Conrad once wrote. Reading is fundamental, not only to the development of our hearts, minds, and spirits but also to Democracy with a capital *D*.

This book is not about "academic" or "literary" criticism, semiotics, or deconstructionism. It is certainly not about starting an argument. It is about the pleasure and value of reading great fiction. And it is meant to start a good conversation—about books.

GREAT

SHORT

BOOKS

Agostino

— 1945 —

Alberto Moravia

New York: New York Review Books, 2014; translated from the Italian by Michael F. Moore; 102 pages

FIRST LINES

In the early days of summer, Agostino and his mother used to go out to sea every morning on a small rowboat typical of Mediterranean beaches known as a *pattino*. At first she brought a boatman along with them, but Agostino gave such clear signs of annoyance at the man's presence that the oars were then turned over to him. He rowed with deep pleasure on the smooth, diaphanous, early-morning sea, and his mother, sitting in front of him, would speak to him softly, as joyful and serene as the sea and sky, as if he were a man rather than a thirteen-year-old boy.

PLOT SUMMARY

"A man rather than a thirteen-year-old boy" sums it up. In this quintessential coming-of-age tale, the fatherless Agostino worships his well-to-do widowed mother, "a big and beautiful woman still in her prime." In the casting game that readers play, it is easy to envision Sophia Loren or perhaps Penélope Cruz as this iconic figure: Madonna and object of desire.

Agostino proudly knows this: "All the bathers on the beach seemed to be watching, admiring his mother and envying him."

But his pride and joy will soon disappear. When a tanned, dark-haired young man arrives on the scene, Agostino must accept being replaced as his mother's boating companion. Jilted, Agostino joins a group of local boys—tough sons of boatmen and lifeguards—and their older leader, a Fagin-like character with six fingers on each hand.

Though repelled by these boys and their coarse ways, the effete Agostino is nonetheless irresistibly drawn to them, even as they snicker and force him to imagine what his mother and the young man might be doing on the boat.

ABOUT THE AUTHOR: ALBERTO MORAVIA

Born Alberto Pincherle in Rome on November 28, 1907, Moravia—his pen name was linked to a family surname—became one of Europe's most prominent twentieth-century writers. At his death in 1990, he was the most widely read Italian novelist and essayist of the century.

The son of a prosperous Jewish architect and painter and a Catholic princess, Moravia contracted tuberculosis at the age of eight and was bedridden for long stretches, spending two years in a sanatorium. Learning German, French, and English from governesses, he spent much of his solitude reading, devouring everything from Boccaccio to James Joyce.

"My education, my formal education that is, is practically nil," Moravia once told an interviewer. "I have a grammar-school diploma, no more. Just nine years of schooling. I had to drop out because of tuberculosis of the bone. I spent, altogether, five years in bed with it, between the ages of nine and seventeen—till 1924." By then, Mussolini had taken power in Italy.

Tuberculosis and Fascism, said Moravia, were the most important facts of his life. He began writing at the dawn of Fascist rule and in 1929 self-published a first novel, *Gli indifferenti* (*The Time of Indifference*), a story of moral decadence that became a sensation. Politically and sexually daring, his next two novels were censored or confiscated by the Fascists during the 1930s and placed on the Vatican's Index of Forbidden Books.

In 1941, Moravia and his wife, the writer Elsa Morante, moved to the island of Capri, where he wrote *Agostino* in the space of a month. Rejected by Fascist censors, it went unpublished. When Moravia learned his name was on a list of subversives, he and Morante fled to the mountains near Fondi, south of Rome.

After Rome's liberation in 1944, the couple returned to the city and *Agostino* was published in 1945. Moravia's international reputation grew with a subsequent book, *La Romana* (1947), a provocative story of a prostitute entangled with the Fascists. Later translated as *The Woman of Rome*, it sold more than 1 million copies in the United States.

Moravia's star continued to rise with *Il conformista* (*The Conformist*, 1951), his third novel. It told of a sadistic man who becomes a Fascist assassin while concealing his sexual orientation. A story collection, *I racconti* (*Stories*), won Italy's prestigious Strega Prize in 1952. A few years later, Elsa Morante also won the Strega for *L'isola di Arturo* (*Arturo's Island*, 1957). The couple separated in 1961 but never formally divorced.

Moravia's fame grew as his books, including *Agostino*, were adapted to the screen in Italy and abroad. Based on his time in hiding, *La ciociara* was published in 1957 and filmed under its English title, *Two Women*, by director Vittorio De Sica; Sophia Loren won an Academy Award for her role in the 1961 film. In 1970, *The Conformist* was adapted and filmed by director Bernardo Bertolucci.

Nominated for the Nobel Prize fifteen times, Moravia never won. He continued to write well into the 1970s and 1980s, but his later works never equaled the earlier acclaim. In 1990, he was found dead, at age eighty-two, of an apparent heart attack in his Rome apartment.

WHY YOU SHOULD READ IT

A classic coming-of-age story, *Agostino* is both painful and candid. It peels back the moment when a young boy is forced—quite literally—to look at his mother, and all women, in a new light. "Like many a forlorn poet, the narrator suffers the afflictions of unrequited love," translator Michael F. Moore wrote, "but the object of his affection, scandalously, is his mother. Rather than seek to elevate her, like Petrarch's Laura, he is intent on debasing her, repeating like a mantra, 'She's only a woman.'"

I discovered the book after reading *The Conformist* and wished I had read *Agostino* first. Compressed into one hundred pages, Agostino's story pulses with raw, erotic energy as it explores two fundamental themes of twentieth-century literature: social class and sexuality. Dispensing with academic and political jargon, Moravia delves into the realms of Marx and Freud, distilling philosophical ideas into a story of an affluent adolescent's singular summer mixing with rough boys from the working class.

Moravia rejected the flowery style that dominated classical Italian fiction. His stark language and focus on social injustice and class distinctions herald what would become the signature of Italy's postwar, neorealist filmmakers—Roberto Rossellini, Vittorio De Sica, and Luchino Visconti, among them—who depicted working-class Italy in bluntly unromantic terms.

In a career spanning six decades, Alberto Moravia was prolific. He wrote many novels, short stories, and essays on politics and literature. But an ideal follow-up to *Agostino* is *The Conformist*. In fact, the teenage Agostino hints in some ways at Marcello, the character who is the "Conformist" of the title.

Opening around 1920, before Mussolini's rise to power, the novel follows Marcello from his troubled youth, in which he goes from killing lizards and a cat to committing a more serious crime. From childhood, Marcello desires to feel "normal," which he equates with behaving in conformity with other people.

After the Fascists take power in 1922, Marcello's quest leads him to a post in Mussolini's regime and then to an assignment to assassinate a former professor who opposes the Fascists. Marcello's craving to conform through unquestioned loyalty to a ruthless leader and murderous cause is very much a story of our time.

Also worthy of attention are Moravia's postwar novels *The Woman of Rome*, a complex story of characters, including a prostitute, who must deal with the Fascist regime, and *Two Women*, a wrenching tale of the horrors endured by a widowed shopkeeper and her daughter in the last days of the war.

Animal Farm: A Fairy Story

— 1945 —

George Orwell

New York: Berkley, 2020; 75th Anniversary edition with a foreword by Ann Patchett, an introduction by Téa Obreht, and an afterword by Russell Baker; 97 pages

* Number 31 on the Modern Library list of 100 Best Novels *
* TIME: "All-TIME 100 Novels" *

FIRST LINES

Mr. Jones, of the Manor Farm, had locked the hen-houses for the night, but was too drunk to remember to shut the pop-holes. With the ring of light from his lantern dancing from side to side, he lurched across the yard, kicked off his boots at the back door, drew himself a last glass of beer from the barrel in the scullery, and made his way up to bed, where Mrs. Jones was already snoring.

PLOT SUMMARY

First things first. George Orwell may have subtitled his brief allegory *A Fairy Story* when it was published in England. But *Animal Farm* is assuredly NOT a children's book. Unlike the barnyard paradise of *Charlotte's Web* (see entry), Orwell's "Fairy Story" depicts a barnyard hell.

The story is simple enough. At Manor Farm, the animals rise up to throw off their human overlords. "The Rebellion" comes after Old Major, a "majestic-looking pig," asks the gathered animals, "Is it not crystal clear, then, comrades, that all the evils of this life of ours spring from the tyranny of human beings?"

But as suddenly as this uprising liberates the barnyard's residents from their two-legged masters, the utopian ideal of "All animals are equal" is overturned. Under its new leaders, two pigs named Napoleon and Snowball, a new order prevails and a shifting set of commandments is posted. One of these reads:

ALL ANIMALS ARE EQUAL

BUT SOME ANIMALS ARE MORE EQUAL THAN OTHERS

ABOUT THE AUTHOR: GEORGE ORWELL

Very few novelists' names become adjectives, as in "Orwellian." Let's agree that "Blairian" doesn't have quite the same ring.

Born Eric Arthur Blair in British colonial India in 1903, George Orwell was the son of an official in the Opium Department of the civil service. He gained literary immortality under his chosen pen name: George for England's patron saint and its king at the time and his surname derived from the river Orwell in East Anglia.

In 1911, at age eight, Eric Blair was sent to an English boarding school where, as a boy, he observed the sharp differences that class endowed and wealth ensured. He later remarked that his family was in the "lower-upper-middle class."

With a scholarship, Blair finished his education at Eton, where Aldous Huxley was one of his masters. Too poor to attend university, Blair instead joined the Imperial Police and was assigned to Burma (now Myanmar).

While on leave in England in 1927, Blair chose not to return to Burma. He resigned from the police to pursue his dream of becoming a writer, moving to live among the working classes in East London and, for a time, Paris.

Under his pen name, Orwell's nonfiction account of working as a penniless dishwasher was published in 1933 as *Down and Out in Paris and London*. It was followed by an autobiographical first novel, *Burmese Days* (1934), based on his unhappy time in the British colonial police. Two more novels followed and then Orwell went to reside with the destitute miners of northern England, an experience he described in another nonfiction work, *The Road to Wigan Pier* (1937).

By the time that book appeared, Orwell and his wife had joined an anti-Fascist militia after the outbreak of the Spanish Civil War in 1936. While fighting against Franco's Fascists, Orwell was shot in the throat and nearly killed in 1937. He eventually left Spain over conflict within the anti-Fascist movement as the Soviet dictator Joseph Stalin set out to wrest control of all opposition to Franco's forces. This experience led to Orwell's nonfiction account of the war, *Homage to Catalonia* (1938), considered one of his best books. He was also left with a lifelong dread of communism, and in particular Stalinist communism.

Back in England during World War II, Orwell served in the Home Guard and continued to work as a journalist and broadcaster for the BBC. He also finished *Animal Farm*, which appeared in 1945 and was widely viewed as an anti-Stalinist allegory when it was published. Today Stalin is recognized as a genocidal dictator. But at the time, Orwell's criticism of Stalin was controversial; the master of the Soviet Union was still viewed favorably as a crucial ally in the defeat of Hitler's Germany, not as a murderous tyrant. Still, the book brought Orwell his first popular success.

In 1949, *Nineteen Eighty-Four*, Orwell's dystopian masterpiece about a future world dominated by three constantly warring totalitarian states, was published, cementing Orwell's reputation.

Since his death, it has been revealed that Orwell provided a list of names of supposed Soviet sympathizers to British government sources in the Cold War era. "The author of '1984' maintained that he 'named names' not because of any private vendetta or opposition to dissent," wrote Timothy Naftali in the *New York Times*, "but because totalitarianism posed a greater threat to liberty than providing information on those with a history of supporting the Soviet Union. This was a hard-won conviction, born of his experience with Stalinism in the Spanish Civil War."

Orwell died on January 21, 1950, at age forty-six, of tuberculosis.

WHY YOU SHOULD READ IT

Orwell was devoted to British socialism and insisted, according to the *New York Times* columnist Russell Baker, "that he had no intention of damaging the 'socialist' cause." But this cautionary story of the rebellion at Manor Farm unmistakably refers to the rise of the Soviet Union. It mirrors how Stalin ruthlessly consolidated his power over the Soviet Union following the Russian Revolution and the death of Lenin in 1924. Old Major stands in for Karl Marx, the German-born theoretician of communism, and Napoleon is Stalin. And the pig Snowball is modeled on Leon Trotsky, Stalin's chief rival, who was first expelled from the Communist Party, later exiled, and then assassinated in Mexico City by a Soviet agent in 1940.

While its depiction of the ruthlessness with which the Russian Revolution was transformed into Stalin's murderous regime is still significant, *Animal Farm*'s value as a piece of history is only a part of its genius. Orwell demonstrated more broadly and in the simplest terms how an idealistic movement is co-opted by a murderous strongman.

The techniques he described, in which truth, facts, reality, loyalty, and a communal spirit are turned upside-down, make Orwell's "Fairy Story" a potent cautionary tale in our time. In an introduction to *Animal Farm*, novelist Téa Obreht—born in the former Yugoslavia—writes, "The notion that Western countries are clever and strong enough to both recognize and resist the grip of totalitarianism is a dangerous myth. A fairy story, if you will."

WHAT TO READ NEXT

Published in 1949, Orwell's dystopian masterpiece is *Nineteen Eighty-Four*. At more than three hundred pages, it was too long to place among these great short books. But this is a no-brainer if you haven't read it yet. And if you last read *Nineteen Eighty-Four* in high school, it is well past time to reread it.

In it, Orwell describes a totalitarian world in which individuality is crushed by the Party and both history and language are strictly controlled to maintain the state's total grip on the people. Both *Animal Farm* (#31) and *Nineteen Eighty-Four* (#13) were included in the Modern Library list of the 100 Best Novels of the twentieth century. Deservedly so.

Orwell's three nonfiction books—*Down and Out in Paris and London, The Road to Wigan Pier*, and *Homage to Catalonia*—help seal his place as one of the most influential writers of modern times.

I can also recommend one of his essays, "Politics and the English Language." In it, he wrote, "Modern English, especially written English, is full of bad habits which spread by imitation and which can be avoided if one is willing to take the necessary trouble." Orwell's essay formulated rules for writing that were not merely about points of literary style but reflected a route to better thinking—a defense against the authoritarianism that Orwell feared and opposed with his timeless literary crusade.

Another Brooklyn

— 2016 —

Jacqueline Woodson

New York: Amistad, 2017; 175 pages

FIRST LINES

For a long time, my mother wasn't dead yet. Mine could have been a more tragic story. My father could have given in to the bottle or the needle or a woman and left my brother and me to care for ourselves—or worse, in the care of New York City Children's Services, where, my father said, there was seldom a happy ending. But this didn't happen. I know now that what is tragic isn't the moment. It is the memory.

PLOT SUMMARY

Set in Brooklyn in the 1970s, this is the poetic, elegiac story of the life stage in which the Woman emerges from the Girl-Child, an account of the perils and pressure of growing up in that chrysalis time of transformation.

It opens as August, an Ivy-educated anthropologist, returns to Brooklyn for her father's funeral. As memory takes over, the story moves back to pre-gentrified Brooklyn in a time when white flight is ongoing and the streets are filled with young Black men whose experience in Vietnam has left them addicted—or otherwise damaged, like August's father, who lost two fingers in the war.

In brief, verse-like vignettes, August recalls growing up without a mother against a backdrop of a neighborhood that is both vibrantly alive yet filled with threats: of men who lurk in corridors; of "Son of Sam," the notorious mass killer who terrorizes the city; of the cheerleader forced to "go South" to have her baby. Facing the turmoil, August and her friends—Sylvia, Angela, and Gigi—aspire to futures that may seem out of reach. They share that link between teenage friends that seems unbreakable but will be tested by their sometimes-unforgiving world.

As August says, "Sylvia, Angela, Gigi, and I came together like a jazz improv—half notes tentatively moving toward one another until the ensemble found its footing and the music felt like it had always been playing."

As she and her brother grow up, August also remembers leaving behind her mother and their Tennessee home. Brought to Brooklyn by their father as small children, August and her brother wait expectantly for her mother to join them. Will she come to Brooklyn? When?

ABOUT THE AUTHOR: JACQUELINE WOODSON

In her 2014 award-winning verse memoir *Brown Girl Dreaming*, Woodson poetically and poignantly described the details of her birth. She wrote of being born on February 12, 1963, in Columbus, Ohio, near the place where her great-great-grandparents were enslaved and worked the land, "unfree" and "unpaid."

Transplanted from Ohio to South Carolina and then later to Brooklyn—where her character August lives—Woodson has emerged as one of the most critically acclaimed and best-selling authors of our time, with more than two dozen award-winning books and an impressive collection of accolades and prizes.

A four-time National Book Award finalist, a four-time Newbery Honor winner, a two-time NAACP Image Award Winner, and a two-time Coretta Scott King Award winner, Woodson received the National Book Award in 2014 for her best-selling memoir, *Brown Girl Dreaming*. In 2018, Woodson was appointed the National Ambassador for Young People's Literature, a position created in 2008 by the Library of Congress.

In 2020, she was named a MacArthur Fellow—the so-called genius award. That same year, she received the Hans Christian Andersen Award, an international honor recognizing lifetime achievement given to authors and illustrators "whose complete works have made an important, lasting contribution to children's literature."

On her website, Woodson recalls the moment she knew she could achieve something:

> I remember my fifth grade teacher, the way her eyes lit up when she said "This is really good." The way I—the skinny girl in the back of the classroom who was always getting into trouble for talking or missed homework assignments—sat up a little straighter, folded my hands on the desks, smiled, and began to believe in me.

Raised in the Jehovah's Witness faith, Woodson later broke with her family's religious tradition. Eventually, she came out to them, telling an interviewer, "That kind of choice was not an option." She lives in Brooklyn with her wife and their two children.

Read it for many reasons.

Read it because it is a compact but engrossing coming-of-age story that plumbs the painfully powerful pull of both family and future during that agonizing time when friendship seems to be the only thing that matters.

Read it because the transition to the adult world and the complexities of family, and sex, and identity are universal experiences. Despite differences in time, place, and race, everyone must make this passage.

Read it because Woodson's novel is a haunting, lyrical work that strikes the many chords of memory, childhood, friendship, and family.

As an author who has written nonfiction for adults often read by younger readers and books for younger readers often read by adults, I believe the distinction between these two categories can be fuzzy—and misleading. "Young adult" once meant roughly twelve to eighteen. But that definition has evolved. That is one reason that so many young adult novels have recently crossed over to find adult readers. It is the same reason that books as diverse as *A Tree Grows in Brooklyn*, *To Kill a Mockingbird*, and *The Catcher in the Rye*—not originally written for young people—are now part of the modern student's canon.

Another Brooklyn falls into this crossover category. Clearly aimed at an adult audience, it will attract younger readers, especially those who already know Woodson's earlier work.

WHAT TO READ NEXT

Woodson's most recent novel for adults, *Red at the Bone*, would make a good next choice. Published in 2019, it became a best seller and was named a *New York Times* "Notable Book of the Year." Set in Brooklyn, it opens in 2001—some thirty years after the events in *Another Brooklyn*—and centers on two Black families who come together when Iris, a girl in high school, becomes pregnant by her boyfriend Aubrey.

Also try Woodson's 2014 verse memoir, *Brown Girl Dreaming*, a signature achievement and winner of the National Book Award. Reviewing the book in the *New York Times*, Veronica Chambers wrote, "This is a book full of poems that cry out to be learned by heart. These are poems that will, for years to come, be stored in our bloodstream."

The Awakening

— 1899 —

Kate Chopin

New York: Signet Classics, 1976; edited with an introduction by Barbara H. Solomon and published as The Awakening and Selected Stories of Kate Chopin; *137 pages*

FIRST LINES

A green and yellow parrot, which hung in a cage outside the door, kept repeating over and over:

"*Allez vous-en! Allez vous-en! Sapristi!** That's all right!"

He could speak a little Spanish, and also a language which nobody understood, unless it was the mocking-bird that hung on the other side of the door, whistling his fluty notes out upon the breeze with maddening persistence.

---

* "Get out! Get out! Damnation!"

PLOT SUMMARY

If it does not already exist, we might label an entire literary genre "Dangerous Beach Holidays." And I don't mean *Jaws*.

Sun, sand, and surf can be far more threatening than sharks. And they are in Kate Chopin's *The Awakening*. Published in 1899, this novel about a married woman dipping her toes into the waters of independence and infidelity is a nineteenth-century example of a distinct category that includes *Agostino*, *Death in Venice*, *On Chesil Beach*, and *The Stranger* (see entries).

The Awakening opens as twenty-eight-year-old Edna Pontellier summers with her two small boys on Grand Island, a seaside resort in the Gulf of Mexico. It is no spoiler to say that the exotic atmosphere of Gilded Age 1890s New Orleans is also key to the novel's sensuous pull.

Married to a well-to-do businessman who leaves his family on Grand Island as he tends to his affairs and card games, Edna stands among literature's unfulfilled women. Think Madame Bovary and Anna Karenina—but Edna is one of the earliest iterations of this fictional icon to have been written by a woman. "In short," writes Chopin, "Mrs. Pontellier was not a mother-woman."

When Robert Lebrun, a young man staying on the island, teaches Edna to swim, it is a liberating act. "She grew daring and reckless, overestimating her strength. She wanted to swim far out," Chopin writes, "where no woman had swum before."

Edna sketches and paints and contemplates having an affair—perhaps with Robert or another man once she has returned to New Orleans—and even leaving her family. As she dips her toes into the Gulf waters, "The voice of the sea is seductive; . . . the touch of the sea is sensuous."

The question is: Will she take the plunge?

ABOUT THE AUTHOR: KATE CHOPIN

Catherine O'Flaherty was born on February 8, 1851, in St. Louis, to a mother of French descent and an Irish-born father. Raised in a slaveholding household, she spoke French and English, read widely, and attended a Catholic school under French nuns who provided girls with an elite education. Her father died when she was five when a railway bridge collapsed during a grand opening. A stepbrother fought in the Civil War with the Confederacy and died in a Union prison.

In 1870, she married Oscar Chopin, a Creole cotton merchant, and settled with him in New Orleans, giving birth to five sons and a daughter. When her husband's business failed, the family moved to northern Louisiana, where Chopin learned more about the Creole culture that would flavor her works. Chopin found herself in difficult straits when Oscar died in 1882. She tried to manage his business, but it was burdened with too much debt.

Returning with her children to live with her mother in St. Louis, she began to write. By the late 1880s, she had successfully sold more than one hundred short stories to prominent magazines of the day like *Vogue* and the *Atlantic Monthly*. A first novel, *At Fault* (1890), received little attention. But two collections, *Bayou Folk* (1894) and *A Night in Acadie* (1897), were popular and won critical praise.

The reception to *The Awakening* was far less favorable. When the novel appeared, it was condemned as "unhealthy," "sordid," "vulgar," and "poison." The few reviews that recognized its literary merit could not rescue Chopin's reputation. Although the book was chaste by later standards, the very ideas of extramarital sex and family abandonment were unacceptable concepts, especially as voiced by a female writer in Victorian America.

While never officially banned, the book was shunned by book-sellers and the public, effectively ending Chopin's career. Her pub-lisher canceled a planned third collection of stories. While visiting the St. Louis World's Fair, Chopin suffered a brain hemorrhage on August 20, 1904, dying two days later at age fifty-four.

WHY YOU SHOULD READ IT

The first question must always be, "Is it great?" If not, the second must be, "Is it important?"

To those questions, my answer is *The Awakening* is very good. It is also very significant. Chopin was ahead of her time, both as a literary stylist writing in the postbellum American South and as a woman novelist voicing discontent. Thirty years before Virginia Woolf published *A Room of One's Own*, Chopin imagined a woman who wanted a house—and a life—of her own.

When it first appeared, *The Awakening* shocked reviewers and readers with its vision of a married woman contemplating the unthinkable—leaving her husband and children and embarking on an illicit liaison.

The Awakening eventually fell out of print and into obscurity, along with its author. However, in the late 1960s *The Awakening* was revived by a generation of readers and scholars who found in Kate Chopin a pioneering voice of early feminism. Her depiction of a woman having desires—artistic and sexual—beyond her role as wife and mother brought *The Awakening* wide readership as the feminist movement accelerated in the 1970s. A woman struggling with discontent and desire, Edna is a figure represented elsewhere in this collection in work by Natalia Ginzburg (*The Dry Heart*), Elena Ferrante (*The Lost Daughter*), Jenny Offill (*Dept. of Speculation*), and Leïla Slimani (*The Perfect Nanny*).

Reading *The Awakening* today raises another question. Written by a southern white woman in the late nineteenth century, the novel refers to its mostly nameless Black characters with cringe-worthy racial pejoratives. But are they disqualifying? When Black writers deploy similar language is that also problematic?

In *Middle Passage* (see entry), Charles Johnson also uses one of these words, and readers may have a different reaction. How do we judge writers of earlier eras in a time when sensitivity toward language has become paramount? In a nation in which freedom of expression is expressly guaranteed in the First Amendment, the chilling effect of sanctioning books and writers can cut in several directions.

The answer lies in what I would call discernment. We might wonder, here, if "offensive" or even "oppressive" language represents the views of the character or of the author. Is the author expressing an overtly racist personal perspective? It is fair to consider the time and place of the writing but also to read with sensitivity into an author's intent—whether it is Kate Chopin, Mark Twain, or Charles Johnson. In some of her other works, Chopin dealt sympathetically with race and intermarriage. But it remains a fair, yet difficult, problem that calls for a judicious and open-minded reader.

One thing is certain. Chopin was a pioneer in American letters. Writing about her career, Barbara H. Solomon concluded, "Chopin, with the same kind of honesty she attributed to Edna, unflinchingly depicted her vision of the paradoxes, complexities, and conflicts of human experience, treating them as no one else had in American fiction." Chopin's life and impact were the subject of a largely admiring PBS documentary, *Kate Chopin: A Re-Awakening*, broadcast in 1999, on the hundredth anniversary of the publication of *The Awakening*.

WHAT TO READ NEXT

Chopin's short stories are widely anthologized. They can be found collected in a single volume by the Library of America and in other published editions of *The Awakening*. Of these stories, "Désirée's Baby" remains one of her most widely read pieces, according to the Kate Chopin International Society. Set before the Civil War and published in *Vogue* in 1893, it is about the birth of a child to a beautiful married woman who was herself a mysteriously abandoned orphan. This brief tale, with its "shock" ending, was certainly ahead of its time in exploring the complexity of racial fear and animus in nineteenth-century America.

The Ballad of the Sad Café

— 1951 —

Carson McCullers

New York: Mariner Books, 2005; published in The Ballad of the Sad Café *and Other Stories; 71 pages*

FIRST LINES

The town itself is dreary; not much is there except the cotton mill, the two-room houses where the workers live, a few peach trees, a church with two colored windows, and a miserable main street only a hundred yards long. On Saturdays the tenants from the near-by farms come in for a day of talk and trade. Otherwise the town is lonesome, sad, and like a place that is far off and estranged from all other places in the world.

PLOT SUMMARY

In an isolated Georgia hamlet, Miss Amelia Evans is an overall-wearing, well-muscled woman who owns the town's general store, makes moonshine, and also lends money. Her store is the center of the small town's circumscribed life, which seems to proceed as if in a fairy tale when a hunchback with a suitcase turns up, claiming kinship with Miss Amelia. To the townsfolk's amazement, she lets him drink from her flask and welcomes him.

When a group of men enters Miss Amelia's store, they are stunned to see the hunchback, Cousin Lymon, now residing with Amelia. As the men gather, Miss Amelia delivers another shock. She had never allowed drinking inside her store. But now she goes to the kitchen and brings out bottles of her moonshine and two boxes of crackers, allowing the men to drink and eat.

And so is born Miss Amelia's café, soon the heart of the town's life, a place to gather "for the sake of pleasure."

But the pleasure is short-lived. This brief idyll crumbles with the return of ex-convict Marvin Macy, Amelia's former husband from a ten-day marriage. His homecoming will violently shatter the harmony and happiness that Amelia's café had bestowed on the town.

ABOUT THE AUTHOR: CARSON MCCULLERS

What a complicated life. It might be called "The Ballad of the Sad Author."

Waiflike and boyish in photographs, Carson McCullers was born Lula Carson Smith on February 19, 1917, in Columbus, Georgia. In her teens, she decided to drop Lula and take the name Carson. "By the time I was six," she later wrote, "I was sure that I was born a man."

With hopes of becoming a concert pianist, she began studying the piano. But rheumatic fever left her unable to practice and she began instead to read voraciously. Given a typewriter, Carson was soon writing plays and stories.

At seventeen, she was given money for a voyage to New York, still intent on studying at the famed Juilliard School. But she lost the five hundred dollars she had carried with her and instead worked various jobs while taking creative writing classes at Columbia University and NYU.

When illness struck again, Carson returned to Georgia. While recuperating she spent time writing, and in 1936 her first short story was published. She was nineteen when "Wunderkind," about a teen-age violinist and a Jewish music teacher, appeared in *Story* magazine. Writer Sarah Schulman later commented that "it was here that McCullers began a lifelong investigation of Jews, blacks, the physically disabled and homosexuals as reflections of an overly self-aware adolescent girl stepping out of her own traditional gender role."

In 1937, she married James Reeves McCullers Jr., an aspiring writer and soldier stationed in nearby Fort Benning; she was twenty, he was twenty-four. "From the beginning," notes Carlos Dews, "the marriage was plagued by alcoholism, sexual ambivalence (both were bisexual), and Reeves's envy of McCullers's writing abilities."

Based on an outline and six chapters of a novel, Carson McCullers received a five-hundred-dollar advance, and the couple later moved to New York when *The Heart Is a Lonely Hunter* was published in June 1940 to immediate success. She was twenty-three.

After Reeves McCullers forged some of her royalty checks, Carson McCullers divorced him in 1941. She later moved into a Brooklyn house rented by George Davis, a prominent literary editor, and shared with the British poet W. H. Auden and his lover. Known as "February House," it emerged as a bohemian commune whose luminary residents included composer Benjamin Britten, the children of Thomas Mann, and poet Paul Bowles. Occasional visitors included Salvador Dalí. The house was underwritten by the famed Gypsy Rose Lee, the burlesque star who had literary aspirations and would become a love interest for McCullers.

It was here, after a night in a Brooklyn bar with Auden, that McCullers was inspired by a dwarf she had seen to write *The Ballad of the Sad Café*.

A second novel, *Reflections in a Golden Eye*, came next. First appearing in two installments in *Harper's Bazaar*, it was published in book form in 1941. A complex exploration of infidelity, set on an army base, it met with mixed critical and commercial success. (It would be filmed in 1967 by legendary director John Huston, starring Marlon Brando and Elizabeth Taylor.)

Following a brief reconciliation, Reeves and Carson became involved in a complicated love triangle with a prominent and openly gay composer, David Diamond. This entanglement, a personal drama partly expressed in *The Ballad of the Sad Café*, was followed by their divorce. The novella appeared first in magazine installments in 1943 and was published in book form in 1951 in a collection with other stories.

McCullers next wrote *The Member of the Wedding* (1946), the story of Frankie Addams, a bored adolescent girl who wants to join her brother's wedding as more than a bridesmaid. Playwright Tennessee Williams encouraged McCullers to write a theatrical adaptation, which opened in 1950. A commercial and critical success, it won the 1950 New York Drama Critics' Circle Award for best American play.

In March 1945, Carson McCullers remarried Reeves, who had re-enlisted during World War II and been wounded on D-Day but continued fighting in France and Germany. After the war, while in France in the early 1950s, Reeves tried to convince Carson to commit suicide with him. Fearing for her life, Carson McCullers returned to the United States. Reeves McCullers committed suicide in a Paris hotel room in November 1953.

Troubled by illness much of her life, Carson McCullers was eventually bedridden after a series of debilitating strokes. Few of her later works equaled the critical or commercial acclaim of her earlier writing. She was sick and in decline when, on August 15, 1967, McCullers suffered another cerebral stroke. Comatose for forty-six days, she died in Nyack, New York, at the age of fifty on September 29, 1967.

WHY YOU SHOULD READ IT

Beneath its inventive charms and memorable characters, epitomizing what is called Southern Gothic, this novella explores the delicate matters of the heart—solitude, isolation, "otherness," and desire—that are central to McCullers's work. It contains this memorable insight into the pained nature of relationships:

> First of all, love is a joint experience between two persons—but the fact that it is a joint experience does not mean that it is a similar experience to the two people involved. There are the lover and the beloved, but these two come from different countries.

Admiring the book as among the best of McCullers's, critic Hilton Als of the *New Yorker* wrote of the book's first lines, "This opening has the power of music, a prelude introducing the story's themes: a far-off place, grief, estrangement from the self, dreams, isolation."

In the end, its comic sensibility gives way to mournful, elegiac notes that linger long after this brief melody ends.

WHAT TO READ NEXT

A novella set on a peacetime army base, *Reflections in a Golden Eye* is a complete departure in tone and style from *Ballad*. I commend it as another short book, but a starkly different and disturbing account of sexual obsession, repressed sexuality, infidelity, and self-harm. It explores the isolation, loneliness, and desperation that animate much of the author's work.

"Outsiderness was McCullers's great theme," comments writer Megan O'Grady, "one that's inextricable from the quest for identity and self-definition, and while none of her protagonists were out of the closet, it's hard to read her work now and not see queerness as a central part. It was her identification with people ill at ease in themselves that made them so relatable to so many."

The much-loved novel *The Member of the Wedding* offers another shift in voice—a coming-of-age tale about a young girl who is in love with her brother and his wife-to-be.

Finally, *The Heart Is a Lonely Hunter* remains Carson McCullers's most popular work and is number 17 on the Modern Library list of 100 Best Novels.

Also set in small-town Georgia, it explores the lives of four people— an adolescent girl with a passion for music, a socialist agitator, a black physician, and a widower who owns a café. Reviewing it at the time of publication, novelist Richard Wright (see entry) wrote:

> To me, the most impressive aspect of *The Heart Is a Lonely Hunter* is the astonishing humanity that enables a white writer, for the first time in Southern fiction, to handle Negro characters with as much ease and justice as those of her own race. This cannot be accounted for stylistically or politically; it seems to stem from an attitude towards life which enables Miss McCullers to rise above the pressures of her environment and embrace white and black humanity in one sweep of apprehension and tenderness.

Big Boy Leaves Home

— 1938 —

Richard Wright

New York: HarperCollins/Olive Editions, 2021; published in the collection Uncle Tom's Children; *with an introduction by Richard Yarborough; 50 pages; originally published in 1938*

FIRST LINES

Yo mama don wear no drawers . . .

Clearly, the voice rose out of the woods, and died away. Like an echo another voice caught it up:

Ah seena when she pulled em off . . .

Another, shrill, cracking, adolescent:

N she washed 'em in alcohol . . .

Then a quartet of voices, blending in harmony, floated high above the tree tops:

N she hung 'em out in the hall . . .

Laughing easily, four black boys came out of the woods into cleared pasture. They walked lollingly in bare feet, beating tangled vines and bushes with long sticks.

PLOT SUMMARY

In the Jim Crow South, four young Black friends have cut school and walk boldly through a white farmer's woods, aware of the danger if they are caught. Taunting one another, full of boyish bravado, they eventually strip down in the heat of the day and jump into a swimming hole.

Suddenly, a young white woman appears. As the naked boys scramble to retrieve their clothes, she screams. They hear the crack of a shot. One body falls. A man in a soldier's uniform appears with a rifle and the scene quickly escalates as Big Boy, strongest and largest of the four, grabs for the weapon. The instant of murderous violence that follows will force Big Boy's parents to make a fateful decision, certain that a lynch mob will soon be hunting their child.

ABOUT THE AUTHOR: RICHARD WRIGHT

One of the most influential American writers of the last century, Richard Wright was born on September 4, 1908, on a Mississippi plantation, to a sharecropper father and a schoolteacher mother. His grandfathers, both born enslaved, had won emancipation fighting for the Union in the Civil War. When Wright was six, his father deserted the family and Wright's mother moved to Natchez, Mississippi, where she took menial jobs. After she was felled by a stroke when Wright was ten, he went to live with his grandmother, a strict Seventh-day Adventist, in Jackson, Mississippi.

A gifted student, at age fifteen Wright had published a story—now lost—"The Voodoo of Hell's Half-Acre," in Jackson's *Southern Register*, a Black newspaper. He was forced to drop out of high school to find work and he took jobs as a porter and bellhop, always facing the threat of racist violence. To use the local library, he had to forge letters pretending that he was checking out books for a white man. But he discovered the work of journalist and cultural critic H. L. Mencken and was profoundly influenced by Mencken's style and withering assault on an anti-intellectual American society including the "low-down politicians, prehensile town boomers, ignorant hedge preachers, and other such vermin" that accepted and celebrated lynching. "He was using words as a weapon," Wright later wrote, "using them as one would use a club. . . . Then, maybe, perhaps I could use them as a weapon?"

At nineteen, Wright moved to Chicago in 1927, where he lived for the next decade, working at a succession of humble jobs: porter, busboy, and post office clerk. During the Great Depression, Chicago was a center of left-wing politics and Wright met a group of radical workers. He joined the John Reed Club, a group of communist writers and artists, and by 1933 had joined the Communist Party. Soon after, his poems and writing began to appear in leftist publications such as *Left Front* and *New Masses*, where he published his first article about boxer Joe Louis. He also worked as a college campus communist organizer and as a reporter for the *Daily Worker*.

In 1935, Wright joined the Federal Writers' Project, a New Deal program to provide work to writers during the Depression by creating city and state guidebooks that collected folklore and oral history. Its projects included the landmark oral history project "Born in Slavery," which included more than twenty-three hundred firsthand accounts of formerly enslaved people. Wright contributed to the guidebooks the project was creating and acted as a supervisor as well. The government work also permitted him to continue his own creative work. Leaving Chicago for Harlem in 1937, he again worked with the Federal Writers' Project and came into contact with other Black writers including Ralph Ellison and a young James Baldwin (see entry).

During this time, Wright unsuccessfully sought to sell a first novel (published posthumously in 1963 as *Lawd Today*). But *Big Boy Leaves Home* appeared in an anthology of Black fiction in 1936 and another prizewinning piece, "Fire and Cloud," appeared in *Story* magazine two years later. These and other novellas were collected in *Uncle Tom's Children* (1938), winning Wright immediate critical renown. In 1940, *Uncle Tom's Children* was reissued with "The Ethics of Living Jim Crow," a stark autobiographical essay underscoring the indignities and violence that Black Americans confronted daily.

Awarded a Guggenheim Fellowship, Wright was able to complete *Native Son*, his first published novel. Released in 1940, it was a landmark work of fiction about Bigger Thomas, a young man growing up in Chicago's Depression-era poverty. A critical sensation, it was chosen as Main Selection by the powerful Book-of-the-Month Club—which demanded the deletion of scenes of masturbation and interracial sex—a major commercial breakthrough for Wright. (Zora Neale Hurston's first novel, *Jonah's Gourd Vine*, had earlier been an alternate selection of the book club.) *Native Son* became the first best seller by a Black writer and was later adapted for Broadway, directed by Orson Welles.

After a brief marriage to ballet dancer and dance teacher Dhimah Rose Meidman in 1939, Wright wed Ellen Poplowitz, a Communist Party member, in 1941. After the birth of their first daughter, Julia, they moved into the Brooklyn home of influential editor George Davis. The large house had become an international literary and artistic commune, with residents including W. H. Auden and Carson McCullers (see entry), whose first novel, *The Heart Is a Lonely Hunter*, Wright had reviewed admiringly before their meeting. By then, a disillusioned Wright had left the Communist Party, rejecting its orthodoxy and the Stalinist purges; a 1944 essay, "I Tried to Be a Communist," which appeared in the *Atlantic Monthly*, was later published in a 1949 collection called *The God That Failed*.

Wright's next book was the memoir *Black Boy*, published in 1945. Selected again by the Book-of-the-Month Club, it remained on the best-seller list for the larger part of that year. But despite Wright's growing fame and success, he was dismayed by the persistent discrimination he and his white wife faced. With the assistance of Gertrude Stein, the thirty-eight-year-old Wright moved his family to Paris in 1946, where a second daughter, Rachel, was born. Richard Wright never returned to America.

Wright found both literary celebrity and acceptance in the French intellectual circle of Camus, Sartre, and Simone de Beauvoir. But over time, he lost much of his American audience. His fellow expatriate James Baldwin later criticized Wright in "Everybody's Protest Novel" and "Many Thousands Gone," essays collected in Baldwin's 1955 *Notes of a Native Son*, which attacked *Native Son* as confirming racist stereotypes of Black people. It ended their friendship.

Three of Wright's novels written in France—*The Outsider* (1953), *Savage Holiday* (1954), and *The Long Dream* (1958)—explored existential themes and were more successful overseas than in the United States. His other books of reportage, political commentary, and autobiography were largely overlooked in the United States. Richard Wright died of a heart attack in Paris on November 28, 1960, at the age of fifty-two.

A second novel unpublished during Wright's life, *The Man Who Lived Underground*, was issued by the Library of America in 2021.

WHY YOU SHOULD READ IT

More than eighty years later, Wright's intense, compact story about a young boy whose life is overturned in a moment of stunning bloodshed remains an electric piece of writing. Wright explores the daily dehumanizing impact of Jim Crow America and the constant threat of violence from white people that Black people endured. Echoes of the story can be found in Colson Whitehead's 2019 novel, *The Nickel Boys*, also included in this collection (see entry). The issues of racism and violence against young Black men are still profoundly timely.

Written largely in dialogue, *Big Boy Leaves Home* remains a vividly arresting work out of the realist-naturalist school. In his introduction to the collection, UCLA professor Richard Yarborough wrote that Wright "was propelled by a fierce determination to break the silence surrounding racism in the United States, a silence maintained in the interest of white supremacy and one to which too many blacks had acceded."

Nevertheless, in an essay written two years after *Uncle Tom's Children* appeared, Wright voiced regret over the collection's publication, contending that he had made it too easy for white readers to assuage their guilt. "When the reviews of that book began to appear, I realized that I had made an awfully naïve mistake," he wrote in "How 'Bigger' Was Born" in 1940. "I found that I had written a book which even bankers' daughters could read and weep over and feel good about. I swore to myself that if I ever wrote another book, no one would weep over it; that it would be so hard and deep that they would have to face it without the consolation of tears. It was this that made me get to work in dead earnest."

Native Son would fulfill Wright's need to write a book that was "hard and deep." But there is no question that *Big Boy Leaves Home* is hardly a story to be read and then "feel good about." Its power lies in the vision of what life meant to be a young Black boy who is thrust suddenly into a world in which he is on his own—an unforgiving world in which survival is finally all that matters.

WHAT TO READ NEXT

The simplest answer is to move on to the other four works collected in *Uncle Tom's Children*, including *Down by the Riverside*, a highly charged narrative of a man desperately struggling to transport his pregnant wife to a hospital during a flood.

Beyond these novellas, Wright's novel *Native Son* and memoir *Black Boy* remain vital parts of the canon of modern American literature.

"Richard Wright was the first African American writer to enter mainstream American literature. A watershed figure in African American literature, he pushed back the horizons for black writers," wrote biographer Hazel Rowley. "At the beginning of the twenty-first century, Wright's writing continued to evoke passionate responses, from deep admiration to vehement hostility. He is an *uncomfortable* writer. He challenges, he tells painful truths, he is a disturber of the peace. He was never interested in pleasing readers. Wright wanted his words to be weapons."

Bonjour Tristesse

− 1954 −

Françoise Sagan

New York: HarperPerennial Modern Classics, 2008; translated from the French by Irene Ash with an introduction by Diane Johnson; 130 pages; originally published in French in 1954; English translation in 1955

FIRST LINES

A strange melancholy pervades me to which I hesitate to give the grave and beautiful name of sorrow. The idea of sorrow has always appealed to me, but now I am almost ashamed of its complete egoism. I have known boredom, regret, and occasionally remorse, but never sorrow. Today it envelops me like a silken web, enervating and soft, and sets me apart from everybody else.

PLOT SUMMARY

"Bonjour tristesse." "Hello, sadness."

Seventeen, bored, and motherless, Cécile is spending the summer on the French Riviera with her father, Raymond, and Elsa, his current girlfriend. At forty, a widower for fifteen years, Raymond is a well-to-do businessman and ladies' man. He has turned Cécile's rearing over to boarding schools and represents the growing amorality and hedonism of a rapidly changing postwar France of the mid-1950s. It might be set today, save that there is no Pill yet.

For Cécile, this enticing summer on the beach only gets better with the appearance of Cyril, a college student a few years older who will teach her how to sail—and maybe more? But their summer idyll is interrupted by the arrival of Anne Larsen. The best friend of Raymond's late wife, Anne is sophisticated, mature, and cultured—the antithesis of Elsa.

As old friends, Anne and Raymond seem well matched, and in short order Anne is in and Elsa is out. Having been godmother of sorts to Cécile, the older woman now takes over cultivating the teenager and ensuring that she studies for a coming exam that she has already failed once.

The new domestic arrangement irks Cécile. She fears that Anne will cramp her style. In particular, Cécile is worried that Anne will disrupt her romance with Cyril. And so she plots to sabotage Anne's plans for a future with her father.

This may sound like it has the makings of the fluffiest of romantic comedies, with swimsuits, beautiful beaches, and Rivera casinos serving as backdrop. But as in other "Dangerous Beach Holidays," bad things can happen at the seaside.

ABOUT THE AUTHOR: FRANÇOISE SAGAN

She was the precocious teenager who would become known as the "Bardot of literature."

Born on June 21, 1935, in Cajarc, France, Françoise Delphine Quoirez was the child of a well-to-do businessman. Educated at private and convent schools, she attended the Sorbonne but was an indifferent student and did not graduate. In time, the lack of a university degree would not matter.

Adopting her pen name from a character in Proust, she claimed to have written the manuscript of *Bonjour Tristesse* in a month's time in August 1953. It was originally published in France in 1954, when she was eighteen. The following year, the English translation reached number 1 on the *New York Times* best-seller list. At nineteen, Sagan was the youngest author to achieve that distinction at the time.

She was ahead of the times. And so was Cécile. Seventeen-year-olds contemplating sex in the Eisenhower fifties were still scandalous. "It was inconceivable," as Sagan was later quoted in the *New York Times*, "that a young girl of 17 or 18 should make love without being in love with a boy of her own age, and not be punished for it."

An international sensation, the book was filmed in 1958, starring a nineteen-year-old Jean Seberg, whose performance made her both a star and a sex symbol. That same year, Françoise Sagan married a book editor twenty years her senior, but divorce followed in 1960. A second marriage took place in 1962, and Sagan had one son, Denis, and just as quickly a second divorce. After that, she would have a series of relationships with both men and women.

With all her attendant celebrity, Sagan continued to write. Among the novels that followed *Bonjour Tristesse* were *Un certain sourire* (1956; *A Certain Smile*), *Les merveilleux nuages* (1961; *Wonderful Clouds*), *Un profil perdu* (1974; *Lost Profile*), *De guerre lasse* (1985; *Engagements of the Heart*, or *A Reluctant Hero*), and *Un sang d'aquarelle* (1987; *Painting in Blood*).

While successful in France, few of these works matched the international notoriety of *Bonjour Tristesse*. Sagan's celebrated personal life became more the focus. A lover of gambling, drinking, and fast cars, she nearly died in 1957 when she flipped her Aston Martin. She later had drug troubles and was convicted twice for narcotics offenses. Convicted of tax fraud in 2002, Sagan was unable to appear in court because of her poor health and received a suspended sentence. Two years later, in September 2004, the writer who shook the world as a teenager died of a blood clot in her lung. She was sixty-nine.

WHY YOU SHOULD READ IT

I took up *Bonjour Tristesse* as one of those cultural mileposts I had missed—a generational novel that struck a chord and became required reading over the years for many young women in particular. I expected a light, saucy, French coming-of-age tale—something like the movie *Clueless*, but with a French Riviera accent instead of California Valley Girl. But it is much more.

Set in the 1950s, Sagan's spirited novel expresses the cynicism and rebellious spirit of the sixties generation that was about to break loose. Far from a period piece, it could easily take place today. The prose carries you along as smoothly as sailing on calm Riviera waters—until Cécile moves from bored teenager to schemer and dangerously rocks the boat.

Many reviewers of the day dismissed the novel, but recent considerations take Sagan and *Bonjour Tristesse* far more seriously. Appraising Sagan as the "great interrogator of morality," critic and novelist Rachel Cusk wrote in 2019, "The hedonism and amorality of 'Bonjour Tristesse' is of a most artistically proper kind. Morality, and its absence, is the novel's defining theme: in this sense, Sagan is far more of a classicist than others of her existentialist brethren, such as Sartre and Camus."

That is pretty heady company.

WHAT TO READ NEXT

Sagan's second novel, *A Certain Smile* (1956), is not a sequel. But it shares many qualities with *Bonjour Tristesse*. Set in Paris in the

1950s, it is told by another Sagan surrogate, Dominique, a young law student bored by her books. Like *Bonjour*'s Cécile, she is restless and curious about love and sex. Although she has a boyfriend, Dominique is drawn to her boyfriend's married uncle, Luc. The older man pursues Dominique even as his kindly wife, Françoise, mothers the young woman.

In her foreword to the 2011 reissue of *A Certain Smile*, writer Diane Johnson notes, "Many found it to be the superior book and preferred it to *Bonjour Tristesse*, finding it less melodramatic, newly compassionate, equally wise, and more realistic, while it exhibited, of course, the same fashionable ennui that readers of the earlier book had found so luridly fascinating."

Apart from Sagan's other novels, the most interesting follow-up to reading *Bonjour Tristesse* might be to set it against the fiction about other young women of Cécile's age: Cait and Baba of *Country Girls* by Edna O'Brien, August in Jacqueline Woodson's *Another Brooklyn*, James Baldwin's Tish (*If Beale Street Could Talk*), and the young woman who narrates Duras's *The Lover* are all around Cécile's age. They live in remarkably different worlds yet must confront so many of the same issues.

Candide, or Optimism

— 1759 —

Voltaire

*New York: Penguin Classics, 2005; translated and edited by Theo Cuffe
with an introduction by Michael Wood; 94 pages*

FIRST LINES

Once upon a time in Westphalia, in the castle of Monsieur the Baron
von Thunder-ten-tronckh, there lived a young boy on whom nature had
bestowed the gentlest of dispositions. His countenance expressed his soul.
He combined solid judgement with complete openness of mind; which
is the reason, I believe, that he was called Candide. The older servants
of the house suspected him to be the son of the Baron's sister by a kindly
and honest gentleman of the neighbourhood, whom that young lady
refused ever to marry because he could only ever give proof of seventy-one

quarterings,* the rest of his genealogical tree having been lost through the ravages of time.

PLOT SUMMARY

Written by one of the most significant French philosophes of the Enlightenment era, *Candide* is a witty, fast-paced, even absurd adventure. But beware: it is no children's story. Far from it. In the world of modern movies, *Candide* would be rated NC-17. Massacres, debauchery, rapes, hangings, and other tortures abound. And yet it is all told so fancifully.

It is the story of the illegitimate Candide, a naïve young hero exiled from the castle in which he was raised. His offense: kissing the hand of his beloved Cunégonde, the daughter of the Baron. After being booted—literally, "with great kicks to his backside"—from the castle, the strapping Candide is conscripted into the army of the King of Bulgars. The head-spinning series of catastrophes that follow carry Candide from Europe to South America, Africa, and Asia. He will be brutalized, flogged, hung, and left for dead through wars, earthquakes, and the Inquisition.

But he suffers it gladly. Miraculously enduring all of these trials and tribulations, the noble Candide has only one goal: to be reunited with his treasured Cunégonde. Candide's beloved is named for Saint Kunigunde (also Cunigunde), canonized for her virgin status in 1200. But in Voltaire's bawdy wordplay, her name also connects to the Latin root for "cunnilingus." Oh, that salty Voltaire.

Through his quest, Candide is guided by the unshakable belief that he lives in "the best of all possible worlds." It is a philosophy

---

* "Quarterings" are divisions in heraldry, indicated on a coat of arms; "seventy-one quarterings" would be an "absurd impossibility," according to translator Theo Cuffe.

instilled by his tutor, Dr. Pangloss (from the Greek "all tongue," or "all talk"), who has instructed his student that everything that happens is for "the best of ends." If Columbus's men had not brought syphilis back to Europe, argues Pangloss, the Old World would not have chocolate, which they also brought back. In other words, good results always follow from bad beginnings. It is that oblivious sense of "Optimism" that inspires the novel's subtitle.

Embracing that excessively positive world view, Candide endures hardships that sorely test his tutor's words.

ABOUT THE AUTHOR: VOLTAIRE

Like so much fiction, *Candide* cannot be separated from the life and extraordinary times of its author, one of the most prominent and influential writers of the Enlightenment (circa 1688 to 1789).

Born near Paris on November 21, 1694, François-Marie Arouet was the son of a well-to-do official in the French legal system. As Voltaire, he later claimed that he was the illegitimate child of a liaison between his mother, who died when he was seven, and a soldier-poet named Rochebrune.

Whatever his parentage, the young Arouet began his studies in 1704 at the Collège Louis-le-Grand, a famous Jesuit college in Paris. He acquired a classical education while developing a love for theater and a skepticism for religious instruction. He watched the fading regime of Louis XIV, "the Sun King," the symbol of absolute monarchy who had brought France to the pinnacle of its power.

Gaining a diplomatic post in Holland, Arouet was sent back to Paris after an intrigue involving a young Dutch woman. He began writing popular poems and aphorisms that made him the wit of Parisian society. But trouble arose when one of his poems satirized a royal family member who was not amused. The poet was exiled, jailed in the Bastille in 1717, and then exiled again in 1718.

Adopting the pen name Voltaire,* he turned to drama and wrote his first play, *Oedipus*, staged with great success in 1718. Three of his plays were performed at the 1725 wedding celebrations of Louis XV, and Voltaire's prominence as a dramatist rose.

At the dawn of the eighteenth-century Age of Reason, he was part of a revolution in intellectual ferment, with such thinkers and scientists as Descartes, Newton, Montesquieu, John Locke, and Benjamin Franklin upending centuries-old views of the universe, human rights, religious authority, and the concept of absolute monarchy.

Voltaire's period of grace ended when a quarrel with another aristocrat forced him into exile in England. Never deterred, he learned English and met and corresponded with such major English literary figures as Alexander Pope and Jonathan Swift, whose *Gulliver's Travels* (1726) Voltaire read and admired.

His return to Paris in 1728 only led to further trouble for the freethinking writer. Voltaire again crossed the powers-that-be with *Letters Concerning the English Nation* (1733), first composed in English, and published in Paris as *Lettres philosophiques* (1734). A collection of fictional letters, it celebrated the general notion of religious tolerance, a heretical notion in the view of church and throne. The French publisher was arrested and the book publicly burned.

Facing arrest himself, Voltaire took refuge in the chalet of his lover, Madame du Châtelet. A mathematician and physicist, she wrote scientific treatises, translated Newton's work into French, and tutored Voltaire in the natural sciences. In 1749, at age forty-two, during an affair with another poet, she died in childbirth. Voltaire had, in the meantime, taken his widowed niece as a lover.

In 1751, the first volume of the *Encyclopédie*, a landmark of the Enlightenment thought, was produced. A collection of articles by

---

* The name Voltaire is thought to have been configured from an anagram of *Arouet le jeune* (i.e., "Arouet the younger") with the *V* derived from an archaic French alphabet, although there are other explanations for the pseudonym.

leading philosophes, it was dedicated to the advancement of science, secularism, and tolerance. Voltaire contributed articles to several early volumes, but publication of the *Encyclopédie* was suspended by the French government in 1757 over its attacks on the Catholic Church and the monarchy.

During this European era of political and religious upheaval, Voltaire moved around the Continent, first to Potsdam and later to Geneva and Frankfurt. In 1758, he acquired a château near Geneva, where he would spend the rest of his life and where he wrote *Candide*, published in early 1759. He spent his last two decades in a crusade against the treatment of French Protestants, attacking the intolerance of the Catholic Church.

Voltaire returned to Paris in 1778 for the first time in nearly three decades for the production of one of his final plays, *Irène*. He died there on May 30, aged eighty-three. But even in death, Voltaire was deemed undesirable by the authorities. His body was smuggled out of the city to avoid the refusal of church authorities to permit his burial and laid to rest in Champagne. But after the Fall of the Bastille and the beginning of the French Revolution in 1789, Voltaire's remains were returned to Paris in 1791 and interred in the Panthéon, a mausoleum for distinguished French citizens.

WHY YOU SHOULD READ IT

It is simple: *Candide*—the oldest novel presented in this collection—is fresh, funny, exciting, and marvelously inventive. There is nothing dated about it. Supposedly written over three days, the story skewers and then roasts all the sacred cows of Voltaire's day: church, priesthood, royalty, government, aristocracy, philosophers, and scientists.

Have I left anyone out? Voltaire did not. Aside from the excessive optimism of Dr. Pangloss, Voltaire went after other philosophers and institutions, including that of African slavery. There is a horrifying moment when an enslaved man whose leg and right hand have been amputated as punishment tells Candide, "It is the price we pay for the sugar you eat in Europe."

Having never read *Candide* previously, I was familiar with it first from seeing an acclaimed production of Leonard Bernstein's operetta, a musical based on the book. Originally written in 1956, it was revived to critical success in 1974. I will leave out the completely sordid details of having read *Candy*, a notorious parody published in 1958, which follows the exploits of a hyper-sexed young woman named, of course, Candy.

Rest assured. At more than 250 years old, *Candide* is no wax museum curiosity. Nor is it stuffy. It is a timeless satire. Imagine Kurt Vonnegut in a powdered wig.

"I think *Candide* is also a lesson in the absurd, a demonstration of the difficulties of making sense of life, of *all* philosophies, of living a meaningful life," said Nicholas Cronk, director of the Voltaire Foundation at the University of Oxford, "—and that is why the book goes on speaking to us, and goes on making us laugh."

So have some fun and get a dose of philosophy too. Reading *Candide* is vastly more entertaining than wading through many of the Enlightenment-era thinkers assigned in Philosophy 101. In the end, you will have new appreciation for the great transformation that the Age of Reason brought about.

WHAT TO READ NEXT

Over a lifetime spanning much of the eighteenth century, Voltaire produced an extraordinary body of work—essays, history, plays, poetry, and fiction. Most of his writing does not translate to modern times as seamlessly as *Candide*, which remains his most widely read book. But I will recommend one title.

Among his most accessible works—Voltaire wanted to be widely understood and wrote for a broad audience—is *A Pocket Philosophical Dictionary* (Oxford University Press, 2011), a collection of short commentary, arranged in alphabetical order, on varied subjects like miracles and tyranny and including commentary on the Bible, church history, and religious fanaticism.

In the entry "Atheism," Voltaire writes:

> Once upon a time anyone who had a secret skill ran the risk of being taken for a sorcerer; every new sect was accused of child sacrifice in the conduct of its mysteries; and philosophers who departed from the jargon of their school were charged with atheism by fanatics and scoundrels, and condemned by fools.

His tone is of clear-eyed, unsparing, and whimsical criticism. "This could have been written in a newspaper today, and it's crucial that the language feels modern," said the Voltaire Foundation's Nicholas Cronk. He continues, "The church in particular hated it because of its sheer cheekiness—its rudeness and brashness, along with its refusal to treat churchmen with the pomp and ceremony they thought they deserved."

Charlotte's Web

— 1952 —

E. B. White
Pictures by Garth Williams

New York: HarperCollins, 2012; 184 pages

FIRST LINES

"Where's Papa going with that ax?" said Fern to her mother as they were setting the table for breakfast.

"Out to the hoghouse," replied Mrs. Arable. "Some pigs were born last night."

"I don't see why he needs an ax," continued Fern, who was only eight.

PLOT SUMMARY

Girls meets pig. Girl falls in love with pig. Pig meets spider. Pig falls in love with spider.

"But it's a children's book," you are probably thinking right now.

That is true. But *Charlotte's Web* is also a perfect book, in oh-so-many ways.

Charlotte's Web, for the uninitiated, is the story of a pig rescued from slaughter by an idealistic young girl named Fern. She names the pig Wilbur and nurses him until Wilbur is eventually sent to live in the nearby barn of Fern's uncle, Homer Zuckerman.

In the extraordinary universe of that barn, Wilbur encounters the sheep, a stuttering goose, and other farm animals who fill his world and his days, along with a memorable scavenger rat named Templeton. And then, longing for a true friend, Wilbur meets one—a spider named Charlotte.

"Charlotte A. Cavatica. But just call me Charlotte."

Charlotte will become Wilbur's best friend. And when he is again threatened by the ax, it is Charlotte who promises to be his savior.

ABOUT THE AUTHOR: E. B. WHITE

"It is not often that someone comes along who is a true friend and a good writer. Charlotte was both."

So, in a sense, was E. B. White.

Elwyn Brooks White was born on July 11, 1899, in Mount Vernon, New York—a small city that is one of the first stops outside New York City on the New Haven train line. It also happens to be my hometown, although I honestly did not know about my geographic connection to the man known as E. B. White until much later. He attended public schools there and then graduated from Cornell University in 1921.

After university, White worked for a series of newswires and local newspapers, and other odd work, even landing a job on a fireboat in Alaska. When White returned to New York City to work in advertising, he submitted an article to the *New Yorker* magazine following its launch in 1925. The magazine's literary editor, Katharine Angell, read it and recommended that Harold Ross, the magazine's legendary founder and editor, hire White. He did, and E. B. White contributed to the magazine for nearly six decades. White helped to shape the magazine's central place in twentieth-century American letters.

White and Katharine Angell later married. In 1938, the Whites moved to a saltwater farm in North Brooklin, Maine, they had purchased in 1933. It was there that he was inspired to write *Charlotte's Web* (1952).

One of White's Cornell professors was William Strunk Jr., the author of a writing manual for his students that was commercially published in 1920. In 1959, White revised and added to Strunk's manual and it was reissued as *The Elements of Style*. A fundamental guide to grammar and writing structure, the book became my introduction to E. B. White as a college freshman. It is still on my bookshelf. It was also named one of the "100 Most Important Nonfiction Books" by *Time* magazine.

E. B. White succumbed to Alzheimer's disease at age eighty-six in North Brooklin, on October 1, 1985. Following his death, *New Yorker* editor William Shawn said:

> E. B. White was a great essayist, a supreme stylist. His literary style was as pure as any in our language. It was singular, colloquial, clear, unforced, thoroughly American and utterly beautiful. Because of his quiet influence, several generations of this country's writers write better than they might have done. He never wrote a mean or careless sentence. He was impervious to literary, intellectual and political fashion. He was ageless, and his writing was timeless.

> E. B. White has passed on. Charlotte and Wilbur live forever.

WHY YOU SHOULD READ IT

I don't know how many times I have read *Charlotte's Web*. But it never gets old. And it never loses its power to move. I dare you to read it and not cry.

Now, there are two animated film versions of this book. But honestly, they pale beside the novel. In "Along Came a Spider," a review of *Charlotte's Web* for the *New York Times* in 1952, novelist Eudora Welty wrote:

> What the book is about is friendship on earth, affection and protection, adventure and miracle, life and death, trust and treachery, pleasure and pain, and the passing of time. As a piece of work it is just about perfect, and just about magical in the way it is done.

Friendship, life and death, trust and treachery, pleasure and pain. These are not the saccharine subjects of children's fiction. They are the enduring issues of literature. But E. B. White crystallized them in a story of such purity and elegant prose, it helps explain why *Charlotte's Web* is sixth on the list of books most checked out in 125 years of the New York Public Library.

WHAT TO READ NEXT

Besides *Charlotte's Web*, White wrote other children's books that became time-honored and much-beloved classics—*Stuart Little* and *The Trumpet of the Swan*. I recommend reading both—either to yourself or to a small person. But much of his fame as a writer rests on his output as a member of the *New Yorker* magazine staff, where he contributed essays for decades. Many of these have been collected and a favorite of mine is *Here Is New York*, a set of essays about the city. And *The Elements of Style* should be on the bookshelf of anyone who writes anything—from an email to a multivolume saga. In the spirit of *Great Short Books*, White wrote this characteristic piece of advice: "Omit needless words."

A Clockwork Orange

— 1962 —

Anthony Burgess

New York: W. W. Norton, 2019; with an introduction by Anthony Burgess;
212 pages

* Number 65 on the Modern Library list of 100 Best Novels *
* TIME: "All-TIME 100 Novels" *

FIRST LINES

"What's it going to be then, eh?"

There was me, that is Alex, and my three droogs, that is Pete, Georgie, and Dim, Dim being really dim, and we sat in the Korova Milkbar making up our rassoodocks what to do with the evening, a flip dark chill winter bastard though dry. The Korova Milkbar was a milk-plus mesto, and you may, O my brothers, have forgotten what these mestos were like, things changing so skorry these days and everybody very quick to forget, newspapers not being read much neither. Well, what they sold there was milk plus something else.

PLOT SUMMARY

Alex is fifteen. With his three friends—his "droogs"—he spends drug-fueled evenings stealing, raping, fighting rival gangs, and terrorizing the population in a future city that seems like Manchester, England, but could be Leningrad or New York.

His excessive criminality falls to what the Beethoven-loving Alex calls being "ultra-violent"—a nasty bit of teenage rebellion in a society in which all work is drudgery, or "rabbiting." In Alex's world, evil is constant and brutality is pervasive. After getting two very young girls drunk, Alex sexually assaults them.

An arrest by the "millicents" lands Alex in prison. There he is offered a stark choice: to serve his full fourteen-year sentence or gain his freedom in exchange for joining a behavior modification program that will erase his violent impulses.

But there is a hitch: the technique, involving drug injections and "viddying" extremely violent movies, is experimental. Will it really change Alex? In this stark, dystopian vision, Burgess poses big questions about free will and virtue. "What does God want? Does God want goodness or the choice of goodness?"

ABOUT THE AUTHOR: ANTHONY BURGESS

Novelist, composer, screenwriter, and literary critic, Anthony Burgess was born John Anthony Burgess Wilson in Manchester, England, on February 25, 1917. Both his mother and an aunt died in the 1918 influenza pandemic. But the boy survived, was raised Catholic, and later was sent to Catholic schools. With no formal musical instruction, Burgess acquired a passion for classical music through a home-built radio and taught himself to play the piano. Graduating from

Manchester University in 1940, he joined the British Army, serving as a musical director of a unit that entertained the troops in Europe during World War II.

During the war, Burgess married Llewela "Lynne" Isherwood Jones. While enduring London's wartime blackout, she was assaulted by American soldiers while pregnant and lost their expected child. This attack, Burgess later said, inspired the brutality he depicted in *A Clockwork Orange*.

Trained in linguistics, Burgess taught after the war, first in British secondary schools and later with the Colonial Service in Malaya and Brunei. While in Malaya, he wrote *Time for a Tiger*, the first of a trilogy of novels set in the British colony.

His teaching career was interrupted when Burgess was diagnosed with a brain tumor in 1959. Told that he had a year to live, Burgess returned to London and began producing novels, essays, and criticism. Working in a frenzy to provide for his wife, he wrote five novels in a year, after which it became apparent that he had been misdiagnosed.

In 1961, he and Lynne took a voyage to Russia that crucially influenced the inventive language and dark social climate that permeate *A Clockwork Orange*. No socialist, Burgess saw the suppression of individuality and state control as dangers and the idea for a novel took hold. This merged with reports of growing teen gang violence in England and a book was born. Burgess later claimed that he wrote *A Clockwork Orange* in three weeks.

"I first heard the expression 'as queer as a clockwork orange' in a London pub before the Second World War," Burgess explained. "It is an old Cockney slang phrase, implying a queerness or madness so extreme as to subvert nature, since could any notion be more bizarre than that of a clockwork orange? . . . I began to write a novel about curing juvenile delinquency. I had read somewhere that it would be a good idea to liquidate the criminal impulse through aversion therapy; I was appalled."

Critical reception was mixed when *A Clockwork Orange* appeared in England in 1962. When an American publisher offered to publish the book on the condition that the final chapter be dropped, Burgess accepted. "I needed money back in 1961, even the pittance I was being offered as an advance," he wrote, "and if the condition of the book's acceptance was also its truncation—well, so be it." Published in the United States in 1963, *A Clockwork Orange* was extolled by a *New York Times* reviewer as "brilliant."

Burgess received five hundred dollars for the movie rights, originally planned as a vehicle for the Rolling Stones with Mick Jagger as Alex. Then Stanley Kubrick took over as director. An initial "X" rating—which meant "No one under 17 admitted" and typically applied to pornographic films—was changed to "R" ("Restricted") after Kubrick deleted some scenes for the 1971 release.

Eventually, Kubrick's "sinny"—the word for a movie, from "cinema" in *A Clockwork Orange*—was nominated for Best Picture and Best Director and garnered awards around the world. Overshadowed by the film's success, Burgess said:

> The film has just been a damned nuisance. I am regarded by some people as a mere boy, a mere helper to Stanley Kubrick, the secondary creator who is feeding a primary creator, who is a great film director. This I naturally resent. I resent also the fact I am frequently blamed for the various crimes which are supposed to be instigated by the film.

Well before the film appeared, Burgess's wife, Lynne, had become an alcoholic and Burgess had begun an affair with Italian translator and literary agent, Liana Macellari. After Lynne's death from cirrhosis in 1968, Burgess married Macellari. During the early 1970s, they moved to the United States, where he taught writing at Princeton University and the City University of New York, among other schools. To avoid England's high tax rate, Burgess and Liana later moved to Monaco while keeping homes in Italy and France.

In addition to his novels, Burgess composed music and wrote more than fifty books, some under a second pseudonym: Joseph Kell. His output includes a biography of Ernest Hemingway and several books about the work of James Joyce: *Here Comes Everybody* (also published as *Re Joyce*, 1965) and *Joysprick: An Introduction to the Language of James Joyce* (1973). Burgess also wrote for film and television, including Franco Zeffirelli's 1977 miniseries, *Jesus of Nazareth*.

In 1980, Burgess's novel *Earthly Powers*, a sweeping saga about a novelist telling his life story, was a finalist for the Booker Prize, which went instead to *Rites of Passage* by William Golding (see entry). Suffering from lung cancer, Anthony Burgess returned to London, where he died on November 22, 1993, at the age of seventy-six.

WHY YOU SHOULD READ IT

Anthony Burgess's most famous book, *A Clockwork Orange* is a riveting exploration of big questions about free will and morality. The devilishly clever narrative brings to life an extraordinary personification of evil in a provocative mixture of action, ideas, and language—its invented slang is central to the book's impact. His created vocabulary includes words like "viddy" for "see," "horrorshow" for "good," "appy polly loggies" for "apologies," and "the old in and out"—you can probably guess its meaning. While challenging, his "Nadsat" has its own compelling logic and exhilarating quality.

Recognizing this hurdle, Burgess wrote:

> It is not the novelist's job to preach; it is his duty to show. I have shown enough, though the curtain of an invented lingo gets in the way—another aspect of my cowardice. Nadsat, a Russified version of English, was meant to muffle the raw response we expect from pornography. It turned the book into a linguistic adventure.

And adventure it is, though a perverse one, vividly reimagined in Kubrick's film classic. If you have never seen it, you should be warned—the film is "ultraviolent" and its treatment of sexual violence in particular is difficult to watch. Read Burgess first for his rich language and audacious vision.

"Like *1984*, this is a book in which an entire social order is implied through language. And what language!" wrote Richard Lacayo in listing the novel among *Time* magazine's All-TIME 100. "Stanley Kubrick's coldly magnificent 'sinny' adaptation has sometimes threatened to overshadow this great novel. Don't let it happen."

I agree. There are some key differences from the novel. The most significant of these is the ending. Kubrick's film was based on the American edition of the novel, which deleted Burgess's final chapter— and Alex's ultimate fate. The revised 1986 American edition restored the novel's missing twenty-first chapter. Which ending is right? Stop after chapter 20, as Kubrick did? Or continue on to chapter 21?

You choose. After all, *A Clockwork Orange* is about freedom of choice. As Burgess put it, "Eat this sweetish segment or spit it out. You are free."

WHAT TO READ NEXT

Having read his books on Joyce, I look forward to reading Burgess's exploration of the life and work of "Papa" Hemingway, *Ernest Hemingway* (1978). Getting one significant novelist's insights into another is an intriguing prospect.

Of Burgess's many other fiction titles, I moved the novel *Earthly Powers* to my To-Be-Read list. Weighing in at nearly seven hundred pages, Burgess's 1980 novel certainly did not make the list of great short books. But it is widely considered his next-best book. The story of an aging gay Roman Catholic novelist, it spans the twentieth century's major events and explores issues of faith, morality, and free will that animate much of Burgess's work. Finally, to follow *A*

Clockwork Orange consider reading several other important great short books in this collection. Burgess explores the same troubling moral landscape investigated by his contemporaries William Golding in *Lord of the Flies*, Doris Lessing in *The Fifth Child*, and George Orwell in *Animal Farm* (see entries).

The Country Girls

— 1960 —

Edna O'Brien

New York: Farrar, Straus and Giroux, 2017; published in The Country Girls: Three Novels and an Epilogue *with an introduction by Eimear McBride; 175 pages*

* BBC: "100 Novels That Shaped Our World" *

FIRST LINES

I wakened quickly and sat up in bed abruptly. It is only when I am anxious that I waken easily and for a minute I did not know why my heart was beating faster than usual. Then I remembered. The old reason. He had not come home.

PLOT SUMMARY

Let's start with this. If the author's parish priest burns a book and politicians condemn it, pay attention: it is probably worth reading. So it was when *The Country Girls* appeared in 1960, shocking an Ireland unready for Edna O'Brien's candid appraisal of sex, church, and the proper place of young women.

The story opens with a fourteen-year-old Caithleen—also Cait or Kate—Brady who resides on a hardscrabble property in a small village in the west of Ireland with her loving mother and Hickey, a farmhand. Her much-absent father, Dada, is reckless with money and a hard drinker. It is her father who has not come home.

Cait's best friend and sometimes antagonist is Bridget "Baba" Brennan, the daughter of the local vet. Baba can be haughty and prone to mischief and bullying. But the pair is inseparable. Both of these "Country Girls" know the world of their remote village in the years after World War II is too small.

After tragedy strikes, Cait and Baba go off to a convent school ruled by the nuns. Chafing against the convent's rigid routine, they plan an escape and end up in Dublin, where the final section of the novel plays out. As working girls living in a boardinghouse, they share talcum powder and perfume. They wear black underwear that they don't have to launder as often.

But Baba is still restless. "We're eighteen and we're bored to death," she tells Cait. ". . . We want to live. Drink gin. Squeeze into the front of big cars and drive up outside big hotels. We want to go places. Not sit in this damp dump."

Both "Country Girls" seek romance, or something like it, in this brilliant novel of longing, desire, and becoming women, first in a trilogy that continues with *The Lonely Girl* and *Girls in Their Married Bliss*.

(Note: *The Country Girls* is not to be confused with Edna O'Brien's 2012 autobiography, *Country Girl: A Memoir*.)

ABOUT THE AUTHOR: EDNA O'BRIEN

Born on December 15, 1930, Josephine Edna O'Brien grew up in Tuamgraney, a village in Ireland's county Clare. Her father, like Cait's, was a profligate drinker. Also, like Cait and Baba, O'Brien was educated in a convent boarding school. Finally, like the "Country Girls," O'Brien left for Dublin as a teenager—in her case to work in an apothecary. There, at eighteen, she met a married writer named Ernest Gébler. He later divorced and they married in 1954, moving to London, where the couple had two sons, and Edna later worked reading manuscripts for a London publisher.

While in London, she first read the work of James Joyce. Realizing that Joyce had turned autobiography into fiction (see *A Portrait of the Artist as a Young Man*), she set out to do the same. Offered a small advance by a publisher, O'Brien is said to have written *The Country Girls* in three weeks.

Published to great critical reception in London and New York, the novel hit Ireland like a thunderbolt. Banned by the official Irish censor, it was also burned by the parish priest in Tuamgraney. Two sequels in the Country Girls trilogy were published in rapid succession in 1962 and 1964; similarly shocking in their day, they were met again with bans in Ireland. (A total of seven of O'Brien's books were banned in her home country.) She then wrote the screenplay for *Girl with Green Eyes*, a 1964 film based on *The Lonely Girl*, her second book. By then, O'Brien's marriage was dissolving. She left her husband and two sons and, after a lengthy court battle, was divorced and won custody of her sons.

Over the next decades, O'Brien was prolific, writing novels, screenplays, short stories, and stage plays, including *Virginia*, a successful 1980 drama about Virginia Woolf staged in London and New York. She also was something of a celebrity—becoming part of what might be called the glitterati, winning friends and admirers among movie stars and celebrated novelists and entering a relationship with a significant British politician who remains unnamed. She was an original panelist in 1979 on a long-running BBC show called *Question Time*, on which prominent people discussed contemporary issues.

In a memoir, Robert Gottlieb, her longtime American editor at Simon & Schuster and Knopf, described her: "She was a glory, with her pale white skin, her flaming red hair and her exotic outfits: ankle-length gossamer skirts, vivid antique lace blouses and layers of baubles, bangles and beads. She dangled and wafted."

And she wrote. And she wrote. Next came *Mother Ireland*, a memoir; a book on Byron, *Byron in Love*; and a biography of James Joyce. O'Brien's focus shifted in the 1990s to fiction based on contemporary events, including *House of Splendid Isolation* (1994) about an Irish Republican Army terrorist; *Down by the River* (1997), inspired by the case of a young Irish rape victim who sought an abortion; and *The Little Red Chairs* (2015), based on war crimes in the Balkan wars. More recently, *Girl* (2019), a novel based on the kidnapping of young women in Nigeria, was published as she neared her ninetieth birthday.

In 2018, the international writers' organization PEN bestowed on Edna O'Brien its PEN/Nabokov Award for Achievement in International Literature. This lifetime award cited O'Brien: "For her powerful voice and the absolute perfection of her prose, and her body of work."

In 2020 she turned ninety, and at this writing she still resided in London.

WHY YOU SHOULD READ IT

In an extraordinary career spanning six decades, O'Brien wrote many great books. But *The Country Girls* remains a touchstone for many readers. In turns touching, comic, poignant, but mostly honest, O'Brien's first novel explored first love, desire, shame, and the overwhelming weight of family and church. Like one of her literary models, James Joyce, O'Brien left Ireland. But the country's character pulses through her work as it does through his.

In an introduction to the trilogy, Irish novelist Eimear McBride wrote that O'Brien and her book "have become era-defining symbols of the struggle for Irish women's voices to be heard above the clamour of an ultraconservative, ultrareligious, and institutionally misogynistic society."

But O'Brien's concerns go beyond Ireland, Catholicism, and gender. Edna O'Brien is, according to her friend the late Philip Roth, "among the handful of most accomplished living writers in the English language."

O'Brien's voice is simply magical. Her concerns as a novelist transcend category and geography. And in these "Country Girls" she created extraordinary characters of depth, empathy, and honesty whose memory lingers long after the reading.

WHAT TO READ NEXT

This one is fairly obvious: move right on to the sequels. *The Lonely Girl* (1962) picks up the story of the women two years later, as Baba and Cait still room together but begin to go their separate ways. The novel is also known as *Girl with Green Eyes*, which was the title of a 1964 film based on the book, for which O'Brien wrote the screenplay.

The trilogy continued with *Girls in Their Married Bliss* (1964), which moves forward several years and shifts the scene to London. O'Brien revised the ending of that novel and then added an epilogue for an omnibus edition published in 1986.

Death in Venice

— 1912 —

Thomas Mann

New York: W. W. Norton, 1994; translated and edited by Clayton Koelb;
63 pages; first published in German in 1912 as Der Tod in Venedig

FIRST LINES

On a spring afternoon in 19—, a year that for months glowered threaten-
ingly over our continent, Gustav Aschenbach—or von Aschenbach, as he
had been known officially since his fiftieth birthday—set off alone from his
dwelling in Prinzregentenstrasse in Munich on a rather long walk. He had
been overstrained by the difficult and dangerous morning's work, which
just now required particular discretion, caution, penetration, and precision
of will: even after his midday meal the writer had not been able to halt the
running on of the productive machinery within him, that "motus animi
continuus" which Cicero claims is the essence of eloquence, nor had he
been able to obtain the relaxing slumber so necessary to him once a day to

71

relieve the increasing demands on his resources. Thus, he sought the open air right after tea, hoping that fresh air and exercise would restore him and help him to have a profitable evening.

PLOT SUMMARY

Lionized in Germany, renowned writer Gustav Aschenbach strolls through Munich. The fifty-year-old author realizes he needs a respite from his work—"a measure he had to take for his health, no matter how much it went against his inclination." After a false start on an Italian island, Aschenbach resolves to go to Venice, "that coquettish, dubious beauty of a city, half fairy tale and half tourist trap."

There, in an elegant beachfront hotel, the writer contemplates his life and art, bounded by "discretion, caution, penetration, and precision of will." He dresses for dinner as he did everything—"slowly and precisely." But as he waits to be seated and observes the other guests, the writer's fastidiously ordered world is shattered. Like a vision, a "perfectly beautiful" young boy appears, a boy with "a face reminiscent of Greek statues from the noblest period of antiquity."

Discreetly observing the boy, known as Tadzio, on the beach, Aschenbach falls under a spell. Obsessed, he follows the boy and his family through Venice. Troubled by poor health and increasingly convinced that Venice is gripped by contagion, Aschenbach learns that the city has been hit by a wave of "Asiatic cholera." In spite of his misgivings, the ailing writer seeks every glimpse of the godlike Tadzio.

As the hotel empties of tourists, the lovesick Aschenbach must choose: Should he stay or should he go?

ABOUT THE AUTHOR: THOMAS MANN

Considered the greatest German novelist of the twentieth century, Thomas Mann was born on June 6, 1875, in Lübeck, Germany, into a fairly prosperous family. After Mann's father died, the family relocated to Munich, where Mann attended the university. Preparing for a career in journalism, he worked briefly for an insurance company before joining a magazine and publishing his first stories, collected in book form in 1898.

Published in 1901, his first novel, *Verfall einer Familie* (*Buddenbrooks: The Decline of a Family*) told the multigenerational saga of a prosperous merchant family that falls from wealth. A great success, the book established Mann's reputation.

A few years later, in 1905, Mann married Katja Pringsheim, and the couple had six children, some of whom also became writers. As Europe moved toward the First World War, *Death in Venice* was published in 1912. That same year, Mann and his wife moved to Switzerland, where she was treated for a lung problem. This became the setting for his novel *Der Zauberberg* (*The Magic Mountain*, 1924), considered one of the most influential works in twentieth-century German literature. On the strength of these three works, Thomas Mann was awarded the Nobel Prize in Literature in 1929.

As Hitler rose to power in 1933, Mann remained in Switzerland, traveling often to the United States. For opposing the Nazis, Mann and his family were deprived of German citizenship in 1936. He moved to the United States in 1938, first settling in Princeton, New Jersey, where he taught at the university. Other members of the Mann family also came to America: brother Heinrich Mann, a writer whose books were burned by the Nazis; son Klaus, most notable as author of *Mephisto*; daughter Erika Mann, a writer and actress; and son Golo Mann, a historian and writer. They were among the many intellectuals fleeing the Nazis, a group that included Hannah Arendt, Bertolt Brecht, and Herman Hesse.

During the war, Thomas Mann made anti-Nazi broadcasts for the BBC, joined the Library of Congress as a Consultant in German Literature, and became a U.S. citizen in 1944. After the war, he refused to return to Germany, although he did visit the divided nation several times. During the anti-communist fervor of McCarthy era, however, Mann would again suffer for his views. He joined protests against the blacklisting of Hollywood writers who were suspected of communist sympathies. For taking that stand, Mann lost his position at the Library of Congress.

Returning to Switzerland in 1952, Mann died, at the age of eighty, near Zurich on August 12, 1955.

WHY YOU SHOULD READ IT

The work of Thomas Mann is challenging and deep. Because of its brevity, simple storyline, and great elegance, *Death in Venice* is perhaps the most approachable of his works and a good entry point.

Its rich, complex prose provides an ideal introduction to Mann's artistic concerns: the life of the artist and his relationship to society; the question of art itself, which Aschenbach likens to "a war"; philosophy and myth; the desperate attempts at love and sex, youth and death; and repressed desire. Mann's diaries later revealed his own apparently unconsummated same-sex desires.

Writing on the one hundredth anniversary of Mann's birth, critic and novelist Elizabeth Hardwick commented, "The description of the young boy Tadzio in 'Death in Venice' surpasses in tenderness and lyricism anything in Mann's work."

Italian director Luchino Visconti's 1971 film version of *Death in Venice* depicts Aschenbach as a composer and conductor. It features the music of composer Gustav Mahler, whose 1911 death played into Mann's conception of the story.

WHAT TO READ NEXT

Thomas Mann created a body of writing—novels, short stories, and essays—that has acquired international status as the work of a genius. After *Death in Venice*, the appropriate next destination is his first novel, *Buddenbrooks*, a landmark of modern literature. The story of four generations of a wealthy family in northern Germany, it is filled with commonplace events—births, marriages, divorces, and deaths. But the saga of the Buddenbrooks family is about their undoing by modernity. Ornate in its detail, it has been judged by some critics as the greatest of Mann's novels, and according to the Nobel Prize committee, this book alone secured his 1929 Nobel Prize.

The other major work Mann wrote prior to the Nobel Prize was *The Magic Mountain*, published in 1924. Originally planned as a novella to follow *Death in Venice*, it was expanded into the coming-of-age story of a young German engineer, who goes to visit a cousin in a tuberculosis sanatorium in the mountains of Switzerland.

A note: both of these Mann works are more than seven hundred pages in length.

During and after World War II, Mann wrote *Doctor Faustus*, a reworking of the Faustus myth. Influenced by Hitler's rise in Germany, it tells the story of a composer who sells his soul to the Devil.

AUTHOR'S NOTE: I used the edition cited on page 71 because it includes valuable notes, essays, and criticism. I do not read or speak German and cannot compare translations. But I will mention that there are many available versions of this book, including this more recent translation: New York: Ecco, 2004; translated by Michael Henry Heim with an introduction by Michael Cunningham; 142 pages.

Dept. of Speculation

— 2014 —

Jenny Offill

New York: Vintage Contemporaries, 2014; 177 pages

FIRST LINES

Antelopes have 10x vision, you said. It was the beginning or close to it. That means that on a clear night they can see the rings of Saturn.

It was still months before we'd tell each other all our stories. And even then some seemed too small to bother with. So why do they come back to me now? Now, when I'm so weary of all of it.

Memories are microscopic. Tiny particles that swarm together and apart. Little people, Edison called them. Entities. He had a theory about where they came from and that theory was outer space.

A young mother, also an ambitious writer, is struggling. She struggles with her baby, who is only quiet when carried through the aisles at Rite Aid. She struggles to write a second book, especially as people keep asking her where it is. And eventually, she struggles in her marriage. It is a perfect trifecta of suffering.

Highly original and deeply felt, this novella is told mostly in a series of brief observations, almost aphorisms. In one of them, the nameless narrator explains:

> The Buddhists say there are 121 states of consciousness. Of these, only three involve misery or suffering. Most of us spend our time moving back and forth between these three.

For the nameless writer-wife-mother—not necessarily in that order—who narrates, the misery and suffering alternate among these three separate identities. She had come to New York to be a writer—an "art monster" with no plans for marriage. Or motherhood. "Women almost never become art monsters because art monsters only concern themselves with art, never mundane things. Nabokov didn't even fold his own umbrella. Vera licked his stamps for him."

But life intruded. First comes love, an apartment, a book, then a baby. As we move through a succession of her sometimes wry, witty, often-poignant thought bubbles, they gather in intensity.

The mood darkens further with the revelation that the narrator-writer's marriage goes rocky. The near-gallows humor of those baby days—when the best part of yoga class is pretending to be dead for ten minutes—is about to be replaced by growing rage.

ABOUT THE AUTHOR: JENNY OFFILL

Look up "Auspicious beginnings" and you might find Jenny Offill, though she would probably disagree. But three at bats and three home runs count as a rather notable statistical average in a novelist's career. Even if it did take fifteen years after the first home run to hit the second.

Born in Massachusetts in 1968, Offill is the child of boarding school teachers. They moved around, and she was raised variously in California, Indiana, and North Carolina, where she finished high school and went to the University of North Carolina at Chapel Hill. She later studied at Stanford as a Stegner Fellow in Fiction. Then, like many aspiring writers, she spent years doing odd jobs, including waitressing, fact-checking, and ghostwriting.

Her first novel, *Last Things* (1999) while not commercially successful, was a critical success, named by the *New York Times* as one of the Notable Books of the Year. *Dept. of Speculation* followed, more than a decade later. During the gap, Offill taught writing at various colleges and universities and produced a children's book.

"There are many autobiographical things in the book," Offill told National Public Radio in a 2014 interview. "The obvious thing that people gravitate towards is whether or not I'm the wife and my husband is the husband. And the truth is really much duller: that we haven't had anything so dramatic happen to us, although, like any couple, of course, we've had our moments where things seem to wobble."

The wait for a third novel was not quite as long. In 2020, she published *Weather*, a book that uses techniques similar to *Dept. of Speculation* to address the climate crisis and nothing less than the fate of the earth.

WHY YOU SHOULD READ IT

It is a fitting accident that this novel follows Mann's. Both explore the writer's challenge—in very different styles and a century apart.

Reading Offill's unique and engaging novella, I felt I was moving through territory also explored by Elena Ferrante in *The Lost Daughter*, Doris Lessing in *The Fifth Child*, and Michael Cunningham in *The Hours* (see entries): the power, weight, and costs of motherhood. Offill probes the burden of this life, as well as the writer's struggle to create, in her peculiarly fragmented yet highly effective style.

"'Dept. of Speculation' is all the more powerful because, with its scattered insights and apparently piecemeal form, it at first appears slight," *New Yorker* critic James Wood wrote. "Its depth and intensity make a stealthy purchase on the reader."

When named one of the "Ten Best Books" of 2014 by the *New York Times*, the paper's critics said of the novel, "Part elegy and part primal scream, it's a profound and unexpectedly buoyant performance."

It works as simply as this. Chapter 22 is headed with the innocuous question "How Are You?" Then, like something from *The Shining*, the answer fills the page with these repeated words:

soscaredsoscaredsoscaredsoscaredsoscared

Motherhood, marriage, and making art are scary.

WHAT TO READ NEXT

The choices for further reading come from a short list. You can begin with Offill's first novel, *Last Things*. It is about an eight-year-old homeschooled child whose mother is an ornithologist and father is a scientist. It poses big questions about life, growing up, and the world around us.

So does her most recent novel, *Weather*. Set around the time of the 2016 presidential election, it is written in a style like that of *Dept. of Speculation* and has received wide praise.

"In both novels, Offill's fragmentary structure evokes an unbearable emotional intensity: something at the core of the story that cannot be narrated directly, by straight chronology, because to do so would be like looking at the sun," wrote Leslie Jamison in a *New York Times* review. "In 'Dept. of Speculation,' that white-hot core was the heartbreak of domestic collapse. In 'Weather,' the collapse exists on a scale at once broader and more abstract: the end of the world itself."

The Dry Heart

— 1947 —

Natalia Ginzburg

New York: New Directions, 2019; translated from the Italian by Frances
Frenaye; 88 pages; originally published in 1947 as È stato cosi *and translated*
into English as That's How It Was *in 1952*

FIRST LINES

"Tell me the truth," I said.

"What truth?" he echoed. He was making a rapid sketch in his notebook and now he showed me what it was: a long, long train with a big cloud of black smoke swirling over it and himself leaning out of a window to wave a handkerchief.

I shot him between the eyes.

PLOT SUMMARY

From its stunning opening scene, Natalia Ginzburg's compact novella—barely ninety pages long—might seem to be on its way to becoming a police procedural about the hunt for a killer. But this is no Agatha Christie whodunit. A woman has just killed her husband of four years.

She then goes out to have a coffee—it is Italy, after all.

The only mystery is "Why?"

Natalia Ginzburg provides the clues to the answer as she portrays the life of a young Italian woman, a schoolteacher living a humdrum life in a boardinghouse with few seeming prospects—"a tiresome and monotonous existence, with worn gloves and very little spending money."

Her life changes when she is introduced to Alberto, a secretive older man who lives with his sick mother—"a very rich but batty old woman who spent her time smoking cigarettes in an ivory holder and studying Sanskrit." Alberto brings the young woman French novels, takes her to the theater, plays the piano, and sketches her. A curious courtship leads to their eventual marriage. But it is not a happy marriage, even after the birth of a daughter.

Alberto often disappears for "business." He is a man with secrets.

With an extraordinary economy of language and a complete lack of pretense or melodrama, the story offers an acute character study of a woman utterly trapped in a world of her dispassionate husband's creation.

Until she finds his revolver.

ABOUT THE AUTHOR: NATALIA GINZBURG

Born in Palermo, Sicily, on July 14, 1916, Natalia Levi was the youngest of five children in a family led by Giuseppe Levi, an eccentric and larger-than-life professor of neuroanatomy. In 1919, he moved the family to Turin, a fairly prosperous center of Italian learning and industry, where he taught at the university.

Giuseppe Levi was a nonpracticing Jew and Natalia's mother, Lidia, was Catholic, but the children were raised as atheists. Natalia did not attend elementary school, as her father believed children picked up germs there, and she later dropped out of college. But she began to write, publishing a novella in a literary journal at the age of eighteen.

After Mussolini seized power in 1922, Turin emerged as a center of anti-Fascist activity and members of the Levi family were involved in opposing Mussolini's regime. Under the Italian dictator's alliance with Hitler, Italian anti-Semitism grew, leading to Italy's 1938 decree that followed Germany's Nuremberg Laws. An era of official anti-Semitism began and Jews could no longer teach. Giuseppe Levi left Turin for a position in Belgium. Two of Natalia's brothers were jailed. Thousands of Italian Jews were later deported to Auschwitz, as portrayed in Primo Levi's *If This Is a Man* (see entry).

In 1938, Natalia married Leone Ginzburg, a Jew born in Odessa, who taught literature at the University of Turin. A leader of Turin's anti-Fascist Giustizia e Libertà (Justice and Liberty), he too was dismissed from the university.

A few years later, in 1940, Leone Ginzburg's political activities resulted in his being sentenced to *confino*, or internal exile. This was the Mussolini regime's initial attempt to deal with dissidents. Natalia and their two children joined Leone in a poor, remote village in Abruzzo, where presumably he could cause no trouble. A third child was born there. In 1942, Natalia Ginzburg's first novel was published under a pseudonym, Alessandra Tornimparte, because Jews were forbidden to publish under Italian racial laws.

In 1943, Leone Ginzburg returned to Nazi-occupied Rome to supervise an underground press. On November 20, 1943, he was arrested, and he died in jail in February 1944, under torture, reportedly including crucifixion, by the Nazis.

After the war, Natalia Ginzburg worked as an editor while continuing to write and translate. Ginzburg later married literature professor Gabriele Baldini, and they had two children. Both were born handicapped: a son who died in infancy and a daughter, Susanna, who ultimately survived her. She briefly joined the Communist Party in the 1980s and was later elected to Parliament as a member of a left-wing independent party.

Natalia Ginzburg died in Rome on October 7, 1991, at age seventy-five. Her place as one of the most prominent and influential Italian writers of the twentieth century has been recently cemented with the reissue of many of her works.

WHY YOU SHOULD READ IT

Provocative yet accessible, *The Dry Heart* is easily read in a single sitting. It is remarkably understated while still dramatic. With a stunning directness, it lays bare the transformation of a woman's dull marriage into a tragedy. Assessing its author, *New York Times* book critic Michiko Kakutani wrote:

> Ms. Ginzburg never raises her voice, never strains for effect, never judges her creations. Though blessed with the rhythms and tensile strength of verse, her language is economical and spare, subordinate to the demands of the story. Like Chekhov, she knows how to stand back and let her characters expose their own lives, their frailties and strengths, their illusions and private griefs.

Family, betrayal, intimacy, and desire are at the heart of Ginzburg's work. But it is not a polemic or an academic exercise. She tells a seemingly simple story that grows more complex and tragic as it unfolds.

In reading it, I was struck by the similarities to the work of Elena Ferrante (see entry). Both writers plumb desire, emotional despair, and dissatisfaction of unhappy marriage. Both explore motherhood and loss.

In *The Dry Heart*, written in 1947, long before the feminist movement flourished and writers such as Betty Friedan explored the "Feminine Mystique," Natalia Ginzburg seized upon the bitterness of an unfulfilled woman. She writes of the tragic loneliness of a woman who says:

> Everything that mattered had happened already, for everything that mattered was Alberto at the moment when I shot him and he fell heavily across the table and I closed my eyes and ran out of the room.

WHAT TO READ NEXT

Widely considered Natalia Ginzburg's masterpiece, *Family Lexicon* is also relatively short, but very different in style and tone from *The Dry Heart*. Winner of the prestigious Italian Strega Prize in 1963, *Family Lexicon* is a frequently comic accounting of Ginzburg's childhood and later life in a remarkable family, coming of age in Mussolini's Italy. While ostensibly a work of fiction, "The places, events, and people in this book are real," Ginzburg wrote in her preface. "I haven't invented a thing."

A collection of essays, *The Little Virtues*, is also worth putting on the To-Be-Read list. It includes "Winter in the Abruzzi," her brief but remarkably vivid account of life as a young mother in *confino*.

Ethan Frome

— 1911 —

Edith Wharton

New York: Penguin Books, 2005; with an introduction and notes by Elizabeth Ammons; 99 pages

FIRST LINES

I had the story, bit by bit, from various people, and, as generally happens in such cases, each time it was a different story.

If you know Starkfield, Massachusetts, you know the post-office. If you know the post-office you must have seen Ethan Frome drive up to it, drop the reins on his hollow-backed bay and drag himself across the brick pavement, to the white colonnade; and you must have asked who he was.

In all likelihood—if you had an American education—you were assigned at some point to read *Ethan Frome*. If you did, read it again. If you didn't, read it now. It is a great short book.

Set in a bleak, wintry Massachusetts village, appropriately named Starkfield, Wharton's compact novella tells a simple, and yes, stark, story about a character who is a "ruin of a man." Wharton explores the cause of that ruin.

Living on his hardscrabble family farm, barely making ends meet, Ethan Frome is descended from people who have worked this hard land for centuries. He lives in "one of those lonely New England farm-houses that make the landscape lonelier."

The farmhouse is visited by the narrator, who arrives in a raging snowstorm, and the story emerges. Ethan Frome is married to Zenobia, a joyless hypochondriac with a constant variety of ills. A suspicious and scornful woman, Zeena seeks a variety of cures that have further reduced Frome's meager fortune.

Enter Mattie, the orphaned daughter of one of Zeena's relatives. The young woman was hired to serve as the couple's live-in housekeeper, but Mattie is never able to please Mrs. Frome. In these close confines, Ethan falls in love with the vivacious Mattie. Obsessed with the young girl, he goes so far as to plot leaving his wife and heading west with Mattie. As events will prove, it is an ill-fated, disastrous dream.

ABOUT THE AUTHOR: EDITH WHARTON

The author who became the first woman to win the Pulitzer Prize for Fiction, Edith Newbold Jones was born on January 24, 1862, into New York's rarefied Knickerbocker society. That upper-crust world of "old money" provided the backdrop for much of her best-known work chronicling America's Gilded Age. But Wharton spent a considerable part of her life abroad.

In 1866, her family moved to Europe, where they lived for the next six years. Upon returning to New York in 1872, Edith was tutored by a governess, read from her father's extensive library, and later secretly wrote a short novel, which went unpublished. Her first published work was a selection of her poems, printed by her mother, one of which later appeared in the *Atlantic Monthly*. "In the eyes of our provincial society," Edith later said, "authorship was still regarded as something between a black art and a form of manual labor."

Making her "social debut" in a Fifth Avenue ballroom preceded the family's return to France in 1881. When her father died in 1882 Edith inherited a considerable sum of money, and she returned in 1883 to the United States. She then met Edward (Teddy) Wharton, a friend of her brother and Boston socialite in Bar Harbor, Maine. Edith married him, at age twenty-three, in 1885. Edith Wharton continued to write and a story, "Mrs. Manstey's View," was accepted for publication in 1890.

Despite the advantages of wealth and society, Edith Wharton suffered personal difficulties that began to grow. Teddy Wharton would prove unfaithful and mentally unbalanced, and their marriage was troubled. Battling depression, she traveled to Italy in 1894 and still managed to write a design guide, *The Decoration of Houses*, with architect Ogden Codman in 1897. After a nervous collapse, Wharton was treated with the "rest-cure."

And still she wrote. A short story collection, *The Greater Inclination* (1899), a novella, *The Touchstone* (1900), and her first full novel, *The Valley of Decision* (1902), appeared in quick succession. In 1902, she moved into The Mount, a home she helped design and had built in Lenox, in the Berkshires region of Massachusetts, the setting for *Ethan Frome*. There she began work on *The House of Mirth*, published in 1905 to critical and popular success.

With Teddy's mental state in serious decline, she returned to Europe and began a three-year affair with Morton Fullerton, a *Times* of London correspondent she had met in 1907 through their mutual friend, Henry James. Around this time, Edith Wharton learned that Teddy had embezzled fifty thousand dollars of her money. Selling her New York apartment, she made France her permanent home and worked toward an eventual divorce in 1913.

In 1911, *Ethan Frome* had been published to admiring reviews. But the world stage was about to be transformed, as World War I broke out in July 1914. In France, Wharton began an ambitious fundraising campaign in support of war refugees, unemployed women, and homeless children. She delivered supplies to the front lines in 1915 and organized a committee to rescue children victimized by the war. For her wartime philanthropy, Wharton was later made a Chevalier of France's Legion of Honor.

In 1920 *The Age of Innocence* appeared, and it won the 1921 Pulitzer Prize, a first for a woman. Wharton's later writing included an autobiography, *A Backward Glance*, and *The Old Maid*, a novella initially rejected by publishers because it dealt with the taboo subject of illegitimate birth. It was later dramatized by playwright and poet Zoë Akins in an adaptation that won the 1935 Pulitzer Prize for Drama.

There was an unsuccessful effort to lobby for a Nobel Prize for Wharton, whose later work paled beside her greatest novels. She would return to the United States only twice—once for an honorary Doctor of Letters from Yale, another first for a woman. In 1937, living at her home in France, she wrote a final short story, "All Souls," before suffering a stroke in June of that year. She died on August 11, 1937, aged seventy-five, and is buried in Versailles.

WHY YOU SHOULD READ IT

When *Ethan Frome* was published in 1911, the *New York Times* called it a "cruel, compelling haunting story." The rest of the notice did not suggest that it would eventually become a staple of American litera-ture. But it surely has. As in several of Wharton's novels, *Ethan Frome* depicts characters trapped in inescapable circumstances, including bad marriages, not unlike Wharton herself.

Read it first for the beauty of the writing, what Harold Bloom described as "sublime eloquence." In prose that is as spare and cold as its New England setting, yet still remarkably sensual, *Ethan Frome* grapples with the seeming impossibility of love. In one scene between Ethan and Mattie, when there still seems a glimmer of hope, Whar-ton writes:

> They had never before avowed their inclination so openly, and Ethan, for a moment, had the illusion that he was a free man, woo-ing the girl he meant to marry. He looked at her hair and longed to touch it again, and to tell her that it smelt of the woods; but he had never learned to say such things.

WHAT TO READ NEXT

Two other short novels by Wharton, *Summer* and *Bunner Sisters*, are often bound with *Ethan Frome*. Though less renowned than *Ethan Frome*, both show Wharton's elegant prose and artistic concerns. Wharton also wrote a great many short stories that are available in collections.

Of course, her two towering works are: *The House of Mirth*, the story of penniless orphan Lily Bart seeking a marriage that will bring her into New York society; and *The Age of Innocence*, the account of an upper-class couple's planned marriage, upset by the arrival of Count-ess Ellen Olenska, the bride's scandal-plagued cousin, and set in the gilded world of Fifth Avenue mansions and Newport "cottages" in which Wharton was raised. The eminent critic Harold Bloom singles out *The Custom of the Country* (1913), the story of Undine Spragg, another woman looking to climb in New York society, as Wharton's best.

Wharton's most famous novels have been brought to screen. Liam Neeson starred in *Ethan Frome* (1993). Martin Scorsese directed *The Age of Innocence* (1993) with Daniel Day-Lewis, Michelle Pfeiffer, and Winona Ryder in the central roles. And a film version of *House of Mirth* (2000) featured Gillian Anderson as Lily Bart.

Evil Under the Sun

— 1941 —

Agatha Christie

New York: William Morrow, 2011; 255 pages

FIRST LINES

When Captain Roger Angmering built himself a house in the year 1782 on the island off Leathercombe Bay, it was thought the height of eccentricity on his part. A man of good family such as he was should have had a decorous mansion set in wide meadows with, perhaps, a running stream and good pasture.

But Captain Roger Angmering had only one great love, the sea. So he built his house—a sturdy house, too, as it needed to be, on the little windswept gull-haunted promontory—cut off from land at each high tide.

PLOT SUMMARY

You were warned about "Dangerous Beach Holidays." Here's another deadly example, opening with the discovery of the corpse of a beautiful woman on a small British island. In Agatha Christie's well-worn fashion, the "Queen of Mystery" throws together a collection of likely suspects, bumps off one of them, and then sets her detective loose.

In this case, the characters include a group of well-to-do vacationers, most British except for a typical—a little loud, a little uncouth—American couple. Safe from the threat of tour buses, they are on holiday on a picturesque island off the coast of England at "an awfully jolly hotel." In their midst stands the famed Belgian detective, Hercule Poirot. When first seen, Christie's hero is "resplendent in a white duck suit, with a panama hat tilted over his eyes, his moustaches magnificently befurled."

After considerable buildup introducing these characters, their quirks, animosities, and, more significantly for some, desires, one of them is found dead on an isolated beach. It lands to Poirot, in his inimitable style, to piece together the puzzle.

ABOUT THE AUTHOR: AGATHA CHRISTIE

What McDonald's is to burgers, Agatha Christie is to books. She sells billions. Agatha Christie stands behind only the Bible and Shakespeare in the history of international book sales. She has sold 2 billion books, half in English and the other half in various translations. The Queen of Mystery officially became a Dame of the British Empire in 1971. Her most famous play, *The Mousetrap*, opened in 1952 and was the longest-running play in history until it closed in March 2020, a victim of the coronavirus lockdown.

Born in Devon, England, on September 15, 1890, Agatha Mary Clarissa Miller was the youngest of three children in a fairly prosperous family. A voracious reader as a child, she was mostly homeschooled.

After her father's death in 1901, Agatha briefly attended a girls' school and was later sent to a boarding school in Paris.

In 1913, she met Archie Christie, a barrister and army officer. Shortly after World War I broke out they married, and during the war Agatha went on to serve as a volunteer nurse and later as an apothecary assistant. During this time, she wrote her first detective novel, *The Mysterious Affair at Styles*. Introducing Hercule Poirot, who had escaped war-torn Belgium for England, it was published in 1920. The rest, as they say, is history.

In all, Agatha Christie wrote more than sixty detective novels, many featuring Poirot or the amateur detective Miss Jane Marple—another much-beloved character.

Perhaps the most tantalizing piece of Agatha Christie's biography is a mystery itself. In 1926, she disappeared. On the night of December 4, carrying only an attaché case, she kissed her daughter good night, drove off, and disappeared. Christie's car was later found abandoned, setting off a nationwide manhunt. By then Christie was a celebrity, and her status as missing person made international headlines.

Nine days after vanishing, Christie was found at a spa, staying under an assumed name and, according to her husband, suffering from a complete loss of memory. It was later revealed that the name she had registered under was that of a woman with whom Archie Christie was having an affair. The Christies divorced not long after this episode.

Although decried by some as a publicity stunt for a new book, Christie's disappearance remained unsolved. "Over 90 years later, biographers and historians are still debating what happened during those days in 1926," Tina Jordan wrote in the *New York Times* in 2019. "Was it revenge, depression or amnesia? Recent biographies . . . shed little light on the episode."

Two years after her divorce, Christie married archeologist Max Mallowan, whom she had met after taking the Orient Express—the setting of one of her most well-known works—to Istanbul and Baghdad.

Arguably her most famous character, Hercule Poirot has a unique distinction. He is the only fictional character to receive a front-page *New York Times* obituary, following his demise in 1975:

> Hercule Poirot, a Belgian detective who became internationally famous, has died in England. His age was unknown. . . . Mr. Poirot, who was just 5 feet 4 inches tall, went to England from Belgium during World War I as a refugee. He settled in a little town not far from Styles, then an elaborate country estate, where he took on his first private case. The news of his death, given by Dame Agatha, was not unexpected. Word that he was near death reached here last May.

Agatha Christie died in 1976 at the age of eighty-five. Yes, from natural causes.

WHY YOU SHOULD READ IT

Not for any probing psychological insights. Not for any profound illumination of the human condition. Not for delving into the enigmas of relationships. Agatha Christie rarely covers these grounds. Nor can she be called a proto-feminist. And certainly not even for a glimpse of history: Published in England's darkest days of World War II, this book offers no hint that London has recently been blitzed and the nation's fate hung in the balance.

You basically read Agatha Christie for the fun of it. It is the literary equivalent of popcorn. Or a trifle—the classic British dessert of sponge cake soaked in rum and topped with jam and cream. You know what you are going to get. It is very pleasing. And it is hard to stop.

In an appreciation of Christie in the *New York Times* in 2020, Tina Jordan commented:

They're comfort books. . . . Yes, they can be dated and fusty. But there's something soothing about the familiar formula. You know there will be at least one murder and quite possibly more. The odds are good that the murder will occur in a bucolic village or someone's country house or on a vacation. And the case will be probably cracked by one of Christie's main detectives, either the portly, mustache-twirling Belgian, Hercule Poirot, or the spinster Jane Marple, who conceals a razor-sharp brain behind a white puff of hair, innocent blue eyes and a pile of knitting.

And from time to time, who doesn't need a comfort book?

WHAT TO READ NEXT

There is obviously plenty to choose from. I selected *Evil Under the Sun* because I wanted a Christie and I wanted a Poirot. But I wanted one I had not read—or previously seen. That eliminated several of the other notable Poirots, starting with the very first, *The Mysterious Affair at Styles*, then *Death on the Nile* and *Murder on the Orient Express*, among many others. All are worth reading.

Another must from the Christie canon is *And Then There Were None* (1939). Renamed because the original title was racist, even more offensive than the later paperback U.S. edition published as *Ten Little Indians*, this is her biggest seller. Also set on a small island off the coast, it commences as eight strangers who have been invited to a house party arrive to find their mysterious hosts absent. Each guest is accused of a terrible crime. Then someone starts to eliminate them, one by one.

Think *Saw* with sherry and biscuits. Or trifle.

The Fifth Child

— 1988 —

Doris Lessing

New York: Vintage International, 1989; 133 pages

FIRST LINES

Harriet and David met each other at an office party neither had particularly wanted to go to, and both knew at once that this was what they had been waiting for. Someone conservative, old-fashioned, not to say obsolescent; timid, hard to please: this is what other people called them, but there was no end to the unaffectionate adjectives they earned. They defended a stubbornly held view of themselves, which was that they were ordinary and in the right of it, should not be criticised for emotional fastidiousness, abstemiousness, just because these were unfashionable qualities.

When Harriet met David.

It was at an office party that they struck a perfect match. Sharing a decidedly conservative outlook, rare in "swinging" 1960s London, they plan to marry and agree to have "six children, at least," or eight or ten. David, an architect, and Harriet, a sales associate, purchase a large Victorian house with an overgrown garden outside London and waste no time: "Harriet indeed became pregnant on that rainy evening in their bedroom."

Soon, the expansive house has become a joyous gathering place for relatives and friends to visit the couple and their growing family:

> That Christmas, Harriet was again enormous, in her eighth month, and she laughed at herself for her size and unwieldiness. The house was full. All the people who were here for Easter came again. It was acknowledged that Harriet and David had a gift for this kind of thing.

But life will take a sharp, disturbing turn. After eight years of marriage and four children, another child is conceived. A painful pregnancy leads to the birth of a son, Ben. The fifth child's arrival marks the onset of misery. Monstrous in appearance, insatiably hungry, and unnaturally strong, Ben shatters the family idyll that Harriet and David had seemingly created, leaving Harriet with an awful choice.

ABOUT THE AUTHOR: DORIS LESSING

Doris May Tayler was born on October 22, 1919, to British parents in Kermanshah, Persia (now Iran), where her father, Alfred Tayler, was a bank official. Alfred had lost a leg in World War I and Doris's mother, Emily, was the nurse who cared for him. When Doris was five, her father uprooted the family from Persia, acquiring a large property in Southern Rhodesia (now Zimbabwe) on a whim, Doris later said, with dreams of becoming a wealthy farmer.

Those dreams were dashed and Lessing's Rhodesian childhood was troubled. After attending convent schools, she dropped out at age thirteen and was subsequently self-educated, becoming an avid reader. At odds with her mother, Doris left home in her teens, working as a nursemaid and later a telephone operator.

At nineteen, she married Frank Wisdom, a civil servant, and they had two children before divorcing in 1943. Doris left the children with their father and became involved with left-wing politics, marrying Gottfried Lessing, a Communist Party leader, in 1943. They had one son, Peter.

Disillusioned with party politics—and having an affair—Doris Lessing divorced her second husband in 1949 and moved to London. Bringing her son Peter, she left behind her first two children with their father.

"For a long time I felt I had done a very brave thing," Lessing later recounted. "There is nothing more boring for an intelligent woman than to spend endless amounts of time with small children. I felt I wasn't the best person to bring them up. I would have ended up an alcoholic or a frustrated intellectual like my mother."

In London, her writing career got underway. She published her first novel, *The Grass Is Singing*, in 1950, recounting the relationship between a white farmer's wife and a Black servant on a farm in South Africa. It was the first of five books known as the Martha Quest or Children of Violence series. Autobiographical works, they explored the clash of cultures and racial injustice Lessing witnessed in Rhodesia. They also led to her being declared a "prohibited alien" in both Rhodesia and South Africa.

Leaving behind social concerns and leftist politics for radical psychology, Lessing took a sharp turn with the publication of *The Golden Notebook* (1962). Featuring strong, independent women characters including writer Anna Wulf, *The Golden Notebook* became a feminist landmark in the 1970s. Novelist Margaret Atwood (see entry) remembered the book's impact and the times:

> It was before widespread birth control. It was before mini-skirts. So Anna Wulf was a considerable eye-opener: she was doing things and thinking things that had not been much discussed at the Toronto dinner tables of our adolescence, and therefore seemed pretty daring.

Following Lessing's introduction to Sufism, a mystical offshoot of Islam, her writing took another sharp turn. She produced a series of five novels she termed "space fiction." Collectively called *Canopus in Argos: Archives,* the series commenced with *Shikasta* (1979). Many reviewers found it hard to swallow and dismissed the work. Lessing's legions of admirers were also dismayed at this new direction.

But Doris Lessing was largely indifferent to critics. She marched to the beat of her own drum, eventually submitting two novels under a pseudonym in an experiment to see how difficult it was to be published. They were rejected, although both novels were later published.

In the late 1990s Lessing suffered a stroke and she no longer traveled. And then, in 2007, came news that she had been awarded the Nobel Prize in Literature. At eighty-nine, the oldest person to receive the prize to date, Doris Lessing was, according to the Nobel Committee, "that epicist [a writer of epic poetry and fiction] of the female experience, who with scepticism, fire and visionary power has subjected a divided civilisation to scrutiny." Her own reaction at the time was to say, "Oh, Christ! I couldn't care less."

Outspoken, opinionated, difficult to pigeonhole, and often uninhibited, Doris Lessing died in London in November 2013, aged ninety-four.

WHY YOU SHOULD READ IT

"It's an absolutely horrible book," Doris Lessing told a *New York Times* interviewer. "And, it has a very strong effect on people."

I disagree with the author that *The Fifth Child* is horrible. But it is horrifying. Lessing was admirably forthright about the novel's effect. *The Fifth Child* is jarring, weighty, and provocative. I recommended it to a friend—a mother with a young child—with a cautionary note. It is a deeply disturbing piece of fiction that taps into a parent's worst fear. As Emily Harnett wrote in a recent assessment, it is "a gutting examination of the crucible of motherhood."

One need not know of Lessing's unhappy relationship with her own mother and then leaving behind her first two children to be absorbed by Lessing's narrative force. Other books that deal vividly with the theme of motherhood in this collection are *The Dry Heart, Dept. of Speculation, The Hours, The Lost Daughter,* and *Lucy.*

As Lessing moves from a fairly tidy domestic drama into the territory of a psychological thriller, the writing is enthralling. But if Agatha Christie offers a "comfort book," this is a "discomfort book." It builds toward Harriet's crucial moment of decision, and the novel's scope is broader than examining a family affair. Through Harriet, Lessing is looking at a changing society and wondering where the world is going. Like Mary Shelley's Frankenstein monster, the child Ben takes the reader into dark territory.

WHAT TO READ NEXT

Lessing continued this foreboding, somewhat twisted family narrative with a sequel, *Ben, in the World* (2000), which begins with Ben as an eighteen-year-old (and which I look forward to reading). When it was published, reviewer Michael Pye wrote:

> At times, Lessing's spare, sharp prose lets you see things as Ben sees them, as you have not seen things before. The book shares that uncanny effect with the best fiction.

Lessing's early works, the Martha Quest novels, are still considered among her best work.

But her most famous and most popular novel remains *The Golden Notebook*. Daring when first published in 1962, it attracted not just readers but devoted followers. Loosely autobiographical, it explores the inner lives of women who, unencumbered by marriage, are free to choose the work and sexual lives they desire.

The Ghost Writer

— 1979 —

Philip Roth

New York: Vintage International, 1995; 180 pages

FIRST LINES

It was the last daylight hour of a December afternoon more than twenty years ago—I was twenty-three, writing and publishing my first short stories, and like many a *Bildungsroman* hero before me, already contemplating my own massive *Bildungsroman*—when I arrived at his hideaway to meet the great man.

PLOT SUMMARY

A budding writer. A literary giant. And a mysterious young woman. These are the components in the first of Philip Roth's books featuring Nathan Zuckerman. Literary alter ego of one of the most prominent and prolific writers in modern American letters, Zuckerman eventually appeared in nine Roth novels.

An ambitious writer embarking on his career—like Roth, Jewish and from Newark, New Jersey—Nathan has come to visit his idol, E. I. Lonoff. Making his pilgrimage to the reclusive writer's Berkshires home on a snowy evening, Zuckerman is like a supplicant approaching a high priest.

And Nathan is worshipful. He exclaims, "I loved him! Yes, nothing less than love for this man with no illusions: love for the bluntness, the scrupulosity, the severity, the estrangement; love for the relentless winnowing out of the babyish, preening, insatiable self; love for the artistic mulishness and the suspicion of nearly everything else; and love for the buried charm, of which he'd just given me a glimpse."

As he seeks insight into the great man's secrets—and perhaps his blessing—Zuckerman meets another houseguest. Alluring, mysterious, with an indeterminate European accent, Amy Bellette is a former student, now organizing Lonoff's papers. Entranced, Zuckerman muses about Amy's relationship with the elderly writer. Are they lovers? What about Hope, Lonoff's long-suffering wife? And just who is Amy? After a hilarious eavesdropping scene, Zuckerman has a stunning insight into this captivating woman's secret. Revealing her identity would count as a Major Spoiler.

Set against Zuckerman's admiration of Lonoff and lust for Amy is the young writer's crisis: he has written a story that his family does not want him to publish. Doing so will put Jews in a bad light. Defiant, Zuckerman asks, "Hadn't Joyce, hadn't Flaubert, hadn't Thomas Wolfe, the romantic genius of my high-school reading list, all been condemned for disloyalty or treachery or immorality by those who saw themselves as slandered in their works?"

Will he conquer Amy? Will he publish his story? Will Lonoff like it?

ABOUT THE AUTHOR: PHILIP ROTH

"In the course of a very long career, Mr. Roth took on many guises," wrote Charles McGrath in the novelist's 2018 *New York Times* obituary, "mainly versions of himself—in the exploration of what it means to be an American, a Jew, a writer, a man."

Philip Roth was born on March 19, 1933, in Newark, New Jersey, the son of Bess and Herman Roth, an insurance salesman who thought his being a Jew kept him from rising in a world of WASPs. After high school, Roth went to Bucknell University, graduating magna cum laude. On a scholarship, he attended the University of Chicago, where he received his M.A. In 1955, he enlisted in the army, a stint cut short by a back injury.

Roth married Margaret Martinson Williams in 1959. It was a stormy relationship and the marriage ended in separation and divorce. "When Roth learned, in 1968, that his ex-wife had been killed in a car crash," wrote the *New Yorker*'s David Remnick, "his grief was less than crippling."

After he published some short stories, Roth's grand entrance came with *Goodbye, Columbus* (1960), a novella that depicted the materialism of a wealthy Jewish suburban family. Published along with four stories, it earned the twenty-six-year-old Roth the first of two National Book Awards, as well as a torrent of complaints from the Jewish community accusing Roth of cultural treason.

Two novels, *Letting Go* (1962) and *When She Was Good* (1967), based in part on his unhappy marriage to Williams, followed the success of *Goodbye, Columbus* but failed to reach the same levels of acclaim.

Then came Portnoy. Roth reached new heights of success with *Portnoy's Complaint* (1969), sections of which had earlier appeared in *Esquire* and other magazines. A comic monologue, its portrayal of a young Jewish man obsessed with sex was "filthy and hilarious," noted Charles McGrath, and "surely set a record for most masturbation scenes per page." The book, says David Remnick, "made him wealthy, celebrated, and notorious."

A cultural landmark in its time, *Portnoy's Complaint* was followed by *The Breast* (1972), *My Life as a Man* (1974), and *The Professor of Desire* (1977). During this time, Roth began living part of the year in London with the actress Claire Bloom. They married in 1990 but divorced four years later. In a memoir, Bloom depicted Roth as a misogynist and control freak who didn't allow her daughter from an earlier marriage to live with them.

Introduced in *The Ghost Writer* in 1979, Nathan Zuckerman appeared in two successive novels, *Zuckerman Unbound* (1981) and *The Anatomy Lesson* (1983), and Roth regained his stride. All three books were published together with a short novella, *The Prague Orgy*, as *Zuckerman Bound* in 1985. In 1995, *Sabbath's Theater*, about a lecherous former puppeteer, won Roth his second National Book Award. *American Pastoral* (1997) followed and received the Pulitzer Prize, the first of three books narrated by Zuckerman; the others were *I Married a Communist* (1998) and *The Human Stain* (2000).

In *The Plot Against America* (2004), Roth presented an alternative American history in which Charles Lindbergh, the heroic aviator turned disgraced Nazi admirer, is elected president. Defeating Franklin D. Roosevelt in 1940, Lindbergh leads America into an alliance with the Nazis and an eventual pogrom of Jewish Americans. (It was made into an HBO miniseries in 2020.) Continuing to work into the early 2000s, Roth produced several more novels, including *Everyman*, a 2006 meditation on aging that won the PEN/Faulkner Award, and *Exit Ghost* (2007), the final Zuckerman novel. In 2012, he announced he would retire from writing fiction.

Philip Roth died in Manhattan in May 2018, aged eighty-five.

WHY YOU SHOULD READ IT

It is great storytelling. It builds to a wonderful reveal. It is funny. And it is a richly realized work about the collision between literature and life. In this novel, David Remnick wrote in 2021, "Roth regained his footing. Zuckerman, Roth's most Roth-like surrogate, was a perfectly pitched instrument."

At the conclusion of the extraordinary scene in which Nathan is desperately trying to eavesdrop on Lonoff and Amy, Zuckerman proclaims:

—Oh, if only I could have imagined the scene I'd overheard! If only I could invent as presumptuously as real life! If one day I could just *approach* the originality and excitement of what actually goes on!

But, of course, Roth is just toying with us. That is exactly what he has done.

WHAT TO READ NEXT

Where to begin? In 2021, the *New York Times* offered its roundup of what to read in "The Essential Philip Roth."

Here's mine. Start at the beginning with *Goodbye, Columbus* (1960), a novella published with four short stories that trumpeted Roth's arrival when it won the National Book Award.

The immediate sequels to *The Ghost Writer* continue Zuckerman's story in *Zuckerman Unbound* (1981) and *The Anatomy Lesson* (1983).

Of the more recent Zuckerman novels, *The Human Stain* has acquired new relevance as it is the story of a distinguished professor who is forced to resign after being accused of sexual harassment and racism. The late Harold Bloom marked *Sabbath's Theater*, also a National Book Award winner, Roth's best work, calling the novel "a tragicomedy, and its Shakespearean reverberations are legitimate and persuasive."

But the first Roth I ever read remains a must: *Portnoy's Complaint* was a cultural marker in the early 1970s, one of those best sellers that everyone was talking about. It stands at number 52 on the Modern Library list of 100 Best Novels. As a *New York Times* reviewer put it at the time it was published, the novel is "a deliciously funny book, absurd and exuberant, wild and uproarious."

Like its author, it is all those things.

The Great Gatsby

— 1925 —

F. Scott Fitzgerald

New York: Scribner, 2018; 180 pages

* Number 2 on the Modern Library list of 100 Best Novels *

FIRST LINES

In my younger and more vulnerable years my father gave me some advice that I've been turning over in my mind ever since.

"Whenever you feel like criticizing anyone," he told me, "just remember that all the people in this world haven't had the advantages that you've had."

PLOT SUMMARY

The plot is simple. Boy meets girl. Boy loses girl. Boy finds girl again.

Set on Long Island and in New York City in 1922—as the twenties begin to "roar"—*The Great Gatsby* is a love story at heart. It recounts the obsessive love of the mysterious and mysteriously rich Jay Gatsby for Daisy Buchanan, the wife of the also very rich Tom Buchanan. Gatsby and Daisy had met five years earlier when Gatsby was a young officer preparing to head for the trenches of World War I. In the intervening years, Daisy had married Tom, who is having a not-very-secret affair with the wife of a local car mechanic.

Against scenes of lavish parties on Gatsby's sprawling estate, where Prohibition has little impact on the flow of alcohol, the guests wonder where the shadowy Gatsby made his money. This Jazz Age drama is seen through the eyes of Nick Carraway, a Yale grad, World War I veteran, and novice bond trader. Gatsby's next-door neighbor and Daisy's distant cousin, Nick becomes the go-between and not-disinterested narrator of this tale.

It is a three-act tragedy that underscores something Fitzgerald wrote in a later story: "Let me tell you about the very rich. They are different from you and me."

ABOUT THE AUTHOR: F. SCOTT FITZGERALD

Born into a middle-class family in St. Paul, Minnesota, on September 24, 1896, he was named Francis Scott Fitzgerald after a distant ancestor, Francis Scott Key, author of "The Star-Spangled Banner." Known as Scott, Fitzgerald attended prep schools before heading to Princeton. There he befriended future literary critic Edmund Wilson and fell in love with a beautiful socialite named Ginevra King—something of a model for Daisy. On academic probation, he dropped out and joined the army after the United States declared war on Germany in April 1917.

Stationed in Alabama, Scott met and fell in love with Zelda Sayre, the debutante daughter of a wealthy family in Montgomery. With ambitions to write, but dim prospects after the war, Fitzgerald wrote ad copy for laundry detergent and sold a few short stories. That was not a formula for winning Zelda.

Returning to Minnesota, he wrote his first novel, *This Side of Paradise* (1920), a thinly veiled autobiographical story about a Princeton man. Championed by the legendary editor Maxwell Perkins, it was an immediate success and gave Fitzgerald entrée into literary circles and better rates for his short stories. Its publication was also the hurdle he had to leap to marry Zelda. In 1921, their only child, a daughter named Frances Scott (called Scottie), was born.

Fitzgerald followed with another popular hit, *The Beautiful and Damned* (1922), exploring New York's café society in the 1920s. Success turned Scott and Zelda Fitzgerald, who began to publish her own short stories and articles, into Jazz Age celebrities, whose hard-drinking and stormy relationship became the stuff of gossip columns.

But their bright-burning star soon dimmed. Having completed *The Great Gatsby* while on the French Riviera, Fitzgerald received good reviews but surprisingly disappointing sales when the novel appeared in 1925. Soon after, Scott and Zelda moved to Paris, where he and Ernest Hemingway became friends and joined the "Lost Generation"—the expatriate artists and writers flocking to Paris and Gertrude Stein's famous salon.

Returning to America in 1926, Fitzgerald headed deeper into alcoholism while Zelda, who had taken an overdose of sleeping pills in France, became more erratic with growing signs of mental illness. Obsessed with ballet, she sometimes practiced eight hours daily, according to biographer Nancy Milford. Though Zelda was invited to join an Italian opera ballet company, mental and physical exhaustion led to her eventual admission to a French sanatorium in 1930.

With his drinking interfering with his work, and struggling financially, Fitzgerald needed ten years to complete his next novel, *Tender Is the Night* (1934). The story of a psychiatrist who marries one of his patients, it was also a commercial disappointment.

By this time, Fitzgerald was deep in debt and an alcoholic, while Zelda was in and out of clinics. During one stay, she had written *Save Me the Waltz* (1932), a thinly disguised portrayal of the couple's relationship. The effort added friction to their marriage and proved a critical and commercial failure. Looking to earn more money, Scott moved to Hollywood in 1937 to work as a studio scriptwriter, while Zelda continued to be intermittently hospitalized.

"Whenever he was drunk," Arthur Mizener, a biographer, later wrote, "he would insist on telling people who he was and pressing them to recognize him—'I'm F. Scott Fitzgerald. You've read my books. You've read "The Great Gatsby," haven't you? Remember?'"

A 1939 trip to Cuba with Zelda was the last time they were together. After a long struggle with alcoholism, F. Scott Fitzgerald died of a heart attack in Hollywood in December 1940, at the age of forty-four. His *New York Times* obituary read, in part:

> Roughly, his own career began and ended with the Nineteen Twenties. "This Side of Paradise," his first book, was published in the first year of that decade of skyscrapers and short skirts. Only six others came between it and his last. . . . The promise of his brilliant career was never fulfilled.

An unfinished novel based on his Hollywood experience was completed from his notes by longtime friend Edmund Wilson and published after his death as *The Last Tycoon* (1941).

Zelda, in the meantime, had again been in and out of institutions. In 1948 while she was awaiting electroshock therapy in a North Carolina hospital, a fire broke out. Zelda Fitzgerald was one of nine women who died in the disaster.

By then, the couple who had epitomized Jazz Age high living had been largely forgotten. *The Great Gatsby* was dismissed as "a period piece that had almost entirely disappeared."

But then came a stroke of good fortune. During World War II, the book was issued as part of the Armed Services Editions, a publishing industry program that provided American GIs with free paperbound books shipped overseas. Selected from publisher submissions, the titles were chosen by a committee. Hundreds of thousands of copies of these stapled, digest-sized editions were distributed, helping create a postwar surge in Fitzgerald's—and Gatsby's—literary fortunes.

WHY YOU SHOULD READ IT

Okay. What's so great about *Gatsby*?

Honestly, when I set out on this project, the choice of Fitzgerald—and specifically *The Great Gatsby*—for my list of great short books was up in the air.

Everyone has read it already. Right? Or seen one of four Hollywood treatments. Was it dated? A bit clichéd?

And then came news late in 2020 that *The Great Gatsby* was going out of copyright and entering the public domain. That milestone occasioned conversation about the book's place in American letters. As Parul Sehgal of the *New York Times* framed it:

> With "The Great Gatsby," the question is simpler and stranger: Can Fitzgerald write? Is the book a masterpiece—what T. S. Eliot called "the first step that American fiction has taken since Henry James"— or, as Gore Vidal put it, as Gore Vidal would, the work of a writer who was "barely literate"?

I am now firmly in the camp that considers it a great short book, full of lyrical prose and memorable characters. It is a signature touchstone in American popular culture, especially evocative of the extraordinary decade between the end of World War I and the Great Depression. Evidence of that comes from a planned musical version, with lyrics and music composed by Florence Welch of Florence + the Machine fame. But it is more.

"This is a book that endures, generation after generation," wrote novelist Jesmyn Ward, "because every time a reader returns to *The Great Gatsby*, we discover new revelations, new insights, new burning bits of language. Read and bear witness to the story's permanence, its robust heart. Read and bear witness to Jay Gatsby, who burned bright and bold and doomed as his creator. Read."

I agree that the writing is often seamlessly brilliant. And, as a fable of striving, obsessive love, and the perils associated with excess, its moral holds true. It is timeless and timely. Consider this passage, much quoted in recent years:

> They were careless people, Tom and Daisy—they smashed up things and creatures and then retreated back into their money or their vast carelessness, or whatever it was that kept them together, and let other people clean up the mess they had made.

WHAT TO READ NEXT

Among Fitzgerald's other completed novels, good choices are *This Side of Paradise*, about a handsome, spoiled young man at Princeton University; and *The Beautiful and Damned*, about another handsome young man and his beautiful wife who party self-destructively through the Jazz Age. Finally, many critics consider Fitzgerald's short stories among his best work. *All the Sad Young Men* (1926) collected many of his finest pieces. A story set after the Stock Market Crash of 1929, "Babylon Revisited" is also considered among his most memorable short works.

The Hour of the Star

— 1977 —

Clarice Lispector

New York: New Directions, 2011; translated from the Portuguese by Benjamin Moser with an introduction by Colm Tóibín; 77 pages; originally published as A hora da estrela *in 1977*

FIRST LINES

All the world began with a yes. One molecule said yes to another molecule and life was born. But before prehistory there was the prehistory of prehistory and there was the never and there was the yes. It was ever so. I don't know why, but I do know that the universe never began.

Make no mistake, I only achieve simplicity with enormous effort.

PLOT SUMMARY

This novella opens like the Prelude to the Gospel of John rendered by Samuel Beckett or James Joyce. Get the picture? This is tricky.

It is also one of the most dazzling and intriguing works included here.

A simple plot summary dodges the fact that we are inside a dizzying and sometimes-puzzling world, guided by a literary voice that critics have placed beside those of Kafka and other modernist giants. *The Hour of the Star* is, in fact, a novel-within-a-novel, narrated by a man named Rodrigo S.M., who is writing a novel—or trying to—about a young woman:

> To draw the girl I have to get a grip on myself and to capture her soul I have to feed myself frugally with fruits and drink iced white wine because it's hot in this cubbyhole. . . . I've also had to give up sex and soccer.

The narrative shifts abruptly between Rodrigo's struggles to write and scenes of his character, Macabéa, a poor typist who rooms with four other women in a Rio de Janeiro slum. Underfed and sickly, she lives on Coca-Cola and hot dogs. The story is comically punctuated by Rodrigo's difficulties in telling Macabéa's tale.

After losing a would-be boyfriend, Macabéa makes her way to a fortune-teller who will read her cards. Madame Carlota delivers the news: Macabéa's life will change completely. That is, of course, an ambiguous prediction. Will it come true?

ABOUT THE AUTHOR: CLARICE LISPECTOR

Clarice Lispector was born Chaya Pinkhasovna Lispector to Jewish parents in Ukraine on December 10, 1920. It was a violent, murderous moment in Ukraine's history, ending in the Soviet takeover of the country. According to her biographer Benjamin Moser:

> It was a time of chaos, famine, and racial war. Her grandfather was murdered; her mother was raped; her father was exiled, penniless, to

the other side of the world. The family's tattered remnants washed up in northeastern Brazil, in 1922. There, her brilliant father, reduced to peddling rags, barely managed to keep his family fed; there, when Clarice was not quite nine, her mother died of her wartime injuries.

In Recife, in northeastern Brazil, Lispector and her two sisters were raised by their father, who later moved the family to Rio de Janeiro. After reading Hermann Hesse at thirteen, Lispector decided to become a writer. Although she later graduated from a prestigious Brazilian law school—rare for women, rarer still for Jewish women—she worked as a journalist and began to publish short stories in journals.

Her first novel, *Near to the Wild Heart*, was published in 1943 and evoked comparisons to James Joyce, a writer Lispector had not yet read. By the time the book appeared, Lispector had married Maury Gurgel Valente, a Brazilian diplomat. For the next fifteen years, she accompanied him—later with their two sons—to a series of posts in Italy, Switzerland, England, and eventually Washington, D.C. Hating the role of the diplomat's wife and missing Brazil, she chose to break from the life.

Separating from her husband in 1959, Lispector returned with her sons to Rio. Taking odd jobs and doing translation work to survive, she also wrote a woman's advice column under a pseudonym. A collection of stories, *Family Ties* (1960), was followed by two novels, and one of these, *The Apple in the Dark* (1961), was released in the United States in 1967 in translation by Gregory Rabassa, a prominent American translator.

Rabassa later commented that Lispector "looked like Marlene Dietrich and wrote like Virginia Woolf"—a frequently quoted appraisal that appears on the book's jacket but which, according to the *New York Times*, Lispector found sexist. The *Times* reported:

> "I don't like when they say that I have an affinity with Virginia Woolf," Lispector also wrote in one column, adding that she had encountered

Woolf's work only after her own first novel was published. "I don't want to forgive her for committing suicide. The terrible duty is to go to the end."

Her next novel, *The Passion According to G.H.* (1964), was a journey into the landscape of the absurd, a meditation narrated by a woman who crushes a cockroach. Around this time, the American writer Elizabeth Bishop was in Brazil and became aware of Lispector's work, which she began to translate, commenting, "—I think she's a 'self-taught' writer, like a primitive painter."

After taking some sleeping pills in 1966, Lispector fell asleep while smoking and was badly burned in a fire, nearly losing a hand. Undeterred, she continued to write fiction, a children's book, and newspaper columns and became increasingly political, demonstrating against the Brazilian military dictatorship. In 1973, Lispector lost her newspaper job and fell back on writing and translating. *The Hour of the Star* was published in 1977 and, soon after, Lispector was diagnosed with inoperable ovarian cancer. Clarice Lispector died on December 9, 1977, on the eve of her fifty-seventh birthday. Her death went unnoticed by the *New York Times*.

In 2009, Benjamin Moser's critically acclaimed biography, *Why This World: A Biography of Clarice Lispector*—a *New York Times* Notable Book of 2009—drew American attention to the life and work of a writer idolized in Brazil. It was followed by new translations of her books and more attention. The *Times* corrected its oversight in 2020 with a belated obituary.

WHY YOU SHOULD READ IT

While *The Hour of the Star* is a complex story that makes certain demands of the reader, it is also a book in which you can abandon yourself. Move away from the simple desire to follow a linear narrative and get caught up in Lispector's "color outside the lines" vision and style, reflected in the voice of Rodrigo and his character; surrender and go with the flow. Lispector works experimentally with a haunting, hypnotic flair and the story builds to a dazzling conclusion.

Lispector explores the very complexity of literary creation. But this is not an academic's arduous musings. She takes the reader on a roller-coaster ride. It is a wild and unpredictable outing, and elements of Macabéa's life that might seem pathetic, if not tragic, are also very funny in Lispector's hands. In his introduction to the novella, novelist Colm Tóibín comments that the book "moves from a deep awareness about the tragedy of being alive to a sly allowance for the fact that existence is a comedy."

WHAT TO READ NEXT

Many of Clarice Lispector's books have been reissued in new English translations. If you like short stories, try Lispector's eighty-six pieces published in *The Complete Stories*. Prefer longer work? Her first novel, *Near to the Wild Heart*, introduced the literary world to what one Brazilian colleague at the time called "Hurricane Clarice." With its stream-of-consciousness techniques, the book won Brazil's award for best debut novel in 1943 and makes a good starting point. Perhaps her other most acclaimed work is *The Passion According to G.H.*, in which a well-to-do sculptress enters her maid's room, sees a cockroach crawling out of the wardrobe, and, panicking, slams the door on it.

A cockroach. Yes, it is Kafka territory.

The House on Mango Street

— 1984 —

Sandra Cisneros

New York: Vintage Contemporaries, 2009; 110 pages

FIRST LINES

We didn't always live on Mango Street. Before that we lived on Loomis on the third floor, and before that we lived on Keeler. Before Keeler, it was Paulina, and before that I can't remember. But what I remember most is moving a lot. Each time it seemed there'd be one more of us. By the time we got to Mango Street we were six—Mama, Papa, Carlos, Kiki, my sister Nenny and me.

PLOT SUMMARY

In a series of brief, expressive vignettes, a twelve-year-old Chicana named Esperanza Cordero brings us to her Chicago, circa early sixties. Through vivid snapshots, she presents a classic coming-of-age story, lyrical and poignant, that reveals a year of growing up in a very particular place.

As Esperanza's tale begins, her family has moved often from a series of run-down apartments into their own house. It is better than the apartment with broken pipes the Corderos had escaped. But it is not exactly the house of Esperanza's dreams. "It's small and red with tight steps in front and windows so small you'd think they were holding their breath." When a nun, one of her teachers, walks by and makes a dismissive remark, Esperanza says, "it made me feel like nothing."

Esperanza's glimpses of her world are luminous and dynamic. She graduates from the childhood joy of double Dutch to trying on high heels. But there is more than a hint of danger when Mr. Benny, the grocer, asks, "Your mother know you got shoes like that? Who give you those?" Then the "Bum Man" by the tavern says, "Your little lemon shoes are so beautiful. But come closer. I can't see very well. Come closer. Please." He may be a big, bad wolf—but this is not a fairy tale. Later Esperanza describes her embarrassment when she wants to dance with a boy but is ashamed of her scuffed saddle shoes.

In a chapter called "My Name," Esperanza says:

> In English my name means hope. In Spanish it means too many letters. It means sadness, it means waiting. It is like the number nine. A muddy color. It is the Mexican records my father plays on Sunday mornings when he is shaving, songs like sobbing.

ABOUT THE AUTHOR: SANDRA CISNEROS

Born in Chicago on December 20, 1954, Sandra Cisneros became a best-selling and honored poet, essayist, and novelist and was named a MacArthur Fellow in 1995. But success did not come easily.

The daughter of a furniture upholsterer with six older brothers, she grew up in the working-class barrio depicted in *The House on Mango Street*, a place where the streets were filled with the sounds of many voices. It was a poor neighborhood, but she found refuge in the library. According to the *New York Times*, Cisneros's love of language can be traced to her mother, "a self-educated woman who got library cards for the seven Cisneros children long before they could actually read themselves." Cisneros graduated from Loyola University in 1976 and attended the University of Iowa's illustrious Writers' Workshop, where she earned her M.F.A. in 1978.

An early focus on verse resulted in a first book of poetry, *Bad Boys* (1980).

The House on Mango Street followed in 1984, issued by Arte Público, a nonprofit imprint of the University of Houston specializing in U.S. Hispanic writers. Though eventually to become a career milestone, the book did not bring overnight success. Quite the opposite.

"After I published *The House on Mango Street* with a small press, there wasn't enough money to pay my rent," she told *Chicago* magazine. "At 33, I didn't have the things other people had. I didn't have insurance or a car or a house. And I couldn't face borrowing money from my mother and father yet again. It just felt easier for me to think of being dead. I had to call a suicide hotline."

In a dark hour, Cisneros was thrown a lifeline. The National Endowment for the Arts awarded her a twenty-thousand-dollar grant. "Now I could pay all my loans back. More important, someone had decided my writing was worth living for."

Later reprinted by mainstream publisher Vintage Books, *The House on Mango Street* went on to become a *New York Times* best seller that has sold more than 6 million copies. Translated into more than twenty languages, it also became a staple of reading lists, from grade schools through colleges. With its underlying focus on emerging sexuality and sexual violence—suggested rather than explicit—that also meant, predictably, the book was challenged by parents and school boards who found it objectionable.

Cisneros followed with more poetry collections, including *The Rodrigo Poems, My Wicked, Wicked Ways,* and *Loose Woman,* and a children's book, *Hairs/Pelitos* (1994), based on the vignette "Hairs" in *The House on Mango Street:* "Everybody in our family has different hair. My Papa's hair is like a broom, all up in the air."

In 1991 a collection of short stories, *Woman Hollering Creek and Other Stories,* was published, and in 1995 she was named a MacArthur Fellow. In 2002, Cisneros wrote a long, multigenerational family narrative, *Caramelo,* a semiautobiographical work about a Mexican American family and their trips back to Mexico City.

After living in San Antonio, Texas, for thirty years, Cisneros moved to San Miguel de Allende in Mexico and in 2015 published a memoir, *A House of My Own: Stories from My Life.* In 2019, she was honored with the PEN/Nabokov Award for Achievement in International Literature. In recognizing her, the judges said:

> Sandra Cisneros has said that she writes because "the world we live in is a house on fire and the people we love are burning." In a formidable and awe-inspiring body of work, which includes fiction, memoir, and poetry, Cisneros brings us astounding and lyrical voices from burning, maligned, devastated, as well as reassembled houses, and nations.

WHY YOU SHOULD READ IT

First of all, read it because everyone should "Read Banned Books." It is one response to the attempt to limit artistic expression and a visible, viable act of resistance as well as support for writers who are threatened with silencing. *The House on Mango Street* has, over the years, become one of the "usual suspects"—books targeted by parents and school groups for somehow being "objectionable." In

2010, the Arizona legislature included it among the books outlawed from schools for advocating "ethnic solidarity" at a time when Tucson schools banned Mexican American studies.

But there is another reason. Read *The House on Mango Street* because it is a deeply felt work that mixes innocence and insight about that moment of being—on the cusp—between childhood and emerging teenager. Deceptively simple yet nuanced, it explores the adolescent heart, soul, and mind.

Recommending *The House on Mango Street* recently, a *New York Times* writer captured the book's essential spirit. "It's impossible not to root for Esperanza as she figures out who she is and how she fits into the world. You don't have to have a mouthful of braces to appreciate Cisneros's message: Bloom where you're planted—and be brave."

WHAT TO READ NEXT

First published as a poet, Cisneros is still best known for her short stories and novels. The short works collected in *Woman Hollering Creek and Other Stories* (1991) have won high praise. Reviewing the book at the time of publication, writer Bebe Moore Campbell commented, "These stories about women struggling to take control of their lives traverse geographical, historical and emotional borders and invite us into the souls of characters as unforgettable as a first kiss."

To follow *House* with longer fiction, the 2002 novel *Caramelo* offers a more sweeping narrative. Told by Ceyala "Lala" Reyes, it begins as her large extended family packs up three cars in Chicago for their annual pilgrimage to the ancestral home in Mexico to spend summer with her "Awful Grandmother," as she is called. Eventually, it covers one hundred years of Mexican and American history.

Praising the book as "joyful" and bridging popular and literary fiction, critic Valerie Sayers wrote, "Cisneros writes poetry as well as prose and her language—especially in the first section of the novel, mostly set in Mexico—is a lovely fusion of Spanish and English, idea and emotion, geography and spirit."

She concluded that *Caramelo* "is written in a more expansive mode, and it's a delight to see Cisneros stretching, even preening."

If Beale Street Could Talk

— 1974 —

James Baldwin

New York: Vintage International, 2006; 197 pages

FIRST LINES

I look at myself in the mirror. I know that I was christened Clementine, and so it would make sense if people called me Clem, or even, come to think of it, Clementine, since that's my name: but they don't. People call me Tish. I guess that makes sense, too. I'm tired, and I'm beginning to think that maybe everything that happens makes sense. Like, if it didn't make sense, how could it happen? But that's really a terrible thought. It can only come out of trouble—trouble that doesn't make sense.

Today, I went to see Fonny.

PLOT SUMMARY

These opening lines are spoken by Tish, preparing to visit her boyfriend in the Tombs. Fonny is being held in the notorious jail in downtown Manhattan for a terrible crime he did not commit. And in that grim setting, separated by a wall of glass, Tish tells her beloved Fonny that she is going to have his baby.

Friends since childhood, the two are in love. A few years older than the nineteen-year-old Tish, Fonny is an aspiring sculptor who dreams of making art and of a life with Tish, who works at a department store perfume counter. Largely set in Harlem and Greenwich Village in the early 1970s, this story might seem like familiar, star-crossed-lover territory. As Baldwin writes, "When two people love each other, when they really love each other, everything that happens between them has something of a sacramental air."

But the families of these two young people are not the Montagues and Capulets. Tish's family—her mother, Sharon, father, Joseph, and older sister, Ernestine—and Fonny's father, Frank, stand resolutely behind the young lovers. To see the baby born safely and the young lovers reunited and married, they enlist a young, white attorney. But Tish, Fonny, and their families must confront the full force of a system and a white world that oppresses them at every turn.

It is this weight of hopelessness and injustice that places *If Beale Street Could Talk* so very much in the present moment. As Fonny's father says, "They been killing our children long enough."

ABOUT THE AUTHOR: JAMES BALDWIN

James Baldwin, as a PBS documentary described him, was "black, impoverished, gifted, and gay."

Born on August 2, 1924, the oldest of nine children, Baldwin grew up in Harlem at a time when choices for young Black men were few. There was the church—which first called out to young

Baldwin—and few possibilities beyond menial labor for young Black men constrained by a system of racist oppression. Pulled to the pulpit by his minister stepfather, Baldwin was a riveting teenage preacher who mesmerized congregations. At another extreme stood the "Avenue" of pushers and pimps, with its promise and dangers to this fourteen-year-old. Baldwin later wrote:

> What I saw around me that summer in Harlem was what I had always seen; nothing had changed. But now, without any warning, the whores and pimps and racketeers on the Avenue had become a personal menace. It had not before occurred to me that I could become one of them, but now I realized that we had been produced by the same circumstances. Many of my comrades were clearly headed for the Avenue, and my father said that I was headed that way, too.

Drawn instead to books, Baldwin spent considerable time in New York's libraries and began writing at a young age. At DeWitt Clinton High School, he edited the school newspaper, where he met fellow student Richard Avedon—later one of the world's most renowned photographers. (They collaborated on a book of essays and photographs, *Nothing Personal*, in 1964.) In Greenwich Village, Baldwin was later introduced to Beauford Delaney, a painter who impressed upon Baldwin the idea that he could be a literary artist.

Baldwin's professional writing career began in a 1947 essay in *The Nation* magazine. He published his first novel, the semiautobiographical *Go Tell It on the Mountain*, in 1953. By then, Baldwin had already left the United States, moving to France in 1948 to escape the racism and homophobia of his home country.

"I was broke. I got to Paris with forty dollars in my pocket, but I had to get out of New York," he told the *Paris Review* in a 1984 interview. "My reflexes were tormented by the plight of other people. Reading had taken me away for long periods at a time, yet I still had to deal with the streets and the authorities and the cold. . . . I was going to go to jail, I was going to kill somebody or be killed."

The success of his first novel was followed by a collection of essays, *Notes of a Native Son* (1955). A second novel, *Giovanni's Room*, that dealt with coming out, desire, and sexual identity was turned down by Baldwin's American publisher, Knopf, which wanted another novel about Harlem. Baldwin said he was told, "You cannot afford to alienate that audience. This new book will ruin your career." It was published instead by Dial Press in 1956.

As the civil rights movement gathered momentum, Baldwin returned frequently to the United States and became a major voice in the crusade. *Nobody Knows My Name* (1961), a book of essays, further established his place as a passionate spokesman for the movement. *The Fire Next Time* (1963) collected two previously published essays, one a letter to his nephew and namesake, James. The other was "Down at the Cross: Letter from a Region of My Mind," a long essay to which the *New Yorker* had devoted an entire issue; it became a best seller and a classic of American civil rights literature.

If Beale Street Could Talk—the title references a 1917 jazz classic by W. C. Handy—is one of James Baldwin's later novels, published in 1974. By then, Baldwin had been firmly established as one of America's most prominent novelists and essayists, as well as a significant civil rights activist.

"Throughout his lifetime as a novelist, essayist, poet and playwright, Baldwin brilliantly chronicled his tortuous relationship with his stepfather, his crisis of faith, his sexuality, and his intense desire to tell the stories that swirled around in his head," writes Princeton professor Eddie S. Glaude Jr. in his essay "Where to Start with James Baldwin." Author of a Baldwin biography, Glaude continues, "He willed himself into becoming one of the world's most important writers and *the* most insightful critic of American democracy and race this country has ever produced."

James Baldwin died of stomach cancer on December 1, 1987, at age sixty-three, at his home in France. His prominence was recently heightened with the production of the documentary film *I Am Not Your Negro*, which appeared in 2016.

WHY YOU SHOULD READ IT

If Beale Street Could Talk may not be typical of Baldwin's other novels in theme and tone. But it is a great short book, in part because the story he tells is as timely as ever. The oppressive judicial system and racist policing it depicts are certainly at the forefront of America's current racial reckoning.

Some critics dismissed the book as "sentimental," but novelist Joyce Carol Oates is an admirer. At the time of publication, she commented in a review:

> "If Beale Street Could Talk" is a quite moving and very traditional celebration of love. It affirms not only love between a man and a woman, but love of a type that is dealt with only rarely in contemporary fiction — that between members of a family, which may involve extremes of sacrifice.

I think she hit the right notes. Far from sentimental in my reading, *If Beale Street Could Talk* is an emotionally potent novel that made two young people—and their respective families—as poignantly real as fictional characters can be. Baldwin's passion and his intense anger at America's systemic racism never bludgeon the reader. And the novel provides an ideal entrée to Baldwin's other, more challenging fiction.

WHAT TO READ NEXT

James Baldwin's body of work is large, influential, and speaks directly to the nation's recent time of racial reckoning. The best place to begin may be his first novel, *Go Tell It on the Mountain* (1953), a classic coming-of-age account of a teenager in 1930s Harlem contending with questions of family, faith, and sexuality. Its successor *Giovanni's Room*—a candidate for this collection at 169 pages—is also highly recommended. Set in 1950s Paris, it is a portrait of David, a man torn between a woman and another man. Writing about it in 2016, novelist Colm Tóibín commented, "Baldwin . . . made clear that he could work wonders with the light and shade of intimacy, that he could move easily and effortlessly into a whispered prose, into moments where David is frightened into sharp wisdom, and then, with equal facility, evoke the excitement of a crowded bar filled with sexual expectation."

Baldwin's passionate voice is also very clear in his essays, collected in three important books: *Notes of a Native Son* (1955), *Nobody Knows My Name: More Notes of a Native Son* (1961), and *The Fire Next Time* (1963). In all of these books, Baldwin explored essential questions of sexuality, repression, and artistic freedom and of being Black in a white world.

If This Is a Man
[Survival in Auschwitz]

(A work of nonfiction)

— 1947, 1958 —

Primo Levi

New York: W. W. Norton, 2015; published in The Complete Works of Primo Levi, *vol. 1 translated from the Italian by Stuart Woolf with author's appendix and translator's afterword; 165 pages; first published in 1947 and reissued in 1958 in Italian as* Se questo è un uomo; *first translated into English in 1959 as* If This Is a Man; *reissued in English as* Survival in Auschwitz: The Nazi Assault on Humanity *(New York: Touchstone, 1996), translated from the Italian by Stuart Woolf with "A Conversation with Primo Levi by Philip Roth"*

FIRST LINES

I was captured by the Fascist Militia on December 13, 1943. I was twenty-four, with little common sense, no experience and a definite tendency—encouraged by the routines of segregation forced on me during the previous four years by the racial laws—to live in an unrealistic world of my own, a world inhabited by civilized Cartesian phantoms, by sincere male and bloodless female friendships. I cultivated a moderate and abstract sense of rebellion.

PLOT SUMMARY

The story is agonizingly simple. A young chemist, an "Italian citizen of Jewish race," is arrested in December 1943 by Italian Fascists and taken to Campo di Fossoli, near Modena in the north of Italy. Established by the Italians as a prisoner of war camp, it has come to serve as a detention camp for Jews and other political prisoners. Levi is one of them.

After a brief internment there, Levi and hundreds of other Italian Jews are transported to Auschwitz. The journey takes four days and four nights before the train is unloaded and the deportees separated:

> In less than ten minutes all the able-bodied men had been gathered in a group. What happened to the others, to the women, to the children, to the old people, we could establish neither then nor later: the night swallowed them up, purely and simply. Today, we know that in that rapid and summary choice each one of us had been judged capable or not of working usefully for the Reich; we know that of our convoy only ninety-six men and twenty-nine women entered the camps, respectively, of Monowitz-Buna and Birkenau, and that of all the others, more than five hundred in number, not one was alive two days later.

In stunning prose, sprinkled with dark humor, Levi offers an unsparing account of his ten months spent doing hard, dangerous labor in the hell of Auschwitz. Like so much Holocaust literature, the story is harrowing. The fact of his or anyone's else's survival defies reason.

But survive he did. After months of living through degradation, disease, and death, Levi became very ill early in 1945 and was sent to the camp infirmary with scarlet fever. As the Soviet army approached, the Germans abandoned the camp. Levi describes his liberation: "The camp was silent. Other starving specters wandered around like us, exploring: beards unkempt, eyes hollow, limbs skeletal and yellowish in tattered garments."

Levi's final entry comes on the day the Russians arrive on January 27, 1945. He and a companion had just carried out the corpse of a fellow inmate.

ABOUT THE AUTHOR: PRIMO LEVI

Primo Levi was born on July 31, 1919, in Turin to a family of Piedmontese Jews, whose ancestors had escaped the Spanish Inquisition. Except for his time in the camps, he would live and die in the family house where he was born.

By the time Levi went to elementary school and then Hebrew school, Mussolini had come to power and firmly established his Fascist dictatorship. When Levi enrolled in the University of Turin as a chemistry student in 1937, it was just before Italy adopted an anti-Semitic racial code modeled on Nazi Germany's Nuremberg Laws. Jewish students like Levi were allowed to remain in the university, while new Jewish students were no longer admitted. Levi graduated with honors in 1941, but his diploma also noted he was "of the Jewish race."

By then, Italy was at war, allied with Hitler's Germany. Despite his religious heritage, Levi was able to find work as a chemist in Turin and then in Milan with a Swiss drug company. But wartime Italy was divided between Fascists fighting with Nazi Germany and anti-Fascist forces who had made a treaty with the U.S. and British allies. Late in 1942, without training, Levi and some friends joined a group of partisans who were battling the Fascists and Nazis. On a fateful night in December 1943, Levi's luck ran out. He was captured and, after admitting to being Jewish, was detained and ultimately deported to Auschwitz.

Sick and emaciated when the Soviet army liberated the camp in late January 1945, he made his way circuitously back to Italy, starting in Russia and reaching Turin in October 1945. Finding work in a paint factory, Levi began writing a description of his camp experience. Rejected by Natalia Ginzburg (see *The Dry Heart*), then an editor with the prominent publisher Einaudi, Levi's first version of his account was published in 1947 by a small press and went out of print. In 1958, the book was picked up, revised, and republished in a new edition by Einaudi, and it was translated into English the following year as *If This Is a Man*. It attracted little attention in the United States.

While working as a chemist, Levi began a sequel, recounting his return to Italy from Russia. Published in 1963 in Italy as *La tregua* (*The Truce*) and later in America as *The Reawakening*, it preceded Levi's turn to fiction. In 1966, under the pseudonym Damiano Malabaila, he published a group of Kafkaesque science fiction short stories collected in *Storie naturali* (*Natural Histories*).

After retiring from full-time work as a chemist in 1975, Levi wrote another semiautobiographical work, *Il sistema periodico* (*The Periodic Table*), tracing his life from childhood, with each chapter connected to one of the chemical elements. It became his most celebrated work and revived interest in his Auschwitz memoir.

He followed with a 1978 novel, *La chiave a stella* (*The Wrench*, also published in the United States as *The Monkey Wrench*), winner of Italy's prestigious Strega Prize. With the American publication of *The Periodic Table* in 1984, Levi achieved a degree of critical recognition and success he had been missing in the United States.

During the forty years following his Auschwitz experience, Levi wrote memoirs and autobiographies, story collections, and novels. Internationally esteemed, he would be called on to testify in the trials of Auschwitz criminals. In time, he became a major voice in countering Holocaust denialism.

Primo Levi took his own life—it is generally agreed—at the age of sixty-seven on April 11, 1987, though some who knew him have argued his death was an accident. Suffering from severe depression, he died in a fall from the upper floor of a marble staircase in the Turin home where he was born.

WHY YOU SHOULD READ IT

In the extensive and significant world of Holocaust literature—both fictional works and nonfiction—*If This Is a Man* is the most profound work I have yet encountered. While it is somewhat curious to praise a memoir by saying it reads like a great novel, that is the case with Levi's book. Like a great fictional account of a human struggle against unthinkable odds, it is a brutal, chilling, yet ultimately triumphant examination of the human capacity for both evil and survival.

Some very notable Holocaust memoirs have been faulted for their author's selective memory or the interference of an editor. Some critics have also said that no written account—whether memoir or fiction—can make "art" of Auschwitz.

Levi may have anticipated such critiques in his preface to *If This Is a Man*. "The story of the death camps should be understood by everyone as a sinister signal of danger," Levi wrote. He continues:

> The need to tell our story to "others," to make "others" share it, took on for us, before the liberation and after, the character of an immediate and violent impulse, to the point of competing with other elementary needs. The book was written to satisfy that need.

And that is why you should read it.

The obvious next step is to read *The Truce*, Levi's sequel describing his harrowing liberation from Auschwitz and a nine-month trek through Russia and Eastern Europe back to Italy. Near its conclusion, Levi writes, "But only after many months did I lose the habit of walking with my gaze fixed on the ground, as if to look for something to eat or put in my pocket quickly and sell for bread; and a dream filled with fear has not ceased to visit me, at intervals now close, now rare."

The series of stories collected in *The Periodic Table* are autobiographical. But they are told in an imaginative and unique style that combines the chemist's precision with the lyricism of a gifted writer, which Levi was.

All of Levi's writings, spanning decades, were edited by the noted translator Ann Goldstein and collected in *The Complete Works of Primo Levi*, published in 2015. In her introduction to the set, novelist Toni Morrison wrote:

For this articulate survivor, individual identity is supreme; efforts to drown identity inevitably become futile. He refuses to place cruel and witless slaughter on a pedestal of fascination or to locate in it any serious meaning. . . . Time and time again we are moved by his narratives of how men refuse erasure.

July's People

— 1981 —

Nadine Gordimer

New York: Penguin Books, 1982; 160 pages

FIRST LINES

You like to have some cup of tea? —

July bent at the doorway and began that day for them as his kind has always done for their kind.

The knock on the door. Seven o'clock. In governors' residences, commercial hotel rooms, shift bosses' company bungalows, master bedrooms *en suite* — the tea-tray in black hands smelling of Lifebuoy soap.

PLOT SUMMARY

Set in South Africa before the end of apartheid and white rule, this mesmerizing novella presents a vision of a country being torn apart by a racial civil war. As Black rebel forces battle the white minority government, one white family's world is upended.

The narrative plays out as an intensely intimate tale of a white family—architect Bam Smales, his wife, Maureen, and their three children—given shelter in a remote village by their longtime Black servant, July.

To escape the fighting that has engulfed the country, Bam and Maureen Smales grab a few essentials—including Bam's hunting gun— and drive to the remote village where July lives. With children in tow, Bam and Maureen flee in their "bakkie," a small sport truck once used for camping and shooting trips. "The vehicle was bought for pleasure, as some women are said to be made for pleasure," writes Gordimer.

Liberal-minded and privileged, they are soon sharing a thatched hut. The family has been dropped into a world in which none of their previous education or skills has value. Surrounded by an unknown language, with no electric lights or running water and little privacy, the Smales family must adjust to their new reality. Depending on a battery-powered radio that offers sketchy, broken news of the con- flict, they are disoriented and seemingly futureless.

As their children adapt to this new world, Maureen and Bam are increasingly forced to rely for survival upon July, his wife, and the other villagers, as the tables—and their world—have been turned upside-down.

ABOUT THE AUTHOR: NADINE GORDIMER

Novelist, short story writer, essayist, and political activist Nadine Gordimer was born on November 20, 1923, in Springs, a mining town outside Johannesburg. Growing up in a secular Jewish, middle-class family, she began writing at an early age and published a first story at age fifteen.

A collection of Gordimer's short fiction, seen mostly in South African magazines, was published in book form in 1949 as *Face to Face*. It was followed by her first novel, *The Lying Days*, in 1953. Gordimer had married in 1949 and had a daughter, Oriane, before divorcing her first husband three years later.

In 1951, the *New Yorker* published "A Watcher of the Dead" and Gordimer's long relationship with the magazine began. In 1954, she married art dealer Reinhold Cassirer, a German refugee who had fought with the British Army in World War II; they had one son, Hugo, and remained married until Reinhold's death in 2001.

When a friend was arrested during an anti-apartheid protest in 1960, Gordimer became more involved in the South African civil rights movement and national politics. She helped edit the "I am prepared to die" speech of Nelson Mandela, who was tried in 1964 and facing a death sentence. Mandela was spared but spent a total of twenty-seven years and eight months in prison before his release on February 11, 1990.

Gordimer continued to focus on the impact of apartheid, the strictly enforced separation of races that was the foundation of South African society. And each new book earned greater recognition. In 1974, she shared the coveted Booker Prize for *The Conservationist*. This was followed by a series of novels: *Burger's Daughter* (1979), *July's People* (1981), *A Sport of Nature* (1987), and *My Son's Story* (1990). In 1991, she received the Nobel Prize in Literature. The Nobel Committee said:

> For fifty years, Gordimer has been the Geiger counter of apartheid and of the movements of people across the crust of South Africa. Her work reflects the psychic vibrations within that country, the road from passivity and blindness to resistance and struggle, the forbidden friendships, the censored soul, and the underground networks. She has outlined a free zone where it was possible to try out, in imagination, what life beyond apartheid might be like. She wrote as if censorship did not exist and as if there were readers willing to listen. In her characters, the major currents of contemporary history intersect.

In accepting the award, Gordimer said:

> For myself, I have said that nothing factual that I write or say will
> be as truthful as my fiction. . . . I did not, at the beginning, expect
> to earn a living by being read. I wrote as a child out of the joy of
> apprehending life through my senses—the look and scent and feel
> of things; and soon out of the emotions that puzzled me or raged
> within me and which took form, found some enlightenment, solace
> and delight, shaped in the written word.

Gordimer continued to write long after Mandela's release from
jail and eventual election as South Africa's president. Her final novel,
No Time like the Present (2012), follows veterans of the battle against
apartheid as they deal with issues facing modern Africa. Nadine
Gordimer died, aged ninety, in Johannesburg in July 2014.

WHY YOU SHOULD READ IT

Published a decade before Nelson Mandela's release from prison in
1990 and eventual majority Black rule in South Africa in 1994, this
novel would be of enormous value simply for its exploration of an
extraordinary moment in recent world events. The largely peaceful
end of minority white rule in the country was a milestone event in
late-twentieth-century history.

But *July's People* is not simply a marker of a time now past. The
reversal of fortunes experienced by Bam and Maureen Smales as the
onetime servant holds power over his former employers provides
the tension in a compelling, provocative story that underscores the
racial and sexual nature of power. Its riveting exploration of race,
and the complexities of marriage, is why Gordimer's work endures
long after apartheid's end.

WHAT TO READ NEXT

Over more than six decades, Gordimer wrote fifteen novels and produced ten collections of short stories, the format many critics consider her best. The most recent of these is *Beethoven Was One-Sixteenth Black*, thirteen stories collected and published in 2007.

For longer fiction, *The Conservationist* (1974), a joint winner of the Booker Prize, is a complex novel about a wealthy white South African tycoon on whose property a dead African is found. It was lauded for its theme of Africa being returned to Africans, as well as Gordimer's richly detailed descriptions of the natural world.

Of her other novels, *Burger's Daughter* is widely considered among her best. Once banned in South Africa, it is set in the seventies and details the story of a family of anti-apartheid activists. Of it Gordimer wrote:

> In 1979, I wrote a novel, "Burger's Daughter," on the theme of the family life of revolutionaries' children, a life ruled by their parents' political faith and the daily threat of imprisonment. I don't know how the book, which was banned in South Africa when it was published, was smuggled to Mandela in Robben Island Prison. But he, the most exigent reader I could have hoped for, wrote me a letter of deep, understanding acceptance about the book.

The Lathe of Heaven

— 1971 —

Ursula K. Le Guin

New York: Scribner, 2008; 184 pages

FIRST LINES

Current-borne, wave-flung, tugged hugely by the whole might of ocean, the jellyfish drifts in the tidal abyss. The light shines through it, and the dark enters it. Borne, flung, tugged from anywhere to anywhere, for in the deep sea there is no compass but nearer and farther, higher and lower, the jellyfish hangs and sways; pulses move slight and quick within it, as the vast diurnal pulses beat in the moon-driven sea. Hanging, swaying, pulsing, the most vulnerable and insubstantial creature, it has for its defense the violence and the power of the whole ocean, to which it has entrusted its being, its going, and its will.

Dreams do come true. And be careful what you wish for.

In postapocalyptic Portland, Oregon, George Orr has trouble sleeping. Or more accurately, his problem is dreaming. George believes he possesses a power he doesn't want. His dreams come true, altering reality, not just for himself but for the entire world.

Seeking help, George consults Dr. William Haber, a psychiatrist who specializes in dreaming. Initially treating George as a psychiatric case, Haber comes to understand George's ability and the immense power he holds. Using a machine he has devised, Haber is able to direct George's dreams.

Certain that he is being manipulated, George Orr asks attorney Heather Lelache to intercede. A strong-minded, no-nonsense woman, Lelache takes his case and sits in on one of George's therapy sessions, witnessing how intensely his dreams actually alter reality. And that is where the action really begins.

In a compellingly compressed narrative, the acclaimed novelist, poet, and essayist Ursula K. Le Guin offers a complex interpretation of "The Monkey's Paw," a famous story in which a person's wishes are granted with dreadful results.

ABOUT THE AUTHOR: URSULA K. LE GUIN

Early in 2021, the U.S. Postal Service announced a stamp honoring Ursula K. Le Guin, making her the thirty-third author to achieve this distinction. It placed her alongside such names as Twain, Wharton, and Whitman. It was one of many accolades for an influential writer who balked at being narrowly cast as a science fiction novelist.

Born Ursula Kroeber in Berkeley, California, on October 21, 1929, she was the youngest of four children and the only daughter of two prominent anthropologists, Alfred L. Kroeber and Theodora Kracaw Kroeber. An expert on California's Native Americans, Ursula's father was one of the leading cultural anthropologists of his time. Her mother wrote *Ishi in Two Worlds* (1961), a notable book about the life of the last surviving member of the Yahi people, known widely as "the last wild Indian."

As a child, Ursula was immersed in legends and mythology, especially Norse and Irish tales, the *Iliad*, and the Native American myths her father told. She also read the science fiction magazines of the day but outgrew these pulp tales featuring men with death rays doing interplanetary battle.

Heading east, she graduated from Radcliffe College in 1951, earned a master's degree in romance literature of the Middle Ages and Renaissance from Columbia, then won a Fulbright Fellowship to study in Paris. Sailing for Europe, she met Charles Le Guin, another Fulbright scholar, and they married in Paris in 1953.

When she returned to the United States, Le Guin dropped her graduate studies to raise two daughters, the first of three children. Later settling in Portland, where her husband taught at Portland State University, the couple had a third child, a son. Juggling motherhood with her literary ambitions was a struggle. Five novels she wrote went unpublished. But she persisted.

Her breakthrough came in 1966 with her first published novel, *Rocannon's World*, the first of a connected series later called the Hainish Cycle. Asked to write a book aimed at teenagers, she published *A Wizard of Earthsea* in 1968. A coming-of-age tale featuring wizardry and magic, it was more fantasy than science fiction and aimed at young adult readers. The book successfully crossed over to an adult audience and was the first of the novels that became the Earthsea Cycle.

Le Guin's next work raised her reputation to a new level. Published in 1969, *The Left Hand of Darkness* is set on the planet Gethen, where people are neither male nor female. Exploring gender through a science fiction lens, the book won the Hugo and Nebula awards, science fiction's two major prizes. But it also broke genre barriers.

After completing two more Earthsea novels, in 1974 Le Guin published *The Dispossessed*, an "anarchist utopian allegory." It won the major science fiction awards that year and cemented her place as a novelist beyond the limitations sometimes placed on genre fiction.

"I don't think *science fiction* is a very good name for it, but it's the name that we've got," she told the *Paris Review* in 2013. "It is different from other kinds of writing, I suppose, so it deserves a name of its own. But where I can get prickly and combative is if I'm just called a sci-fi writer. I'm not. I'm a novelist and poet. Don't shove me into your damn pigeonhole, where I don't fit, because I'm all over. My tentacles are coming out of the pigeonhole in all directions."

In April 2000, Le Guin was named a Living Legend by the U.S. Library of Congress. At the 2014 National Book Awards, Le Guin was given the Medal for Distinguished Contribution to American Letters. She accepted the award on behalf of her fellow writers of fantasy and science fiction, who, she said, had been "excluded from literature for so long." In 2016, she achieved another distinction: the first of several volumes of Le Guin's works was published by the Library of America, a series of books usually reserved for "classics" by dead writers.

Many readers felt that Le Guin's best work had come during the 1970s. But others saw her later work as opening up possibilities beyond the strict genre category that often defines writers. Writing in the *New Yorker* in 2016, Julie Phillips commented, "By breaking down the walls of genre, Le Guin handed new tools to twenty-first-century writers working in what [Michael] Chabon calls the 'borderlands,' the place where the fantastic enters literature."

In January 2018, Ursula K. Le Guin died at age eighty-eight in her Portland home. The following year, public television featured her life, work, and influence in its *American Masters* series. "Ursula was a seer and what she called a Foreteller," critic Harold Bloom wrote after her death. "Ursula was an exquisite stylist. Every word was exactly in place and every sentence or line had resonance. She was a visionary who set herself against all brutality, discrimination, and exploitation."

WHY YOU SHOULD READ IT

Read it because her prose can approach poetry. Read it because she was a visionary who used—and broke—the conventions of science fiction to explore environmental threats, racism, authoritarian power, spirituality, and human psychology.

These are all very large concerns. But in *The Lathe of Heaven* they are still expressed in a narrative that builds in tension and excitement. The novel reaches a pounding level of intensity as George Orr's directed dreams turn disastrous, leading to scenes reminiscent of *The War of the Worlds*. For all of her intriguing and consequential themes, this is where Le Guin also proves that she is a masterful storyteller.

WHAT TO READ NEXT

With more than twenty novels, hundreds of short stories, poetry collections, essays, and children's books written over six decades, Le Guin produced a vast library. Start with her groundbreaking success, *The Left Hand of Darkness*. Writing in the *Paris Review* in 2013, John Wray commented, "No single work did more to upend the genre's conventions than *The Left Hand of Darkness* (1969)."

The five books in the Earthsea Cycle—consisting of *A Wizard of Earthsea*, *The Tombs of Atuan*, *The Farthest Shore*, *Tehanu*, and *The Other Wind*—are still among her most popular and topical works. Imagine that: a series of successful books about a boy learning to become a wizard and battling dark forces.

Finally, *The Dispossessed*, a 1974 dystopian work that moves between two planets, was a response to Vietnam. According to Le Guin, "I needed to understand my own passionate opposition to the war that we were, endlessly it seemed, waging in Vietnam, and endlessly protesting at home."

After Le Guin's death, Margaret Atwood called her one of the literary greats of the twentieth century:

> In all her work, Le Guin was always asking the same urgent question: what sort of world do you want to live in? Her own choice would have been gender equal, racially equal, economically fair and self-governing, but that was not on offer. It would also have contained mutually enjoyable sex and good food: there was a better chance of that.

Lord of the Flies

— 1954 —

William Golding

New York: Penguin Books, 2016; 202 pages

* Number 41 on the Modern Library list of 100 Best Novels *
* BBC: "100 Novels That Shaped Our World" *
* TIME: "All-TIME 100 Novels" *

FIRST LINES

The boy with fair hair lowered himself down the last few feet of rock and began to pick his way toward the lagoon. Though he had taken off his school sweater and trailed it now from one hand, his grey shirt stuck to him and his hair was plastered to his forehead. All round him the long scar smashed into the jungle was a bath of heat. He was clambering heavily among the creepers and broken trunks when a bird, a vision of red and yellow, flashed upwards with a witch-like cry; and this cry was echoed by another.

This one you may know. Nobel laureate Golding's most famous work is still required reading for most American students as well as young readers around the world. As it should be.

Following a plane crash, a group of British schoolboys is left stranded on an uncharted island. Celebrating their new-found freedom, the boys begin to organize a basic society to ensure their survival. It is all very civilized. At first.

Fair-haired Ralph and an overweight, bespectacled boy christened Piggy find a conch shell that will be used to call the surviving boys and establish a sort of order. The leader of a robed group of choirboys, Jack proclaims his group the hunters. As the boys divide into groups stratified along power lines, a caste system develops. In a series of stunning steps, the order they have created begins to collapse into primal terror:

> *"Kill the beast! Cut his throat! Spill his blood!"*
> The movement became regular while the chant lost its first superficial excitement and began to beat like a steady pulse. Roger ceased to be a pig and became a hunter, so that the center of the ring yawned emptily. Some of the littleuns started a ring of their own; and the complementary circles went round and round as though repetition would achieve safety of itself. There was the throb and stamp of a single organism.

The boys' descent into tribalism leads to violence and a heart-racing conclusion. Will the boys be rescued? Will they all survive?

ABOUT THE AUTHOR: WILLIAM GOLDING

Born on September 19, 1911, in Cornwall, England, William G. Golding was the son of a schoolteacher father and a mother who campaigned for suffrage. Growing up in a fourteenth-century house beside a graveyard, he attempted to write a novel at the age of twelve, but it would be years before he found his way into print.

He graduated from Oxford in 1934 and began teaching school in 1935. Soon after the outbreak of World War II, he joined the Royal Navy, eventually serving on a destroyer and then commanding a ship that took part in the 1944 D-Day Normandy landings.

The reality of war, and teaching English when it was over, led to his first and most recognized work. Golding related how things got out of hand when he allowed a group of schoolboys complete freedom in a debate and anarchy prevailed in the classroom. The incident, along with his wartime experience, helped inspire *Lord of the Flies*. "World War II was the turning point for me," Golding later said. "I began to see what people were capable of doing. Anyone who moved through those years without understanding that man produces evil as a bee produces honey, must have been blind or wrong in the head."

Clearly, many publishers were blind to Golding and the value of *Lord of the Flies*. After multiple rejections, the book was accepted and published in England in 1954. William Golding's first novel became an almost immediate success. It has gone on to become a global cultural touchstone, selling more than 25 million copies in English, with translations in every major language, as well as Georgian, Basque, and Catalan.

Although his succeeding works never matched the impact or enormous success of his first book, Golding continued to write. His immediate works after *Lord of the Flies* included *The Inheritors* (1955), about Neanderthals confronted by "new people," and *Pincher Martin* (1956), which records the thoughts of a drowning sailor.

With the success of *Lord of the Flies*, Golding stopped teaching in 1961. By 1971, however, suffering from writer's block, his life had become "unendurable" and Golding "took to drink," according to his biographer John Carey. Extended treatment by C. G. Jung resolved some of Golding's troubles but not his writer's block. It took years to complete *Darkness Visible* (1979), which opens during the wartime Blitz of London and explores a different sort of evil—sexual abuse. In 1980, *Rites of Passage* won the Booker Prize, Britain's premier literary award. Set in the nineteenth century, it was the first of a trilogy about a ship sailing for Australia and the cast of characters thrown together on board.

In 1983, Golding was awarded the Nobel Prize. Comparing him to Herman Melville, the Nobel citation said:

> William Golding's novels and stories are not only somber moralities and dark myths about evil and about treacherous, destructive forces. As already mentioned, they are also colourful tales of adventure which can be read as such, full of narrative joy, inventiveness and excitement.

After winning the prize, he completed the trilogy begun in *Rites of Passage*, which became the basis for *To the Ends of the Earth*, a BBC series that aired in 2005 and on PBS in the United States in 2006.

William Golding died in June 1993, aged eighty-one, of heart failure. A novel in draft form was published posthumously as *The Double Tongue*.

WHY YOU SHOULD READ IT

If you were assigned to read it in school—or have only seen one of the film versions, one in 1963 and another in 1990—it is time to revisit Golding's coral island world. It is, first of all, a thrilling read. The final section of the book, in which the boys' descent into primal violence is fully realized, is a heart-pounding page-turner.

But the book's concern with the violence that may lie within us all is what has made it a modern classic. And in our own times—when political tribalism has become so pronounced—it is timelier than ever. We have seen "the throb and stamp of a single organism" on the steps of the U.S. Capitol. An angry political mob is a mere stone's throw from Golding's imaginary island.

In an introduction to an anniversary edition of the novel published in the U.K., Stephen King wrote:

> To me, *Lord of the Flies* has always represented what novels are for, what makes them indispensable. Should we expect to be entertained when we read a story? Of course. An act of the imagination that doesn't entertain is a poor act indeed. But there should be more. A successful novel should erase the boundary-line between writer and reader, so they can unite. When that happens, the novel becomes a part of life.

It should be noted that Castle Rock, a site on Golding's island, inspired the name of the Maine town where more than fifteen of Stephen King's novels are set (see *Rita Hayworth and Shawshank Redemption*).

WHAT TO READ NEXT

To continue with the theme of a group of people thrown together on the ocean, *Rites of Passage* describes a nineteenth-century voyage to Australia, depicting the conflicts among the ship's passengers. It is told through the journal kept by one of them; *Close Quarters* and *Fire Down Below* completed the trilogy.

The 1979 novel *Darkness Visible* is an intensely visceral novel that is also unfortunately of the moment. Opening in World War II London, it tells of a boy who is disfigured in the Blitz, then turned over to a school where he is sexually abused. "Cruelty and lust," writes A. S. Byatt in an introduction to the novel, "both go hand and hand with darkness in Golding."

Assessing his own works, Golding said his favorite book was *The Inheritors*, about the destruction of Neanderthal man by *Homo sapiens*.

The Lost Daughter

— 2006 —

Elena Ferrante

New York: Europa Editions, 2008; translated from the Italian by Ann Goldstein; 140 pages; first published in 2006 in Italian as La figlia oscura

FIRST LINES

I had been driving for less than an hour when I began to feel ill. The burning in my side came back, but at first I decided not to give it any importance. I became worried only when I realized that I no longer had the strength to hold onto the steering wheel. In the space of a few minutes my head became heavy, the headlights grew dimmer; soon I even forgot that I was driving. I had the impression, rather, of being at the sea, in the middle of the day.

PLOT SUMMARY

A forty-eight-year-old divorced professor of literature, Leda sets off to spend several weeks at a small beach town in the south of Italy. Her two grown daughters have gone to live with their father in Canada and Leda is feeling liberated. "For the first time in almost twenty-five years," Leda says, "I was not aware of the anxiety of having to take care of them."

Her daily ritual of sunning, reading, and quiet contemplation is soon broken when a large, boisterous family arrives. She is annoyed and unsettled by the group, which reminds her of her own childhood and her family's beach outings.

But she is also intrigued. A young woman and her small daughter are part of the large group. Leda observes them from a distance until a busy Sunday when the child disappears on the crowded beach. While the child is soon found—no spoiler—life takes a sharp turn for the professor and the young mother as their paths intersect and become increasingly tangled. In befriending the other woman, Leda must confront her childhood memories and her own role as a mother.

ABOUT THE AUTHOR: ELENA FERRANTE

As the creator of an international literary sensation called the Neapolitan Quartet, Elena Ferrante is a phenomenal worldwide success. Not only have her books sold millions of copies in many languages, but they are also the basis for the critically acclaimed HBO series *My Brilliant Friend*.

The four books recount a decades-long saga of two women, friends from an insular Naples neighborhood, whose lives are completely entwined and who are widely beloved and well-known within their community. But Elena Ferrante is not. She is a mystery. The name is a pseudonym. While there has been considerable speculation and even journalistic investigations into her true identity, the author has remained mostly silent on the question of who she is.

What is known is that Elena Ferrante was born in Naples and has written, in addition to *The Lost Daughter* and the Neapolitan series, three other novels and a collection of essays and letters, *Frantumaglia*. According to the *New Yorker*'s James Wood, she has provided some clues to her past in written answers to journalists' questions and essays over the years. "She has a classics degree; she has referred to being a mother," writes Wood. In addition, she has revealed, "I study, I translate, I teach."

And that may be all one needs to know. Reading her work without knowing her biography is a very good case for separating the artist from the art. The reader need not be aware of this author's biography to appreciate the depths of the writing and the insights she brings to the complexities of life and intimate relationships.

WHY YOU SHOULD READ IT

This is no idealized portrait of a liberated wife and mother rediscovering herself on, yes, another Beach Holiday. In a short space, in prose that is crystalline, Ferrante lays bare, with brutal honesty, the inner world of a woman unsettled by the outside world. Her thoughts of her children and motherhood go against the traditional grain. They are delivered in a story that is direct, candid, even blunt—and thought-provoking.

As a man who spent the first years of my two children's lives as a "stay-at-home dad," I found Ferrante's description of the anxiety and stress of caring for children cut very close to the bone. It is Ferrante's fierce candor that elevates her fiction.

"Her novels are intensely, violently personal, and because of this they seem to dangle bristling key chains of confession before the unsuspecting reader," James Wood wrote in the *New Yorker* profile of Ferrante. He adds:

More than these occasional and fairly trivial overlappings with life, the material that the early novels visit and revisit is intimate and often shockingly candid: child abuse, divorce, motherhood, wanting and not wanting children, the tedium of sex, the repulsions of the body, the narrator's desperate struggle to retain a cohesive identity within a traditional marriage and amid the burdens of child rearing.

Ferrante takes these very raw materials and, with a clarity and directness of prose—in Ann Goldstein's translation—turns them into a work of piercing revelation.

An English-language film version set in Greece instead of Italy, marked the directorial debut of Maggie Gyllenhaal, and made its premiere at the Venice Film Festival in 2021 to considerable acclaim, receiving an award for best screenplay, and later three Academy Award nominations.

WHAT TO READ NEXT

For those who have not experienced the Neapolitan Quartet, get ready to take the plunge. Be prepared to put your life on hold and binge-read, as many Ferrante admirers have. The four books beginning with *My Brilliant Friend* are extraordinary. Once started, they are difficult to put down. In my view, they are Dickensian in sweep.

Beginning in the late 1950s, in a close-knit Naples neighborhood, the four novels—the other three are *The Story of a New Name*, *Those Who Leave and Those Who Stay*, and *The Story of the Lost Child*—play out over decades. They are focused almost entirely on two characters: Elena, or Lenù, and Rafaella, or Lila. Both born in 1944, the girls become lifelong friends as children. While they take very different paths, Lenù and Lila are soul mates whose lives are inseparably entwined.

Ferrante creates an unforgettable world in their rough-and-tumble, working-class Naples neighborhood. While the settings eventually move to other parts of Italy, pitched against the sweep of contemporary Italian history, the story is ultimately centered in the small universe in which these two women were born. Though the books plumb many contemporary issues, at their heart they are about friendship, love, betrayal, and self-discovery.

Ferrante has also written two other excellent short novels, both made into films in Italian. *Troubling Love* (*L'amore molesto*, 1999; English translation, 2006) was her first novel and helped establish Ferrante's reputation. *The Days of Abandonment* (*I giorni dell'abbandono*, 2002; English translation, 2005) was her best-known work before *My Brilliant Friend* and begins starkly, "One April afternoon, right after lunch, my husband announced that he wanted to leave me."

Like much of Ferrante's writing, the brilliant directness of that opening draws readers into a much more complex and exquisitely detailed world.

I thought Ferrante's most recent novel, *The Lying Life of Adults (La vita bugiarda degli adulti*, 2019), did not reach the high bar she set in earlier work. But in a review author Merve Emre wrote:

> Always, Ferrante's fiction reminds us that sometimes you need someone else to help gather the scattered fragments of your existence. A writer is a friend who can find the thread of your story when you are too blinded by your lies to grasp it yourself. She can give you the beginning and end you need—if not in life, then in fiction.

The Lover

— 1984 —

Marguerite Duras

New York: Pantheon, 1997; translated from the French by Barbara Bray with an introduction by Maxine Hong Kingston; 117 pages; published in French as L'Amant

FIRST LINES

One day, I was already old, in the entrance of a public place a man came up to me. He introduced himself and said, "I've known you for years. Everyone says you were beautiful when you were young, but I want to tell you I think you're more beautiful now than then. Rather than your face as a young woman, I prefer your face as it is now. Ravaged."

PLOT SUMMARY

The taboo relationship between a French teenager and an older Chinese man is at the heart of this complex, intense novel. Largely set in the 1930s, during the French colonial era in what is now Vietnam, it is recounted much later by a Frenchwoman—who says at the opening she is "already old."

The premise of the narrative is simple: lovers from two different worlds embark on a doomed relationship. The story centers on a poor and fatherless teenage schoolgirl who encounters a man twelve years older than she is. The unnamed man, son of a wealthy Chinese businessman, sees the girl on the ferry she rides to school. She wears gold lamé shoes—"Bargains, final reductions bought for me by my mother"—and a brownish-pink fedora. The man offers her a ride in his limousine.

What ensues is an obsessive sexual liaison between the two. The girl's impoverished family, her mother and two brothers, grudgingly accepts and even encourages this relationship—in essence, prostituting the girl—as the man buys them dinner. The couple's furtive meetings continue until the day the girl is sent to France to attend university.

Plot is secondary to style here. The narrative flows, almost hypnotically, with little concern for chronological fidelity, as the author recalls both the passionate intensity and enormous despair of her youth.

ABOUT THE AUTHOR: MARGUERITE DURAS

Born in French Indochina on April 4, 1914, Marguerite Donnadieu was the daughter of the headmistress of a girls' school and a mathematics professor. Suffering from dysentery, Marguerite's father returned to France and died there in 1918, while Marguerite remained in Vietnam with her mother and two brothers. The family's savings were lost in a disastrous rice-farming venture and they were left desperately poor—and often hungry. The young Marguerite sometimes hunted birds and small game to survive.

Many of these biographical details align closely with those of the character in The Lover. At the age of fifteen, Marguerite also had met a wealthy man who became her lover. In 1932, she left Indochina and went to France to study. "Later, Duras said the depiction in 'The Lover' was her actual childhood," critic and novelist Rachel Kushner wrote in 2017, "but those who knew her best suggest she had begun to confuse her fiction with reality."

In France, Duras took her pen name from her father's hometown. She married her first husband, writer Robert Antelme, in 1939, the year World War II began, and her first book, *Les Impudents*, was published in 1943, the same year that the couple joined the French Resistance. Robert Antelme was captured and held in Dachau, the Nazi concentration camp, as a political prisoner. He nearly starved to death before being liberated.

While her husband was still a prisoner, Duras began an affair with French writer Dionys Mascolo. After Robert recovered, they ended up in a ménage à trois. In 1947, Duras divorced Robert and married Mascolo, with whom she had one child.

After the war, Duras went on to join the Communist Party, from which she was later expelled. She wrote novels, essays, and plays, winning a loyal but relatively small readership. Her breakthrough came with the original screenplay she wrote for *Hiroshima mon amour* (1959), a landmark in modern French cinema. Set in 1959 in the city leveled by the atomic bomb, the movie explores the relationship between a French actress and a Japanese architect, identified only as *Elle* (Her) and *Lui* (Him).

The publication of *The Lover* when she was seventy years old catapulted her to new heights. The book won France's chief literary award, the Prix Goncourt, and became an international best seller, selling millions of copies, both in France and in translation into forty languages, according to Pantheon, her American publisher.

For much of her life, Duras struggled with alcoholism and emphysema, which left her in a coma for five months in 1988. Despite the hardships, she said she found love again in a relationship with a younger gay man, Yann Andréa Steiner, a writer with whom she shared her final years.

In a 1990 interview quoted in her *New York Times* obituary, she said:

> I write about love, yes, but not about tenderness. I don't like tender people. I myself am very harsh. When I love someone, I desire them. But tenderness supposes the exclusion of desire.

Marguerite Duras died in her Left Bank home in Paris on March 3, 1996, aged eighty-one.

WHY YOU SHOULD READ IT

The jacket of one paperback edition of the novel promises something of a "disturbing, erotic" sensation. If you are expecting *Fifty Shades of Grey*—or even *Lady Chatterley's Lover*—you may be disappointed. *The Lover* is demure by contemporary standards. Far from explicit, its action and even the protagonist's youth were hardly shocking when it first appeared.

The novel is not well-dressed pornography. It is a woman's reflection, in her old age, of the force of youthful passion and the loss of something irretrievable. As the girl departs by ship for France, she hears a Chopin waltz. Duras writes:

> There wasn't a breath of wind and the music spread all over the dark boat, like a heavenly injunction whose import was unknown, like an order from God whose meaning was inscrutable. And the girl started up as if to go and kill herself in her turn, throw herself in her turn into the sea, and afterwards she wept because she thought of the man from Cholon.

Shortly after Duras died, *New York Times* book critic Parul Sehgal wrote an appraisal:

Name a current literary trend, and the French writer Marguerite Duras almost certainly got to it first—and took it further than anyone working today. The melding of memoir and artifice called autofiction; the fondness for fragments; the evasive, obliquely wounded female narrator; the excavations into trauma, addiction, maternity.

Many of these ingredients can be found in *The Lover*, which novelist and critic Rachel Kushner calls "disclosure," in an introduction to an edition of Duras's notebooks. Kushner writes:

> Duras became a huge star. Readers were eager to wade into a steamy vision of a colonial childhood and to presume it was her life. As a novel it is no more conventional than her others, but in its vivid compactness, the way it marbles and integrates the close and distant sensations and memories of one mind, it is a kind of artistic zenith.

With a narrative style that does not follow a straight timeline, it is a challenging read. Brooding and intense, it is far from a lighthearted or sentimental reflection on "lost innocence." Nor is it a romantic tale of first love remembered like something out of Nicholas Sparks. Duras is, as she described herself, "harsh." And *The Lover* is a stark—yes, in the author's word, "harsh"—reflection on passion, despair, sex, and death.

WHAT TO READ NEXT

The Lover, Wartime Notebooks, Practicalities is a single volume that collects the novel with essays and journals by Duras. Begin with that edition if you are interested in deeper insight into this influential writer's life and work.

To delve further into her fiction, consider *Hiroshima mon amour.* Before *The Lover* became a literary sensation, Duras was most famous for the screenplay of this modern classic of French New Wave cinema. Nominated for an Academy Award for Best Original Screenplay, the script is available in book form.

Among Duras's many other works, the earlier novel *The Ravishing of Lol Stein* (*Le ravissement de Lol V. Stein* in French, 1964; English translation, 1966) recounts a woman who returns to the scene of her past breakup with a lover and attempts to re-create this moment from the past.

Lucy

— 1990 —

Jamaica Kincaid

New York: Farrar, Straus and Giroux, 2002; 164 pages

FIRST LINES

It was my first day. I had come the night before, a gray-black and cold night before—as it was expected to be in the middle of January, though I didn't know that at the time—and I could not see anything clearly on the way in from the airport, even though there were lights everywhere. As we drove along, someone would single out to me a famous building, an important street, a park, a bridge that when built was thought to be a spectacle. In a daydream I used to have, all these places were points of happiness to me; all these places were lifeboats to my small drowning soul, for I would imagine myself entering and leaving them, and just that—entering and leaving over and over again—would see me through a bad feeling I did not have a name for.

PLOT SUMMARY

Set mostly in a large, unidentified North American city, this compressed and compelling account of a teenager who leaves the West Indies for life as an au pair was written more than thirty years ago, in 1990. But its concerns are as timely as ever. Its narrator, Lucy, is nineteen when she arrives in America, circa 1969. She has been hired to care for the four daughters of Mariah and Paul. Wealthy, white, beautiful, liberal-minded, they seem to have it all.

"The husband and wife looked alike and their four children looked just like them," Lucy comments after settling into the household. "In photographs of themselves, which they placed all over the house, their six yellow-haired heads of various sizes were bunched as if they were a bouquet of flowers tied together by an unseen string."

As she observes and takes part in the lives of this family, Lucy sees beyond their perfect picture of privilege. Her relationship to them, especially with Mariah, who tries so hard to befriend Lucy, is complex. As the young woman navigates this new world, she is emotionally tied to her old one.

Observing the cracks in this "perfect" family makes Lucy reflect on her own family in the West Indies. She cuts herself off from that past, refusing to open her mother's letters and never writing in return. Coming to terms with her own dreams and desires as her sexual self emerges is part of Lucy's struggle. She will bitterly confront the complexities of her emotional connection to her native island, its colonial history, and her own family.

ABOUT THE AUTHOR: JAMAICA KINCAID

Like the fictional Lucy, Jamaica Kincaid came to America as a nanny, or au pair, arriving in 1966. She was born Elaine Potter Richardson in Antigua on May 25, 1949, when the island and its small neighboring

island, Barbuda, were British colonies that would not gain independence until 1981.

Elaine Potter Richardson was raised in relative poverty. Her father
was a carpenter and her mother kept house in a home with no
electricity or running water. She excelled at the colonial British
schools she attended and was an avid reader. As she recalled to an
interviewer in 1990:

> When I was a child I liked to read. I loved "Jane Eyre" especially and
> read it over and over. I didn't know anyone else who liked to read
> except my mother, and it got me in a lot of trouble because it made
> me into a thief and a liar. I stole books, and I stole money to buy
> them. . . . Books brought me the greatest satisfaction. Just to be alone,
> reading, under the house, with lizards and spiders running around.

When she was nine, the first of three brothers was born. Although
a gifted student, she was taken out of school and sent to New York
at age seventeen to work as a nanny for a suburban couple. She was
expected to send money home. But like Lucy, she never did.

In and out of college, she returned to New York and began freelance writing for magazines, including teen monthlies, *Ms.*, and
the New York alternative weekly *Village Voice*, adopting the name
Jamaica Kincaid in 1973. Eventually discovered by the *New Yorker*
writer George W. S. Trow, to whom *Lucy* is dedicated, Jamaica Kincaid
was launched on a long relationship with the magazine, eventually
becoming a staff writer and contributing to its renowned "Talk of
the Town" column. In June 1978, her first piece of fiction, called
"Girl," appeared in the *New Yorker*.

In 1979, Kincaid married composer Allen Shawn, a professor
at Bennington College and son of the longtime *New Yorker* editor
William Shawn, who had hired Kincaid. They had two children
before divorcing in 2002.

Publishing short fiction in the *New Yorker* and the *Paris Review* led to a collection of ten stories called *At the Bottom of the River* (1983). Another set of stories published in the *New Yorker* about a young girl growing up in Antigua became chapters in the novel *Annie John* (1985). *A Small Place* (1988) is a nonfiction collection that explored colonialism, racism, corruption in the Antiguan government, and ecological damage done to the island. Then in 1990, after appearing as chapters in the *New Yorker*, *Lucy* was published in book form.

After twenty years as a staff writer at the *New Yorker*, Kincaid left the magazine in 1996, disagreeing with the direction the magazine had taken under new editor Tina Brown. Kincaid has since written several more novels, including one about a brother who died of AIDS, as well as nonfiction, including a work on gardening. Jamaica Kincaid is, at this writing, also Professor of African and African American Studies in Residence at Harvard University.

WHY YOU SHOULD READ IT

Let me make a prediction. After you read *Lucy*, you will not think of "I Wandered Lonely as a Cloud"—Wordsworth's famous poem about daffodils—in quite the same way. A classic of Romantic poetry, it becomes an ode to colonialism in Kincaid's novel. The words are bitter in Lucy's mouth as she is forced to recite the poem in school.

This is what a great book can do: make us look at those things we often don't question with different eyes. More than thirty years after it was published, *Lucy* has lost none of its timeliness. Or its intensity. Through Lucy, Kincaid explores the inescapable weight and consequences of colonialism. And of sex, race, privilege, class, and women living in a patriarchy.

There is certainly anger in Lucy. But it is such beautiful anger. In some moments, Kincaid's prose is absolutely cool. At others, it burns white-hot. Shortly after she settles into her new room—the "maid's room"—we hear Lucy:

What a surprise this was to me, that I longed to be back in the place that I came from, that I longed to sleep in a bed I had outgrown, that I longed to be with people whose smallest, most natural gesture would call up in me such a rage that I longed to see them all dead at my feet.

Over her career, Kincaid has been dismissively referred to as an "angry Black woman." But though Lucy sometimes seethes with anger, it always seems an entirely appropriate response to the world and the life she is in.

WHAT TO READ NEXT

Start with *At the Bottom of the River*, the first collection of stories that heralded Kincaid, then best known for her nonfiction in the *New Yorker*, as an accomplished writer of fiction. These stories have a dreamlike quality, quite different from the sharp realism of *Lucy*. Or follow with *Annie John*, a finalist for the 1985 Ritz Paris Hemingway Award. Set in Antigua, it focuses on a young girl's fierce conflict with her mother as she grows up. Clearly presaging *Lucy*, the girl in *Annie John* eventually leaves home as a young teenager, both an exile and an escape. It is more or less the very point at which *Lucy* begins.

Maus I: A Survivor's Tale: My Father Bleeds History

— 1986 —

Art Spiegelman

New York: Pantheon Books, 1986; 159 pages

FIRST LINES

Rego Park, N.Y. c. 1958

 It was summer, I remember. I was ten or eleven . . .

 "Last one to the schoolyard is a rotten egg!"

 . . . I was roller skating with Howie and Steve . . .

 . . . 'til my skate came loose.

 "Ow!

 Hey! Wait up fellas!"

 "Rotten egg! Ha Ha!"

"W-wait up!"

"SNK, SNF"

My father was in front, fixing something . . .

"Artie! Come to hold this a minute while I saw."

"SNRK?"

"Why do you cry, Artie? Hold better on the wood."

"I- I fell, and my friends skated away w- without me."

He stopped sawing.

"Friends? Your friends? . . .

If you lock them together in a room with no food for a week . . . .

THEN you could see what it is, FRIENDS!"

PLOT SUMMARY

The first installment of what became a two-volume work, *Maus I: A Survivor's Tale: My Father Bleeds History* is an account of the Holocaust, told in comic book–style panels, in which Jews are depicted as mice, Germans as cats, and Poles as pigs.

The Holocaust? As a cartoon strip? Yes, it is included here for both its intrinsic literary value as well its place in publishing history. Before *Maus*, few graphic novels or comic books of any kind were accorded the status of literature. *Maus* changed that.

Through this landmark combination of words, art, history, and biography, author and cartoonist Art Spiegelman recounts the story of his parents, Vladek and Anja. Polish Jews, they are depicted in the years before the war begins and then during Vladek's brief stint in the Polish army when Germany invades Poland in 1939.

Vladek and Anja are forced into hiding with the approach of the Holocaust until—and this is no spoiler—Vladek is unloaded from a truck at the gates of Auschwitz. Set against that story, *Maus* also explores the troubled relationship between father Vladek and son Artie, who is trying to comprehend his mother's suicide.

ABOUT THE AUTHOR: ART SPIEGELMAN

Art Spiegelman was born on February 15, 1948, in Stockholm, Sweden, and was brought to the United States in 1951 as a toddler by his parents, survivors of Auschwitz. An older brother had died during the Holocaust before Spiegelman was born. The family eventually settled in Queens, New York. While attending New York City's High School of Art and Design, Spiegelman began selling illustrations to newspapers and later designed art for Topps Chewing Gum. While in college, he helped develop the successful "Garbage Pail Kids" and "Wacky Packages" trading cards.

Spiegelman later told the *New York Times* that after he showed his father one of his first comics, "his only response was, 'From this you make a living?'"

After his mother's suicide in 1968, Spiegelman left the State University of New York at Binghamton and began contributing to the alterative comics scene pioneered by R. Crumb. In 1972, two groundbreaking strips were published. The first was *Maus*, originally appearing as a three-page story. The second, *Prisoner on the Hell Planet*, dealt with the suicide of Spiegelman's mother. In 1980, he founded *Raw*, an underground comics anthology, with his wife, Françoise Mouly, later the art editor of the *New Yorker*. In *Raw*, they pioneered graphic novels and "comix" (comics written for a mature audience).

Spiegelman continued to tell the story in *Maus* in serial fashion. Attempting to sell the series in book form, Spiegelman was rejected by many mainstream publishers. But a newspaper article praising the project led to its eventual publication in book form by Pantheon in 1986.

A second volume, *Maus II*, published in 1991, was accorded a prestigious front-page review in the *New York Times Book Review*. It went on to become a *New York Times* best seller initially on the Fiction list and later moving to the Nonfiction list. The two works were awarded a special Pulitzer Prize citation in 1992. Spiegelman's art for *Maus* was also given an exhibition at the Museum of Modern Art.

Spiegelman went on to work as an illustrator for the *New York Times* and *Playboy* and as a staff artist and writer for the *New Yorker*. In 2004, Spiegelman published *In the Shadow of No Towers*, his reflection on the destruction of the World Trade Center on 9/11. It was selected as one of the "100 Notable Books of the Year" in 2004 by the *New York Times*.

WHY YOU SHOULD READ IT

There is, of course, an extraordinary range and sweep of Holocaust literature, in both fiction and nonfiction. John Hersey's *The Wall*, a fictional account of the Warsaw uprising, left an indelible impression on me as a young person. And such novels as *Sophie's Choice*, *Schindler's Ark (Schindler's List)*, and *The Reader*, as well as Elie Wiesel's many books, including *Night*, and Primo Levi's memoir (see *If This Is a Man*), are central to the historical memory of the Holocaust.

But as Lawrence L. Langer wrote in reviewing *Maus II* in the *New York Times* in 1991: "Perhaps no Holocaust narrative will ever contain the whole experience. But Art Spiegelman has found an original and authentic form to draw us closer to its bleak heart."

On my second reading, I was struck by the significance of the difficult relationship between father and son, a level of emotion that a focus on the Holocaust material tends to overlook. A brilliant blend of memoir and history, *Maus* is presented in a visual format that makes the humanity of Spiegelman's cartoon "animals" all the more vivid. To a German reporter who once asked if his depiction of Auschwitz was in bad taste, Spiegelman replied, "No, I thought Auschwitz was in bad taste."

Early in 2022, *Maus* made international headlines when a school board in Tennessee removed the book from the school curriculum, provoking an outcry over censorship. That decision came in the midst of a wave of book bannings across America, many of them directed at books written by and about gays and people of color, as well as nonfiction focusing on gender issues, teen sexuality, slavery, and racism in America.

WHAT TO READ NEXT

Obviously, the answer is *Maus II*, which continues the saga of Artie's parents, his fraught relationship with his father, and his own sense of guilt and loss. Reviewing it in 1991, *New York Times* critic Michiko Kakutani wrote, "In recounting the tales of both the father and the son in 'Maus' and now in 'Maus II,' Mr. Spiegelman has stretched the boundaries of the comic book form and in doing so has created one of the most powerful and original memoirs to come along in recent years."

In the Shadow of No Towers emerged from his experience living near the World Trade Center towers struck on September 11, 2001. Depressed and obsessed with the attack and its aftermath, he spent several years drawing the panels, which were serialized in Europe before being published in the United States in 2004. While he was working on the project, he told an interviewer:

> It's hard to explain why these drawings that everybody thinks you scrawl on the side of a math test should take so long to put into shape for publication. I think it's useful to think of them as haikus.

Middle Passage

— 1990 —

Charles Johnson

New York: Scribner, 2015; with an introduction by Stanley Crouch; 206 pages

FIRST LINES

Of all the things that drive men to sea, the most common disaster, I've come to learn, is women. In my case, it was a spirited Boston schoolteacher named Isadora Bailey who led me to become a cook aboard the *Republic*. Both Isadora and my creditors, I should add, who entered into a conspiracy, a trap, a scheme so cunning that my only choices were prison, a brief stay in the stony oubliette* of the Spanish Calabozo (or a long one at the bottom of the Mississippi), or marriage, which was, for a man of my temperament, worse than imprisonment—especially if you knew Isadora.

---

* An oubliette is a dungeon with a trapdoor in the ceiling as the only way in or out.

PLOT SUMMARY

A roguish thief and roustabout, Rutherford Calhoun is a freedman living in New Orleans with all of its attendant temptations. Intelligent and erudite, Calhoun was educated by the Reverend who had enslaved and then emancipated him. But when high-minded Isadora Bailey tries to force him to settle down, Rutherford chooses escape. Stowing away on the *Republic* as it sails, he is unaware that he has joined an illegal slave ship. Spared being pitched overboard, Calhoun becomes a cook and confidant of the ship's notorious dwarfish Captain Ebenezer Falcon.

Set in 1830, well after the international slave trade was outlawed in America, the novel follows the misadventures of Calhoun, the morally repugnant Falcon, and the rest of a motley crew as they sail for an African slaver's fort. There they take on board a group of Allmuseri, a legendary African people famed for their mystical powers, to be carried across the ocean to the slave blocks.

Making the perilous Middle Passage on the *Republic*, Calhoun sees the grim atrocities of the slave trade. Then a greater force intervenes. When Calhoun learns that Captain Falcon—who also traffics in stolen artifacts—has another prize in a crate belowdecks, the novel moves into the realm of the supernatural. As the crew and captives threaten rebellion, the voyage home becomes a nightmarish odyssey of Homeric dimensions.

ABOUT THE AUTHOR: CHARLES JOHNSON

Esteemed as a novelist, essayist, philosopher, literary scholar, screenwriter, and university professor, Charles Johnson first aspired to be a cartoonist. Born on April 23, 1948—Shakespeare's birthday, he notes in a memoir—in Evanston, Illinois, he demonstrated a talent for drawing at an early age and had visions of working for Marvel.

At one point, he talked with his father about a career. "He didn't understand the arts. But he supported me," Johnson recalled to a *Chicago Tribune* interviewer in 2021. "He paid for my art lessons. He supported me on something he didn't understand and to me, that's real love—supporting someone because you can see how passionate they are. I mean, he didn't think Black people were allowed to be cartoonists."

Through college at Southern Illinois University, where the novelist and critic John Gardner was a mentor, Johnson drew cartoons. His first two books were cartoon collections. And in 1970, Johnson created and hosted *Charlie's Pad*, an early public television series that consisted of fifteen-minute lessons in cartooning. He also wrote six novels that went unpublished.

After earning degrees in writing and journalism, Johnson received a Ph.D. in philosophy. In 1976, he joined the faculty at the University of Washington, teaching writing and literature. By then, he had published his first novel, *Faith and the Good Thing* (1974), a story that brought together philosophy, Black folklore, and surrealism. It followed a woman named Faith, raised in the Deep South, who moves to a world of prostitution and drugs in Chicago. It was praised in a *New York Times* review that called Johnson's first fiction "a many-splendored and ennobling weaving-together of thought, suffering, humor and magic." A second novel, *Oxherding Tale* (1982), merged Johnson's studies in Buddhist philosophy with the story of an enslaved man's journey toward freedom.

American slavery became the centerpiece of his masterwork, *Middle Passage*, published to acclaim in 1990 and winner of the National Book Award that year.

Over a long career, Johnson has produced more than two dozen books, including novels, cartoon collections, and works of philosophy. He has published three story collections: *The Sorcerer's Apprentice* (1986), *Soulcatcher: And Other Stories* (2001), and *Dr. King's Refrigerator and Other Bedtime Stories* (2005). His nonfiction includes

Being and Race: Black Writing Since 1970 (1988), *King: The Photobiography of Martin Luther King, Jr.* (2000), and *Turning the Wheel: Essays on Buddhism and Writing* (2003). In *The Way of the Writer: Reflections on the Art and Craft of Storytelling* (2016), Johnson describes reading his first copies of Mary Shelley and Shakespeare when his mother brought home books discarded by women in a sorority house where she worked as a cleaning woman and where Jewish and Black people would never be admitted as members. Johnson also collaborated on *Africans in America: America's Journey Through Slavery* (1999), a book based on the six-hour PBS series of the same name chronicling slavery in America.

The breadth of Johnson's accomplishments and intellectual appetite is one hallmark of his career. "I have been opposed to being put into boxes my whole life. Those boxes are artificial," he told an interviewer in 2021. "A creative spirit is wider. It holds something one day, something else the next. I realize people identify me very simply as the award-winning author of 'Middle Passage,' this adventure set during the North Atlantic slave trade. . . . I've had to reinvent myself three times in 73 years. I started as a cartoonist and worked intensely seven years that way. Then I was seduced by philosophy. But at school we were told: There will be no jobs in philosophy."

In 1998, Johnson was awarded the prestigious MacArthur Fellowship. He continued teaching until his retirement in 2009 and resided in Seattle, Washington, at this writing.

WHY YOU SHOULD READ IT

Echoing the great American nautical literary tradition of Melville, Jack London, and Richard Henry Dana—along with touches of Twain, Homer, and Voltaire's *Candide* (see entry)—Johnson's novel is a tour de force that ultimately explores slavery as the American heart of darkness. Its narrator, Rutherford Calhoun, is one of those brilliant fictional characters who can be placed beside Melville's

Ishmael, Twain's Huck, and Candide as an improbable but unforgettable guide.

Steeped in the romance of sea yarns, Johnson's novel is an exciting picaresque that also evokes elements of history—the events on the *Republic* recall an actual mutiny by African captives in 1839 on the *Amistad*, a case that landed before the U.S. Supreme Court and was a landmark in the abolition movement.

But no small part of the electricity and excitement of this novel is Johnson's ability to weave in a measure of the supernatural, or magical realism. That element places this novel in the realm of mythic allegory. And naming the slave ship *Republic* is no accident. The book is about the American republic's original sin: slavery.

Writing that Johnson "combines the physical realities with the internal mysteries of sensibility so well," the late critic Stanley Crouch also commented, "His command of the language is so omni-directional that he creates a nineteenth-century seaman and adventurer, a curious minded man in a time when the world was made to heel before technology, mystic explanations, and the intertwined facts of slaving and slavery."

It might be odd to consider that a work about the horrors of slavery could be comic, and perhaps "tragicomic" is more fitting. But Johnson seamlessly interweaves moments of humor in a story that exposes the brutality of America's original sin and the cruelty of human nature.

WHAT TO READ NEXT

In the catalog of Charles Johnson's fiction, I would next turn to *Soulcatcher: And Other Stories* (2001), stories based on the history of slavery in America, including Martha Washington's dealings with the enslaved servants she managed after George Washington's death. Another collection to consider, *The Sorcerer's Apprentice*, was nominated for the prestigious PEN/Faulkner Award. Reviewing these stories in 1986, *New York Times* critic Michiko Kakutani wrote, "Mr. Johnson has used his generous storytelling gifts and his easy familiarity with a variety of literary genres to conjure up eight moral fables that limn the fabulous even as they remain grounded in the language and social idioms of black American communities."

If you are interested in writing fiction, Johnson's *The Way of the Writer* is one of those rare instructional guides that offer a rigorous, provocative approach to the exercise of practicing the craft.

In addition to reading Johnson's other work, I highly recommend Marcus Rediker's nonfiction book *The Slave Ship: A Human History* (2007) for anyone interested in learning more about the history of the slave trade and the Middle Passage. In excruciating detail, Rediker describes what life aboard these ships was like for crews and their human cargo.

Mrs. Dalloway

— 1925 —

Virginia Woolf

New York: Harvest, 1981; foreword by Maureen Howard; 194 pages

* TIME: "All-TIME 100 Novels" *

FIRST LINES

Mrs. Dalloway said she would buy the flowers herself.

For Lucy had her work cut out for her. The doors would be taken off their hinges; Rumpelmayer's men were coming. And then, thought Clarissa Dalloway, what a morning—fresh as if issued to children on a beach.

PLOT SUMMARY

Nearly one century after it was published, Virginia Woolf's novella remains a landmark in twentieth-century literature. It is a simple story. On a single London day in June 1923, Clarissa Dalloway makes preparations for a party she will host that evening. At every step along the way, as Big Ben tolls the hours, she is reminded of moments from her past and the choices she has made.

Against her story is that of a stranger she passes. A veteran of World War I, Septimus Smith has been left deeply damaged by the war—what was then described as shell shock—and is tended by his wife, Lucrezia. Although Mrs. Dalloway never actually meets Septimus, their paths cross and lives converge on this fateful day.

As the novel moves toward Mrs. Dalloway's dinner party, the book is dominated by these two characters and their thoughts. But we are also in the minds and observations of other various characters, especially those in Mrs. Dalloway's life, through the "stream of consciousness" technique that Woolf practiced.

Michael Cunningham, author of the Pulitzer Prize–winning *The Hours* (see entry), wrote, "Virginia Woolf's 'Mrs. Dalloway' is a revolutionary novel of profound scope and depth, about a day in the life of a woman who runs a few errands, sees an old suitor and gives a dull party. It's a masterpiece created out of the humblest narrative materials."

ABOUT THE AUTHOR: VIRGINIA WOOLF

What a brilliant, complicated, and tragic life.

Born on January 25, 1882, in London, Adeline Virginia Stephen was the daughter of Leslie Stephen, a prominent figure in English letters. Both her father and mother, Julia Jackson, had previous marriages, but both of their spouses died. With four children between them, they married in 1878, and four of their own children followed: Vanessa—who would become a modernist painter—a son, Thoby, Virginia, and Adrian.

At nine, Virginia began writing a newspaper, filled with family anecdotes. But her mother's death in 1895, when Virginia was thirteen, ended this endeavor, and she sunk into depression. In 1897, one of her half sisters died at age twenty-eight, deepening Virginia's emotional despair.

Encouraged by her father, she began to write anonymous reviews for the *Times Literary Supplement* and other journals. Then, following the death of her father in 1904, Virginia had a nervous breakdown. The death of her brother Thoby by typhoid in 1906 added to her emotional despair. Her diaries would reveal that she was also the victim of sexual abuse as a child by her older half brothers.

Virginia and other members of the Stephen family later moved to the bohemian Bloomsbury section of London, where they would form an artistic and literary society known as the Bloomsbury Group, which became a center of modernist thought in art, literature, politics, and social and sexual attitudes.

The group included, among others, novelist E. M. Forster, economist John Maynard Keynes, art critic Clive Bell—who had an open marriage with Virginia's sister Vanessa—the critic and gallerist Roger Fry and painter Duncan Grant, who both became Vanessa's lovers, and essayist Leonard Woolf. In 1912, Virginia married Woolf, also a civil servant and political theorist. Despite their apparently happy marriage, Virginia Woolf attempted suicide in 1913. Her first novel, *The Voyage Out* (1915), was followed by another suicide attempt.

In 1922, Virginia met an aristocratic writer named Vita Sackville-West and they began a friendship that became a sexual relationship. It was during these years that Woolf published some of her most significant work through the Hogarth Press she had established with Leonard in 1917: *Mrs. Dalloway* (1925), *To the Lighthouse* (1927), *Orlando* (1928), and *The Waves* (1931).

As the 1930s marched toward World War II, Woolf found herself unable to write. There has been much conjecture about her self-doubt, bouts of depression, possible bipolar disorder, and history of sexual abuse. Whatever the reasons, on March 28, 1941, Virginia Woolf walked down to the river Ouse, filled the pockets of her over-coat with stones, and drowned herself. She was fifty-nine years old.

I first encountered Virginia Woolf's remarkable June day while in college in the 1970s—and had to read it at least twice. Once for a course on women in fiction and again for a seminar on the twentieth-century novel. Long overlooked, Woolf experienced a great revival as the feminist movement awakened interest in her pioneering work in fiction and essays.

Returning to it many years later is something of a revelation. This is the essence of what Italo Calvino, cited in my introduction, meant when he wrote, "Even if the books have remained the same (though they do change, in the light of an altered historical perspective), we have most certainly changed, and our encounter will be an entirely new thing."

In an introduction to a reissue of *Mrs. Dalloway*, novelist Jenny Offill (see entry) addressed this experience as she described the process of rereading it. "Each time, I have found shocks of recognition on the page, but they are always new ones, never the ones I was remembering," writes Offill. "Instead, some forgotten facet of the story comes to light, and the feeling is always that of having blurred past something that was right in front of me. This is because 'Mrs. Dalloway' is a remarkably expansive and an irreducibly strange book. Nothing you might read in a plot summary prepares you for the multitudes it contains."

In my rereading, the brilliance of Woolf's prose now seems more sharply defined, even if it is also demanding. Her descriptions of the most ordinary moments on a London day—the sounds, textures, sights—are a pleasure. But the revelation in this reading was found in the depths of Septimus Smith's reveries. Perhaps understanding more fully about World War I and its madness makes the tragedy of his story even more compelling.

The War had taught him. It was sublime. He had gone through the whole show, friendship, European War, death, had won promotion, was still under thirty and was bound to survive. . . . For now that it was all over, truce signed, and the dead buried, he had, especially in the evening, these sudden thunder-claps of fear. He could not feel.

As Michael Cunningham, who reshaped *Mrs. Dalloway* into his Pulitzer Prize–winning *The Hours* (see following entry), put it:

The book encompasses, as well, almost infinite shades and degrees of happiness, loss, satisfaction, regret and tragedy. It invokes, over and over, the choices we make, those that are made for us by others, and their sometimes lifelong ramifications, many of which we could not possibly have imagined at the time.

A new and lavishly illustrated *Annotated Mrs. Dalloway* was published in 2021. While its photography, artwork, and copious notes are fascinating and may add to an appreciation of the book, some readers might find them distracting and prefer simply reading the text alone.

WHAT TO READ NEXT

The list of Woolf's titles in the front pages of *Mrs. Dalloway* is daunting. There are novels, criticism, book-length essays, collected essays (four volumes), and the diary (five volumes). To move beyond Clarissa Dalloway, an important first step might be *A Room of One's Own*, an extended essay based on lectures delivered to women at Cambridge University in 1928 and published in 1929. In it, Woolf argues that women needed space, literally and figuratively, not just to write but to be able to fully participate in society. Their status often resulted in poverty, she argued, trapping them. She also hinted discreetly at lesbianism, still a taboo in literature and society. Her lover, Vita Sackville-West, was in the audience when she presented her lecture.

For her fiction, an important next step is *To the Lighthouse* (1927), the novel that followed *Mrs. Dalloway*. It recounts the visits of a family to the Isle of Skye in Scotland over a decade. It is ranked number 15 on the Modern Library list of 100 Best Novels.

Finally, *Orlando: A Biography* (1928) is very different in style and is one of Woolf's most popular books. Inspired by and dedicated to her friend and lover Vita Sackville-West, it describes the adventures of a poet who changes sex from man to woman and lives for centuries. It also opens with a delightfully hard-to-resist first line: "He—for there could be no doubt of his sex, though the fashion of the time did something to disguise it—was in the act of slicing at the head of a Moor which swung from the rafters."

Orlando is on the BBC list of "100 Novels That Shaped Our World."

The Hours

— 1998 —

Michael Cunningham

New York: Picador USA, 1998; 226 pages

* 1999 Pulitzer Prize for Fiction *

FIRST LINES

She hurries from the house, wearing a coat too heavy for the weather. It is 1941. Another war has begun. She has left a note for Leonard, and another for Vanessa. She walks purposefully toward the river, certain of what she'll do, but even now she is almost distracted by the sight of the downs, the church, and a scattering of sheep, incandescent, tinged with a faint hint of sulfur, grazing under a darkening sky. She pauses, watching the sheep and the sky, then walks on. The voices murmur behind her; bombers drone in the sky, though she looks for the planes and can't see them.

PLOT SUMMARY

Inspired by Virginia Woolf's *Mrs. Dalloway*, Cunningham's *The Hours* explores three lives ultimately entwined with the fictional Mrs. Dalloway. Brilliantly conceived and executed, the novel follows three women on a single day in three different times and settings.

One of the women is the novelist Virginia Woolf herself, who is first seen in the act of committing suicide in 1941. The story then flashes back and Woolf appears in 1923 as she begins to write the book that will become *Mrs. Dalloway*. Next is Clarissa Vaughan, a fiftyish book editor in 1990s Manhattan, who is preparing a party to celebrate her ex-lover, a poet dying of AIDS, who once nicknamed her Mrs. Dalloway. And the third is Laura Brown, a suburban Los Angeles housewife in 1949, who is preparing a birthday party for her husband but who really wishes only to keep reading *Mrs. Dalloway*.

In exquisitely written alternating chapters, each of these women moves through the hours of their days, busying themselves with seemingly ordinary details—buying flowers, making cakes, having tea with a sister. But all the while, they contemplate the meaning of their families, loves, and lives.

ABOUT THE AUTHOR: MICHAEL CUNNINGHAM

Born on November 6, 1952, in Cincinnati, Ohio, and raised in Pasadena, California, Cunningham is a novelist, screenwriter, and short story author. He studied literature at Stanford University and was a Michener Fellow at the University of Iowa Writers' Workshop, where he received his MFA. While a student, he wrote short stories that appeared in the *Atlantic Monthly* and *Paris Review*. His story "White Angel" appeared in the *New Yorker* and was chosen for inclusion in *The Best American Short Stories, 1989*. It later became a chapter in his 1990 novel *A Home at the End of the World*, a novel about three people—a gay man, his bisexual friend, and a straight woman—who form a family together.

Among numerous awards, Cunningham received a Guggenheim Fellowship in 1993. His novel *Flesh and Blood* (1995), a multigenerational saga of a Greek family, was followed by *The Hours*, which won the 1999 Pulitzer Prize as well as a PEN/Faulkner Award for Fiction. In 2002, *The Hours* was filmed with the central roles played by Meryl Streep, Julianne Moore, and Nicole Kidman, who won an Academy Award for her portrayal of Virginia Woolf.

Cunningham's later novels are *Specimen Days* (2005), *By Nightfall* (2010), and *The Snow Queen* (2014), along with a collection of short fiction, *A Wild Swan and Other Tales* (2015).

Besides the novels and short stories, Cunningham has written a nonfiction book, *Land's End: A Walk in Provincetown* (2002), and two screenplays: one for his novel *A Home at the End of the World* (2004) and one for *Evening* (2007), based on a novel by Susan Minot. At this writing, Cunningham was teaching creative writing at Yale University and lived in Manhattan.

WHY YOU SHOULD READ IT

This is a great short book inspired by another great short book. So, question number one is obvious: Must one read *Mrs. Dalloway* before reading this book?

The honest, short answer is: No. With a bit of guidance, you could read *The Hours* without reading *Mrs. Dalloway*. But why would you?

Mrs. Dalloway is about one woman, Clarissa Dalloway, going about her day in London in June 1923 as she plans for a party that same evening. Simple.

An homage to the genius of Virginia Woolf and her novel, *The Hours* is masterful in its own right, fathoming art, love, life, and death—and flowers and parties. Like a talented musician performing variations on a theme by another composer, Cunningham takes the notes and pauses of Virginia Woolf and makes something new and different.

In an essay on Virginia Woolf published in *The Guardian*, Cunningham described reading *Mrs. Dalloway* at age fifteen—"to impress a girl who was reading it at the time." While shaping him as a reader, the experience made a deep artistic impression. "In *Mrs Dalloway*, Woolf asserts that a day in the life of just about anyone contains, if looked at with sufficient penetration, much of what one needs to know about all human life, in more or less the way the blueprint for an entire organism is present in every strand of its DNA," wrote Cunningham. "In *Mrs Dalloway*, and other novels of Woolf's, we are told that there are no insignificant lives, only inadequate ways of looking at them."

Apart from its three vividly drawn central characters and its large, grave concerns, *The Hours* is filled with finely crafted passages, delicious in their weight—sometimes ethereal, sometimes dense. As Laura Brown makes a birthday cake in her 1949 kitchen, with the help of her three-year-old son, she thinks:

> She is going to produce a birthday cake—only a cake—but in her mind at this moment the cake is glossy and resplendent as any photograph in any magazine; it is better, even, than the photographs of cakes in magazines. She imagines making, out of the humblest materials, a cake with all the balance and authority of an urn or a house. The cake will speak of bounty and delight the way a good house speaks of comfort and safety. . . . Wasn't a book like *Mrs. Dalloway* once just empty paper and a pot of ink?

It is Cunningham's inventiveness and exquisite skill as a novelist that makes this sort of passage *referential* without making it *derivative*. And that is no small part of the artistry of *The Hours*.

WHAT TO READ NEXT

Cunningham wrote two novels before *The Hours*. Both were much admired by critics and both explore family, sex, and relationships. In *A Home at the End of the World* (1990), two men and a straight woman try to raise a child in a mini-commune in upstate New York. *Flesh and Blood* (1995) is about the Stassos family, several generations of Greeks ruled by a patriarch. It was lauded by novelist Meg Wolitzer, who wrote, "Grand themes of love, death and loyalty are all played out here at length."

Written after *The Hours*, Cunningham's *By Nightfall* (2010) also brings together a trio of people—he is clearly interested in sets of three. A New York couple in their forties are unsettled by the unexpected arrival of the wife's younger brother. Reviewing the book, novelist Jeanette Winterson (see entry) summed up Cunningham's work:

> Cunningham writes so well, and with such an economy of language, that he can call up the poet's exact match. His dialogue is deft and fast. The pace of the writing is skilled—stretched or contracted at just the right time. And if some of the interventions on art are too long—well, too long for whom? For what? Good novels are novels that provoke us to argue with the writer, not just novels that make us feel magically, mysteriously at home.

———————————

AUTHOR'S NOTE: As noted in my Introduction, I am placing this novel after *Mrs. Dalloway*, which inspired Michael Cunningham. As I also explain, one could read *The Hours* first.

The Nickel Boys

— 2019 —

Colson Whitehead

New York: Anchor Books, 2020; 208 pages

FIRST LINES

Even in death the boys were trouble.

The secret graveyard lay on the north side of the Nickel campus, in a patchy acre of wild grass between the old work barn and the school dump. The field had been a grazing pasture when the school operated a dairy, selling milk to local customers—one of the state of Florida's schemes to relieve the taxpayer burden of the boys' upkeep.

PLOT SUMMARY

Inspired by the discovery of a covert cemetery on the grounds of the Arthur G. Dozier School for Boys in northern Florida, this is a fictional account of one of the country's largest and most notorious "reform schools"—and it is riveting. Set mostly in Florida in the early 1960s, it tells the story of the fictional Nickel Academy as seen through the eyes of Elwood Curtis, a young man growing up in in Tallahassee, Florida, still in the Jim Crow era of discrimination, segregation, everyday slights, and daily humiliations.

As Elwood listens to Martin Luther King speak on a phonograph album and watches lunchroom sit-ins, he aspires to follow King's path. Guided by a caring grandmother—his parents have abandoned him—Elwood walks a straight path. He is a promising student, working to save for college. But one day, while on his way to class, he makes a grievous mistake that lands him in Nickel Academy, with its hellish catalog of cruelty, abuse, and corruption.

In this Inferno, Elwood's devotion to Dr. King's words and ideas will be put to an extreme test. He tries to negotiate the reign of terror, including the "White House" where beatings are administered to boys who cross the authorities. But he is traumatized by what he hears and sees—some boys just disappear. The horrors he experiences are not fiction—they are sourced from the testimony of men who survived the Dozier School. This makes the story all the more chilling.

With few allies and little hope, Elwood and his friend Turner, who thinks Elwood is naïvely idealistic, plot their separate approaches to surviving Nickel Academy.

ABOUT THE AUTHOR: COLSON WHITEHEAD

When a *Time* magazine cover declares that you are "America's Storyteller," a novelist is elevated to a lofty place. When two Pulitzer Prizes position that writer alongside Faulkner and Updike as a fairly exceptional repeat winner, he is in rarefied territory. Meet Colson Whitehead.

Born in Manhattan on November 6, 1969, Arch Colson Chipp Whitehead was the third of four children. His parents were entrepreneurs who owned an executive recruiting firm, and White-head attended a private school in Manhattan and then went to Harvard. Thinking it too "preppy," *Time* reported, he dropped "Arch" in favor of "Colson" at age twenty-one.

Returning to New York, Whitehead wrote for the alternative newsweekly *Village Voice*. After multiple rejections of an attempted first novel, Whitehead successfully published *The Intuitionist* (1999), the story of a woman who inspects elevators. The book won crit-ical praise and established his reputation as an emerging talent. He enhanced that standing with a second novel, *John Henry Days* (2001), which draws on the legendary folk hero who wins a contest against a steam-driven rock-drilling machine, and was a finalist for the Pulitzer. In 2002, he was awarded the prestigious MacArthur Fellowship.

Whitehead's talent continued to unfold. His later novels included *Apex Hides the Hurt* (2006), a satirical novel about a man who creates new names for consumer products; *Sag Harbor* (2009), about a Black enclave on Long Island; and *Zone One* (2011), a *New York Times* best seller and Whitehead's take on the well-worn zombie apocalypse theme. He also wrote two works of nonfiction, *The Colossus of New York* (2003), a history of New York City, and *The Noble Hustle* (2014), about the World Series of Poker, as well as short stories.

In 2016, Whitehead reached new heights of critical success with *The Underground Railroad*, a reimagining of the escape route used by enslaved people. An Oprah Book Club selection, praised by President Barack Obama, the book won the Pulitzer Prize and National Book Award among other honors. A ten-part television adaptation of the novel began airing in May 2021 to wide critical acclaim. Whitehead followed with *The Nickel Boys*, which garnered his second Pulitzer Prize.

Whitehead lives in Brooklyn with his wife, a literary agent, and their two children. *Harlem Shuffle*, a work of crime fiction set in the 1960s, was published in September 2021.

Sometimes a novelist unearths "the roots that clutch"—T. S. Eliot's memorable phrase from "The Waste Land." The writer does this through a story and perhaps characters that rumble through a reader's thoughts long after the last page. They take hold and don't easily let go.

The Nickel Boys is one of these books. This riveting, unforgettable novel explores a piece of America's past—the "hard history" still being reckoned with during our very troubled times. As Whitehead told the *New York Times* before publication:

> The book about the Dozier school seemed relevant, just to make sense of where we are as a country. I think we've regressed and I think a lot of normal people and artists are trying to make sense of this moment.

No small part of his achievement in *The Nickel Boys* is Whitehead's hard-edged, sharply focused style. It emerges from the tradition of classic American realism. One key to that style is the understatement he uses to record the cruelty without overly graphic descriptions. The scene he sets is often lean, yet more than enough. It lingers without elaboration.

After interceding in a fight, for instance, Elwood must wait for a beating in the Nickel's notorious White House. He listens as the other boys are beaten. Then comes Elwood's turn:

> The strap was three feet long with a wooden handle, and they had called it Black Beauty since before Spencer's time, although the one he held in his hand was not the original: She had to be repaired or replaced every so often. The leather slapped across the ceiling before it came down on your legs, to tell you it was about to come down, and the bunk springs made noise with each blow.

With such spare prose, Whitehead moves seamlessly through Elwood's nightmarish sentence—with time markers like the famous Clay-Liston heavyweight bout—and then jumps forward to a future in New York City and the ultimate revelations of what has taken place at the school.

Like the best of fiction, Whitehead's novel makes us see. But it is more than the "glimpse of truth." Ultimately, the book raises an issue more important than merely remembering the past: Whitehead demands we ask ourselves how we respond to injustice.

WHAT TO READ NEXT

Among his other works try *John Henry Days*, Whitehead's widely acclaimed second novel that works off the history and legend of the "steel driving man" who supposedly defeated a steam engine in a contest and then collapsed afterward.

As a sucker for postapocalypse zombie fiction, I look forward to reading Whitehead's interpretation, *Zone One*. A reviewer in *Esquire* wrote, "Whitehead brilliantly reformulates an old-hat genre to ask the epidemic question of a teetering history—the question about the possibility of survival."

Whitehead's other Pulitzer winner, *The Underground Railroad*, tells the story of Cora and Caesar, a couple who attempt to escape enslavement in Georgia. In Whitehead's imagining, this becomes an actual rail transport system in addition to the historically accurate series of safe houses used to escape slavery. "The result," wrote Michiko Kakutani in a *New York Times* review, "is a potent, almost hallucinatory novel that leaves the reader with a devastating understanding of the terrible human costs of slavery."

No One Writes to the Colonel

— 1961 —

Gabriel García Márquez

New York: HarperPerennial Modern Classics, 1999; translated from the Spanish by J. S. Bernstein; 64 pages; originally published in 1961 as El coronel no tiene quien le escriba; *published in* Collected Novellas *with* Leaf Storm *and* Chronicle of a Death Foretold

FIRST LINES

The colonel took the top off the coffee can and saw that there was only one little spoonful left. He removed the pot from the fire, poured half the water onto the earthen floor, and scraped the inside of the can with a knife until the last scrapings of the ground coffee, mixed with bits of rust, fell into the pot.

PLOT SUMMARY

It is a simple story. An impoverished, aging, retired colonel, living with his asthmatic wife in a backwater Colombian river town, awaits the arrival of a military pension he had been promised fifteen years earlier. As the elderly couple scrape by, selling off their household items to buy food, he keeps a rooster that belonged to his dead son, killed in Colombia's political turmoil.

The colonel hopes the rooster will win an approaching cockfight. But his wife presses him to sell the rooster so they can buy some food. The weekly arrival of the mailboat at the docks is the key to his other hope, the long-awaited pension:

> The colonel saw it dock with an anguished uneasiness. On the roof, tied to the boat's smokestacks and protected by an oilcloth, he spied the mailbag. Fifteen years of waiting had sharpened his intuition. The rooster had sharpened his anxiety.

Anxiety and waiting. For this aging veteran of Colombia's past wars, these are the things that define his life. Along with hope, which in the colonel's case, is definitely "the thing with feathers"— as Emily Dickinson famously wrote—a rooster he must feed while starving himself.

ABOUT THE AUTHOR: GABRIEL GARCÍA MÁRQUEZ

Born in Aracataca, a small town near Colombia's Caribbean coast, on March 6, 1927, Gabriel García Márquez was the eldest son of a postal clerk, telegraph operator, and pharmacist who could barely support his wife and twelve children. When his father left to take a job in a city pharmacy, García Márquez spent his early childhood living with his maternal grandparents in a large rambling house. His grandfather was a colonel and veteran not unlike the character in *No One Writes*.

This home, his grandparents' remarkable stories, superstitions and old folktales, and this town were the seeds of the mythical village of Macondo that plays such a role in his work. "I feel that all my writing has been about the experiences of the time I spent with my grandparents," the man affectionately known as Gabo would recall.

After his grandfather's death, García Márquez was sent to school in Barranquilla, Colombia. He abandoned law studies for journalism during a violent period in Colombia's history and became a struggling newspaper writer in Barranquilla, where he lived in the garret of a brothel. "It was a bohemian life: finish at the paper at 1 in the morning, then write a poem or a short story until about 3, then go out to have a beer," he said in an interview, according to the *New York Times*. "When you went home at dawn, ladies who were going to Mass would cross to the other side of the street for fear that you were either drunk or intending to mug or rape them."

During the 1950s, García Márquez was a newspaper correspondent living in Paris while reading American authors, like Hemingway and Faulkner, along with Proust, Joyce, and Russian writers. They helped shape his style. As García Márquez would later explain:

> The whole notion that I am an intuitive is a myth I have created myself. I worked my way through literature, reading, writing, reading and writing—it's the only way. . . . [The] tricks you need to transform something which appears fantastic, unbelievable into something plausible, credible, those I learned from journalism. The key is to tell it straight. It is done by reporters and by country folk."

When the newspaper he wrote for shut down, García Márquez was stranded and scrounged for money while working on drafts of a first novel, *In Evil Hour*, and *No One Writes to the Colonel*. Both would be published in the early 1960s in Spanish (later appearing in the United States).

In 1958, he returned to Colombia and married Mercedes Barcha, his childhood sweetheart. The couple had a son, Rodrigo, in 1959, before García Márquez joined Prensa Latina, the official Cuban press agency in New York, after Fidel Castro came to power. His friendship with Castro would cause political problems with the U.S. government, and other writers were critical of his support for Castro, who imprisoned dissidents and writers.

In 1961, García Márquez took his wife and son on a Greyhound bus trip through the American South because he wanted to see "Faulkner country." They moved to Mexico City, where Gonzalo, a second son, was born in 1964. It was there, in 1965, that he began writing *Cien años de soledad* (*One Hundred Years of Solitude*), his masterpiece of "magical realism."

"For 18 months, he had holed up in his office in their home while Ms. Barcha kept the landlord, and the world, at bay," wrote Penelope Green in Mercedes Barcha's *New York Times* obituary in 2020. "When he emerged in late 1966 . . . she asked: 'Did you really finish it? We owe $12,000.' She then pawned her hair dryer and the couple's blender so she could pay the postage to send the manuscript to his Argentine editor."

Published in 1967, it was an immediate success. It would eventually go on to sell more than 50 million copies.

That allowed him to move to Barcelona, Spain, with his family and begin work on his next novel, *The Autumn of the Patriarch* (1975), which told of a dictator in a fantastical Latin American state who rules for so many decades that nobody can recall what life was like before him. Next came the 1981 novella, *Chronicle of a Death Foretold*, which uses journalistic techniques to tell the story of twin brothers who murder the man responsible for taking their sister's virginity.

Hailed by the Nobel Prize committee for novels and short stories that "led us into this peculiar place where the miraculous and the real converge," Gabriel García Márquez was awarded the Nobel Prize in Literature in 1982. In announcing the award, the committee lauded

the extravagant flight of his own fantasy, traditional folk tales and facts, literary allusions, tangible, at times, obtrusively graphic,

descriptions approaching the matter-of-factness of reportage. . . .
With his stories, Gabriel García Márquez has created a world of his
own which is a microcosmos.

Published in 1985, *Love in the Time of Cholera* was García Márquez's
most romantic novel, inspired by his grandparents. It told the story
of the resumption of a passionate relationship between a recently
widowed septuagenarian and the lover she had broken with more
than fifty years before. *The General in His Labyrinth* (1989) conjured
up the last days of Simón Bolívar, the father of South America's
independence from Spain.

After a lymphatic cancer diagnosis in 1999, García Márquez began
work on his memoirs and published another novella. By 2012, he
was suffering from dementia and had stopped writing. He died in
Mexico City in April 2014 at age eighty-seven.

WHY YOU SHOULD READ IT

There is sheer artistry in the writing of García Márquez. This novella
lacks the sense of the fantastical—the essence of the magical realism for which he is most famed. Instead, it is highly realistic, even
while carrying absurd elements. Like many other famous literary
characters who are waiting—expectantly, desperately—the seventy-
five-year-old colonel symbolizes a deeper sense of the weight and
futility of hope.

This is what the Nobel Committee meant when it said:

> A tragic sense of life characterizes García Márquez's books—a sense
> of the incorruptible superiority of fate and the inhuman, inexorable
> ravages of history. But this awareness of death and tragic sense of life is
> broken by the narrative's apparently unlimited, ingenious vitality. . . .
> The comedy and grotesqueness in García Márquez can be cruel,
> but can also glide over into a conciliating humour.

After this novella, read the two short works published in the same collection: *Chronicle of a Death Foretold* (*Crónica de una muerte anunciada*, 1981; English translation, 1982) recounts the murder of a man in a so-called honor killing by twin brothers; *Leaf Storm* (*La Hojarasca*, 1972; English translation, 1972), the author's first novella, introduces the fictional village of Macondo, setting of his most famous work: *One Hundred Years of Solitude*.

Sooner or later, the masterwork *One Hundred Years of Solitude* must be read. As a reviewer put it in the *New York Times*:

> When it gets hot in Macondo, it gets so hot that men and beasts go mad and birds attack houses. A long spell of rain is remembered to have lasted, not weeks, but four years, eleven months and two days. When a plague hits the region, it is no ordinary killer but an "insomnia plague," which gradually causes people to forget everything including the names and uses of the most commonplace objects. In order to combat the memory loss, the villagers label chairs and clocks, and even hang a sign on the cow.

This imaginative world, the creation of Gabo, is what has made his work timeless and why Carlos Fuentes described him as "the most popular and perhaps the best writer in Spanish since Cervantes."

The Old Man and the Sea

— 1952 —

Ernest Hemingway

New York: Scribner, 2003; 127 pages

* 1953 Pulitzer Prize for Fiction *

FIRST LINES

He was an old man who fished alone in a skiff in the Gulf Stream and he had gone eighty-four days now without taking a fish. In the first forty days a boy had been with him. But after forty days without a fish the boy's parents had told him that the old man was now definitely and finally *salao*, which is the worst form of unlucky, and the boy had gone at their orders in another boat which caught three good fish the first week.

PLOT SUMMARY

Man hunts fish. Fish hunts man.

Men in a life-or-death confrontation with large fish have made for some memorable literature over the centuries. There's Jonah in the belly of the whale, of course. Then Captain Ahab in pursuit of the great white killer. *Jaws*. And then there is Ernest Hemingway's old Cuban fisherman.

Told with the simplicity and raw power that are hallmarks of Hemingway's writing, this novella was among the last works by one of twentieth-century America's most celebrated—and notorious—writers. Ernest Hemingway's story of a poor, aging fisherman confronting nature in the form of a great marlin won the 1953 Pulitzer Prize and helped lock down the writer's 1954 Nobel Prize.

The plot needs no lengthy elaboration. Down on his luck, a poor fisherman sets out each day to make a catch that will feed him and bring some needed money. His great pleasure is following news of his favorite baseball team. "The Yankees cannot lose," the old man tells his young friend. He adds, "Have faith in the Yankees my son. Think of the great DiMaggio."

Faith and not losing are what matter here. This man is locked in an existential struggle with the forces of nature when a great fish takes the hook. His battle has just begun as he tries to return to shore. Who will win?

ABOUT THE AUTHOR: ERNEST HEMINGWAY

Sometimes called Papa, the near-legendary novelist, short story writer, and journalist Ernest Miller Hemingway was born on July 21, 1899, in Oak Park, Illinois. The son of a physician and a musician, he was the second of six children. Recent accounts, including a Ken Burns and Lynn Novick PBS documentary, have revealed that his mother raised Ernest and his older sister, Marcelline, as twins until he was five, sometimes dressing him in girl's clothing.

Attending local schools in Illinois, Hemingway wrote for and edited the high school newspaper and yearbook, and after graduating he worked as a cub reporter for the *Kansas City Star*. The paper's style rules influenced Hemingway's work: "Use short sentences. Use short first paragraphs. Use vigorous English. Be positive, not negative."

After the United States declared war on Germany in 1917, Hemingway tried to enlist in the army but was rejected because of poor eyesight. He joined the Red Cross Ambulance Service instead and was sent to Italy. Stationed near Venice, he was seriously wounded in a mortar attack. While recuperating in a Milan hospital, he fell in love with a Red Cross nurse, and the experience fueled his later novel *A Farewell to Arms*.

In 1921, Hemingway married Hadley Richardson, the first of his four wives, and they moved to Paris, where he worked as a foreign correspondent. It was the Paris of the famed "Lost Generation" of artists and writers. Hemingway met and befriended F. Scott Fitzgerald (see entry) and James Joyce (see entry) among others in the expatriate community surrounding Gertrude Stein. Among them was Ezra Pound, who commissioned the stories that would be published in the collection *In Our Time* (1925), which established Hemingway's first literary credentials.

His experiences in Europe, including trips to Spain for the running of the bulls, led to his debut novel, *The Sun Also Rises* (1926). It recounted the story of Jake Barnes, an American war correspondent whose wounds left him impotent, and his relationship with Lady Brett Ashley, a divorcée and thoroughly modern woman.

In 1927, Hemingway divorced Richardson following an affair with wealthy *Vogue* journalist Pauline Pfeiffer, who became his second wife in May 1927. In 1928, Hemingway's father committed suicide.

The following year, *A Farewell to Arms*, the story of a World War I love affair between a wounded American ambulance driver and an English nurse, was published, cementing Hemingway's stature as a major American writer. He returned to Spain to work on a nonfiction account of bullfighting that became *Death in the Afternoon* (1932).

With the outbreak of the Spanish Civil War, Hemingway again went to Spain in 1937 as a war correspondent. While there, he witnessed the battle in which General Franco's Fascist army finally defeated the republican forces. Divorcing Pauline, he married journalist Martha Gellhorn, with whom he had been having an affair, in 1940. That same year, he published *For Whom the Bell Tolls*, based on his experience covering the Spanish Civil War, about an American fighting with the nationalist forces against the Nazi-supported Fascists.

When the United States entered World War II, Hemingway returned to Europe to cover the war. Despite a concussion sustained in a car accident, he was among the correspondents on board a landing craft on D-Day. Although journalists were kept out of the actual fighting on Normandy's beaches, Hemingway was peeved that Gellhorn managed to reach the beach in the guise of a nurse. He returned to Paris when it was liberated in 1944 and then covered the Battle of the Bulge, the last great Nazi offensive of the war. For his wartime service, he was awarded a Bronze Star by the U.S. Army.

In the meantime, he had met *Time* correspondent Mary Welsh. She became his fourth wife in 1946, after he divorced Gellhorn.

After the war, Hemingway's health began to fail; he was overweight, drinking heavily, and suffered from depression and diabetes. Despite these difficulties, *The Old Man and the Sea* was published in 1952 to great success, winning the 1953 Pulitzer, followed by Hemingway's winning the 1954 Nobel Prize.

The same year he received that honor, Hemingway nearly died. After decades of surviving wars and misadventures, he was involved in a pair of plane crashes on successive days in Africa. His injuries left him in pain and ill health for the rest of his life. He was bedridden, drinking heavily, suffering delusions, and would eventually undergo electroshock treatments for his depression and mental state. In the meantime, he had recovered some lost trunks containing notebooks left behind in Paris years earlier. Those notes became the source of his memoir of Paris in the 1920s, *A Moveable Feast.*

That book would be published posthumously in 1964. Early on the morning of July 2, 1961, Hemingway took his life with a shotgun at his home in Ketchum, Idaho. He was sixty-one years old.

WHY YOU SHOULD READ IT

The committee awarding the 1954 Nobel Prize in Literature cited Hemingway "for his mastery of the art of narrative, most recently demonstrated in *The Old Man and the Sea,* and for the influence that he has exerted on contemporary style."

Not everyone agrees on that point. Although an admirer of Hemingway—whom she knew—Irish novelist Edna O'Brien (see *The Country Girls*) dismissed *The Old Man and the Sea* as "schoolboy writing" in a recent Ken Burns-Lynn Novick documentary on Hemingway. With all due respect to O'Brien, I disagree.

Drafted in eight weeks, it is vintage Hemingway. The prose is clean, direct, intense. Resilience in the face of an extreme challenge is the essence of Hemingway, summarized in one of his most famous quotes. In a 1926 letter to F. Scott Fitzgerald, he described "guts"— often cited as "courage"—as "grace under pressure."

Rituals and resilience are central to Hemingway. The old man has careful methods of setting his lines and tending his catch. As he nears the beach and home, we know his thoughts:

Bed is my friend. Just bed, he thought. Bed will be a great thing. It
is easy when you are beaten, he thought. I never knew how easy it
was. And what beat you, he thought.

"Nothing," he said aloud. "I went out too far."

WHAT TO READ NEXT

With a career spanning more than a half century, Hemingway offers
many choices. His early reputation was established with his stories
and Harold Bloom has called Hemingway "the best short story writer
in the English language from Joyce's *Dubliners* until the present."
There are many collections of these stories, including *The Complete
Short Stories of Ernest Hemingway: The Finca Vigía Edition* (1987) and
The Nick Adams Stories (1972).

Today Hemingway's stories demand an honest reckoning. Reading some of them now betrays the racism, sexism, and anti-Semitism
in many of Hemingway's works, mirroring his private views. Discussing the recent PBS Burns-Novick documentary on Hemingway,
the *New Yorker* critic Hilton Als wrote:

> There's ugliness in Hemingway. . . . Hemingway was not above
> the impulse to reduce people to types; nor did he entirely resist the
> pointed, class-informed racism of his time.

His work must be read with this in mind—not to apologize for
it or excuse it, but to understand it.

A Moveable Feast, his posthumously published memoir of Paris in
the 1920s, includes portraits of the expatriate community surrounding Gertrude Stein cited in this guide, James Joyce and F. Scott and
Zelda Fitzgerald among them.

Beyond these, consider two of Hemingway's most enduring
works: *A Farewell to Arms*, his World War I novel (number 74 on the

Modern Library list of 100 Best Novels), and *For Whom the Bell Tolls*, set in the Spanish Civil War.

Finally, without ignoring the anti-Semitism that runs through *The Sun Also Rises*, many critics still consider his first novel among his best. It is number 45 on the Modern Library list of 100 Best Novels. Reviewing it at publication, the *New York Times* critic said:

> No amount of analysis can convey the quality of "The Sun Also Rises." It is a truly gripping story, told in a lean, hard, athletic narrative prose that puts more literary English to shame.

On Chesil Beach

— 2007 —

Ian McEwan

New York: Anchor Books, 2008; 203 pages

FIRST LINES

They were young, educated, and both virgins on this, their wedding night, and they lived in a time when conversation about sexual difficulties was plainly impossible. But it is never easy. They had just sat down to supper in a tiny sitting room on the first floor of a Georgian inn. In the next room, visible through the open door, was a four-poster bed, rather narrow, whose bedcover was pure white and stretched startlingly smooth, as though by no human hand.

PLOT SUMMARY

It is 1962. Beatlemania, the Swinging Sixties, and the Sexual Revolution still lie ahead.

But in the honeymoon suite of a hotel on England's Dorset coast, Florence and Edward, married just hours before, are anxious. As they awkwardly work their way through a dinner served by two local lads, that four-poster bed looms large. A recent university graduate in history who has studied plague, rebellion, and war, Edward is worried about his approaching moment of conquest: "How this was to be achieved without absurdity, or disappointment, troubled him."

For Florence, a talented violinist, the prospect awaiting her is even worse. "In a modern, forward-looking handbook that was supposed to be helpful to young brides, with its cheery tones and exclamation marks and numbered illustrations, she came across certain phrases or words that almost made her gag: *mucous membrane*, and the sinister and glistening *glans*."

From its brilliantly composed opening scene, this exquisite novel travels back to the childhoods, family life, eventual meeting at a "Ban the Bomb" rally, and courtship of Florence and Edward. In crisp, elegant prose, McEwan orchestrates a wedding night to remember. As the opening chapter moves inevitably to a stunning—dare I say it—climax, what will become of this devastatingly awkward moment?

ABOUT THE AUTHOR: IAN MCEWAN

Ian McEwan is among the most prolific, successful, and politically outspoken contemporary British writers. Born on June 21, 1948, in Aldershot, England, McEwan spent part of his childhood moving around the world, following his military father, until he was sent to an English boarding school at ten.

After university, he began writing gothic short stories, many erotically charged, and first collected in *First Love, Last Rites* (1975), winner of the Somerset Maugham Award for young writers. It was followed by a second collection, *In Between the Sheets* (1978).

His next books were novels: *The Cement Garden* (1978), about children who conceal the death of their parents, and *The Comfort of*

Strangers (1981), an unsettling story of a young couple on holiday in Italy. Both were works of psychological suspense, both later made into films that helped establish McEwan's nickname as Ian Macabre. McEwan was later described by an interviewer as "a connoisseur of dread, performing the literary equivalent of turning on the tub faucet and leaving the room; the flood is foreseeable, but it still shocks when the water rushes over the edge."

He shifted style and tone with more historical works: *The Innocent* (1990) and *Black Dogs* (1992), and reached a new level of acclaim with *Amsterdam* (1998)—the story of a euthanasia pact between friends—which won the prestigious Booker Prize. It was followed by his greatest success, *Atonement* (2001), a story about a small girl's dreadful mistake that opens as World War II looms. Short-listed for the Booker Prize, *Atonement* was made into a 2007 film that won the British Academy of Film and Television Awards (BAFTA) Best Picture and was nominated for the Academy Award for Best Picture. That same year, *On Chesil Beach* was published and was also short-listed for the Booker Prize. The film version, for which McEwan wrote the screenplay, was made in 2017.

McEwan holds strong views on climate change, Brexit, artificial intelligence, and Islamic jihadism. He once sheltered his friend and fellow novelist Salman Rushdie, who was forced into hiding after he was threatened with death for writing the novel *The Satanic Verses*. McEwan told the *New Yorker*:

> We stood at the kitchen counter making toast and coffee, listening to the eight-o'clock BBC News. He was standing right by my side and he was the lead item on the news. Hezbollah had put its sagacity and weight behind the project to kill him. I was close to tears, but I didn't want him to see.

Since *On Chesil Beach*, McEwan has written six more novels, most recently *Machines like Me* (2019), an alternative history about artificial intelligence, and *The Cockroach* (2019), a Brexit satire.

Beautifully written, McEwan's delicate, lacerating novella hits on lust, sex, expectations, and, finally, dashed hopes. It is often delightfully awkward, and even comic, as when Edward makes his first attempt at undressing his bride and agonizingly encounters the enigma of the difficult zipper:

> When Edward drew Florence into his embrace, it was not to kiss her, but first to press her body against his, and then to put a hand on her nape and feel for the zip of this dress. . . . But the zip could not be unfastened with one hand alone, at least, not for the first inch or two. You had to hold the top of the dress straight with one hand while pulling down, otherwise the fine material would bunch and snag. She would have reached over her shoulder to help, but her arms were trapped.

Such moments give way to a more disturbing and unsettling tone. And what might be an innocently awkward moment descends into disaster. It is what makes *On Chesil Beach* such a pleasure to read.

WHAT TO READ NEXT

McEwan's work is sometimes divided in two. First, there is the early "Ian Macabre" work found in the story collections and *The Cement Garden* and *Comfort of Strangers*. Both are short novels that I considered including in this collection.

Work in his later period includes another short book, *Amsterdam*, in which two old friends meet for the funeral of another friend. But all of these lead to *Atonement*. Set before and in the early days of World War II, it is about the dreadful mistake made by Briony Tallis, a teenager and future writer, whose accusation of a crime transforms the lives of everyone involved.

No matter what you choose next, McEwan is a writer who examines big themes. But he is also a masterful storyteller and dazzling stylist. As Daniel Zaleski wrote in a lengthy *New Yorker* profile of McEwan:

Although his novels headily explore ideas, and his gift for visual detail approaches that of John Updike (Briony's cousin, fondling a suitcase: "The polished metal was cool, and her touch left little patches of shrinking condensation"), his international success has a lot to do with an old-fashioned talent for creating suspense.

One Day in the Life of Ivan Denisovich

— 1962 —

Aleksandr Solzhenitsyn

New York: Farrar, Straus and Giroux, 2005; translated from the Russian by H. T. Willets with an introduction by Katherine Shonk; 182 pages; originally published in the Russian magazine Novy Mir, *November 1962*

FIRST LINES

The hammer banged reveille on the rail outside camp HQ at five o'clock as always. Time to get up. The ragged noise was muffled by ice two fingers thick on the windows and soon died away. Too cold for the warder to go on hammering.

The jangling stopped. Outside, it was still as dark as when Shukhov had gotten up in the night to use the latrine bucket—pitch-black, except for three yellow lights visible from the window, two in the perimeter, one inside the camp.

Set in one of Stalin's notorious Soviet forced-labor camps, the first novel by Nobel Prize laureate Aleksandr Solzhenitsyn recounts a single day in the brutal existence of a man accused of spying for the Germans during World War II.

Based on Solzhenitsyn's own experiences as a political prisoner, or *zek*, the story follows inmate "Shcha-854"—Ivan Denisovich Shukhov—from the moment he wakes.

Feeling sick, Shukhov lies in his bunk, trying to stay warm, his feet tucked into a sleeve of his coat. As he listens, men carry out heavy latrine buckets. "He heard the orderlies trudging heavily down the corridor with the tub that held eight pails of slops. Light work for the unfit, they call it, but just try getting the thing out without spilling it!"

Another inmate says the temperature is twenty below. The prisoners check the thermometer daily because they don't have to work if the temperature reaches forty-one degrees below.

As Shukhov and his fellow squad members work, they seek any chance to wheedle extra food or a moment's warmth. In direct, straightforward prose, Solzhenitsyn strips bare the struggle to simply live for the next day:

> Shukhov felt pleased with life as he went to sleep. A lot of good things had happened that day. He hadn't been thrown in the hole.... He'd swiped the extra gruel at dinnertime.

ABOUT THE AUTHOR: ALEKSANDR SOLZHENITSYN

Aleksandr Solzhenitsyn was born on December 11, 1918, to a widowed mother. His father, a Cossack army officer, had died in a hunting accident before his birth. The Russian Revolution upended the family's life when their farm was taken by the state. Well-educated and a devout Russian Orthodox, his mother raised him in that faith even after the communist takeover.

Solzhenitsyn attended university, and though he graduated with a mathematics degree, he was always interested in literature. When World War II broke out, he joined the army and rose to the rank of captain. In 1945, he was arrested for writing a letter deemed critical of Soviet dictator Joseph Stalin. Solzhenitsyn spent eight years in labor camps for this offense—the same crime for which Shukhov is sentenced. Once released and "rehabilitated" in 1956, he taught mathematics and began to write.

After Stalin's death in 1953, there was a relaxing of the former dictator's most brutal practices and liberalization in the arts under Nikita Khrushchev. Permission was granted to a literary journal called *Novy Mir* (*New World*) to publish *One Day in the Life of Ivan Denisovich* in 1962, which would have been unthinkable under Stalin. It was a sensation that brought Solzhenitsyn overnight comparisons with Tolstoy and Dostoyevsky, the giants of Russian literature.

But the Cold War-era thaw was brief. The period of liberalization ended and Solzhenitsyn was soon forbidden to publish in the Soviet Union. Some of his work appeared in the clandestine Russian dissident literature known as samizdat. His books were also spirited out of the country and appeared in other markets. Two novels, *First Circle* (republished as *In the First Circle*) and *Cancer Ward*, both appeared in English in 1968 to great acclaim.

In 1970 came word that Solzhenitsyn—on the strength of these works—had been awarded the Nobel Prize in Literature. He chose not to leave the Soviet Union to accept the award, in fear that he would not be allowed to return home. Bestowing the prize in his absence, the award presenter of the Swedish Academy said:

Such are the words of Alexander Solzhenitsyn. They speak to us of matters that we need to hear more than ever before, of the individual's indestructible dignity. Wherever that dignity is violated, whatever the reason or the means, his message is not only an accusation but also an assurance: those who commit such a violation are the only ones to be degraded by it.

Next Solzhenitsyn published a historical epic called *August 1914* (1971), telling of Russia's devastating defeat by Germany in World War I. Even more significantly, in 1973 the first parts of a grand opus exposing Soviet labor camps were sent to publishers in Paris and the United States on microfilm. In three volumes, it revealed the history of the enormous network of prison camps in a monumental literary and historical record that was eventually published as *The Gulag Archipelago*. Soon after, Solzhenitsyn was arrested, charged with treason, and exiled from the Soviet Union in February 1974.

He eventually settled somewhat reclusively in a secluded estate in Cavendish, Vermont. While critical of Soviet communism, Solzhenitsyn did not embrace American democracy. In writings and rare speeches, he was critical of American foreign policy and decried Western consumerism. In one public appearance, he addressed Harvard's 1978 commencement and criticized a country he called spiritually weak and a government that capitulated in Vietnam.

"Many in the West did not know what to make of the man," Michael T. Kaufman wrote in the *New York Times*. "He was perceived as a great writer and hero who had defied the Russian authorities. Yet he seemed willing to lash out at everyone else as well—democrats, secularists, capitalists, liberals and consumers."

In 1994, after the Soviet Union collapsed, Solzhenitsyn returned to an utterly changed Russia. Through initially approving of Vladimir Putin, he later criticized the Russian leader as antidemocratic and in 1994 said the country was an oligarchy. Yet, wrote Michael T. Kaufman, "In the final years of his life, Solzhenitsyn had spoken approvingly of a 'restoration' of Russia under Vladimir Putin, and was criticized in some quarters as increasingly nationalist."

Having far outlived the Soviet Union, he died in Moscow in August 2008 at the age of eighty-nine.

WHY YOU SHOULD READ IT

It is brilliant writing. It is a riveting story of dehumanizing cruelty and human resilience. It is a historical document of enormous importance. These reasons place *One Day in the Life of Ivan Denisovich* among the twentieth century's most significant works of fiction. But the appearance of writing critical of the murderous dictator of the Soviet Union nine years after Stalin's death was even more extraordinary. It made history because Solzhenitsyn laid bare the brutality of the vast network of prison camps, the destructive legacy of collectivization of farms, and the imprisonment of people based on religion or other factors perceived as "disloyal."

On the centennial of the novelist's birth, biographer Michael Scammel wrote:

Solzhenitsyn should be remembered for his role as a truth-teller. He risked his all to drive a stake through the heart of Soviet communism and did more than any other single human being to undermine its credibility and bring the Soviet state to its knees.

This slim volume is one of the most consequential reminders of the great cost of tyranny and the destruction it breeds.

WHAT TO READ NEXT

Alluding to one of Dante's circles of Hell, *In the First Circle* (2009) is a revised version of Solzhenitsyn's highly autobiographical novel first published in 1968 as *The First Circle*. It depicts *zeks* who are prisoners, but instead of doing forced labor they do research and development for the Soviet Union.

In writing about Solzhenitsyn in 1968 in the *New York Times*, Soviet literature expert Patricia Blake summed up the extraordinary impact of both *One Day* and *The First Circle*:

> They compel the human imagination to participate in the agony and murder of millions that have been the distinguishing feature of our age. Such a task could only have been accomplished by literature, performing here what may be, after the historical cataclysm of Stalinism and Nazism, its highest cathartic function.

Oranges Are Not the Only Fruit

— 1985 —

Jeanette Winterson

New York: Grove Press, 1985; 182 pages

FIRST LINES

Like most people I lived for a long time with my mother and father. My father liked to watch the wrestling, my mother liked to wrestle; it didn't matter what. She was in the white corner and that was that.

PLOT SUMMARY

With eight chapters named for books of the Bible—the Old Testament, significantly—Winterson's prizewinning first novel is a frequently laugh-out-loud coming-of-age story. It is also a coming-out story.

Told by an adopted girl not coincidentally named Jeanette, it is about her idiosyncratic family, living in a dreary industrial town in the north of England. As a child, Jeanette's life is dominated by her evangelical mother, who tunes into radio programs plotting the progress of global missionary efforts. There is much churchgoing in a world governed strictly by the mother's views:

Enemies were: The Devil (in his many forms)
               Next Door
               Sex (in its many forms)
               Slugs

Friends were: God
               Our dog
               Auntie Madge
               The Novels of Charlotte Brontë
               Slug pellets

Interspersed with the fairy tales and Arthurian legends that course through Jeanette's imagination, her story moves from grade school, where she scares the other children with stories of Hell, to her plan as a teenager to become a missionary. Those plans change when she sees a girl cleaning fish at the market. "She looked up, and I noticed her eyes were a lovely grey, like the cat Next Door."

The girl from the fish market comes to church. And then comes the sermon on "Unnatural Passions."

A word on the title: it is attributed to a famed eighteenth-century English actress, Nell Gwyn, who started life in the theater as a scantily clad "orange girl," selling fruit to theater patrons, and later became a lover to Charles II. Oranges are cited often, given to Jeanette by her mother, especially when she is ill. The orange motif, which has surely inspired entire dissertations, works on several levels, including the notion that "fruit" is slang for "gay."

ABOUT THE AUTHOR: JEANETTE WINTERSON

It might be best to tell her story as it appears on Winterson's website:

> I was born in Manchester, England, to a young woman who worked
> as a machinist at Marks & Spencer. That was in the days when
> Lancashire was still the textile king of the U.K., and garments for
> M&S were made in their factory in Manchester. Ann was sixteen
> or seventeen when she gave birth to me. She came from an Irish
> family of ten children, and it was decided that adoption was the best
> thing. For me. For her.

Winterson's adoptive parents were Pentecostals, and Jeanette
was raised to be a missionary.

Once you know Jeanette Winterson's biography, you will see that
details from her life correspond closely with those of the fictional
Jeanette in her novel.

In real life, Jeanette Winterson sold ice cream from a van and
worked in a funeral parlor—also delightfully part of the fictional
Jeanette's story. Winterson also escaped her mother, the Pentecostal
church, and cheerless Accrington. But the real Jeanette goes places
her fictional counterpart does not. She studied at Oxford and later
worked in a London theater. After interviewing for a job at a newly
formed feminist press, she was encouraged by its editor to write the
novel that became *Oranges Are Not the Only Fruit*. Published in 1985,
the book won the Whitbread Award for best first novel, becoming
a word-of-mouth best seller. In 1990—the year her mother died—
Winterson adapted the novel for BBC Television.

Two more acclaimed novels, *The Passion* (1987) and *Sexing the
Cherry* (1989), followed and Winterson was freed to write full-time.
In 1994 she bought a property in the Cotswolds, and later she opened
an organic food shop called Verde in the Spitalfields neighborhood
of East London.

Her fiction from this stretch was thought to be uneven. "During the 90s," Stuart Jeffries commented in *The Guardian*, "it became commonplace for critics to argue that Winterson was steadily writing worse novels." Following the end of a long-term relationship, Winterson revealed in an interview that she had considered suicide, spurred by the discovery of her adoption papers. Winterson revisited her early life and coming out in a memoir, *Why Be Happy When You Could Be Normal?* (2011).

"The memoir's title is the question Ms. Winterson's adoptive mother asked after discovering her daughter was a lesbian," Dwight Garner wrote in a *New York Times* review. "This sentence carries a large freight of irony because Ms. Winterson, in this book, seems nearly incapable of happiness, and suspicious of it as well."

In 2009, Jeanette met Susie Orbach, a well-known psychoanalyst and author of *Fat Is a Feminist Issue* and *The Impossibility of Sex*. They married in 2015 but have since separated. In 2019, Winterson's novel *Frankissstein*, a reimagining of Mary Shelley's classic *Frankenstein*, was long-listed for the Booker Prize and in 2021, she published *12 Bytes: How We Got Here. Where We Might Go Next*, a collection of essays on the implications of artificial intelligence.

WHY YOU SHOULD READ IT

First, read it for Winterson's razor-sharp humor. The fictional Jeanette of *Oranges* is an astute observer of the quirks of an idiosyncratic family. Recalling her mother's piety, she says:

> We had no Wise Men because she didn't believe there were any wise men. But we had sheep. One of my earliest memories is me sitting on a sheep at Easter while she told me the story of the Sacrificial Lamb. We had it on Sundays with potato.

And yes, read it as a coming-out narrative. Though it may be of particular interest to readers drawn to LGBT literature, "it's for anyone interested in what happens at the frontiers of common-sense," Jeanette Winterson once stated on her website. "Do you stay safe or do you follow your heart? I've never understood why straight fiction is supposed to be for everyone, but anything with a gay character or that includes gay experience is only for queers. That said, I'm really glad the book has made a difference to so many young women."

Finally, though, read it as a deeply insightful and sharply etched portrayal of a child becoming a young woman—a bright, perceptive young woman who chafes at a prescribed destiny. With mordant wit and a love of language, Winterson does this poignantly. Her deft use of the fairy tales and legends that fill the young fictional Jeanette's thoughts adds resonance to the story. She is on a quest and she has beasts and demons to battle. One of those demons is her mother.

WHAT TO READ NEXT

Winterson has written more than twenty books, including non-fiction and children's books. The two novels that followed *Oranges* are still considered among her best work. *The Passion*, named to the BBC's list of "100 Novels That Shaped Our World," is about a young soldier in the Napoleonic army; *Sexing the Cherry* is about a mother and daughter who time-travel from seventeenth-century London in search of exotic fruits. Yes, fruit again. Both books drew comparisons to García Márquez, though Winterson rejects the label of "magical realism" for her work.

Her 2019 novel, *Frankissstein*, melds an account of Mary Shelley writing her most famous novel with a Brexit-era story about an expert in artificial intelligence and sex toys. Crediting the book "with an intelligent soul," *New York Times* critic Dwight Garner wrote, "This novel is talky, smart, anarchic and quite sexy."

Interviewed at the time the book was published, Winterson said:

The purpose of art changes as society changes. Sometimes art has to break us up—sometimes art has to heal us up. Literature, because it is made of language, returns language to us. If we have the words, we are not silenced, although we learn, through the enforced quiet of reading, what it means to be silent.

Pale Horse, Pale Rider

— 1939 —

Katherine Anne Porter

New York: Harcourt Brace Modern Classic, 1967; collected in Pale Horse, Pale Rider: Three Short Novels; *69 pages*

FIRST LINES

In sleep she knew she was in her bed, but not the bed she had lain down in a few hours since, and the room was not the same but it was a room she had known somewhere. Her heart was a stone lying upon her breast outside of her; her pulses lagged and paused, and she knew that something strange was going to happen, even as the early morning winds were cool through the lattice, the streaks of light were dark blue and the whole house was snoring in its sleep.

PLOT SUMMARY

This is one of the few pieces of fiction that examine the 1918 influenza outbreak—the deadliest pandemic in United States history prior to the Covid pandemic. The story opens in the fall of 1918, after the United States has entered World War I and millions of "doughboys" are shipping off to Europe's deadly trenches. While working in a Denver newsroom, a spirited writer named Miranda meets Adam, an army officer awaiting orders to be sent "over there." They soon fall in love.

As Miranda gets caught up in the country's patriotic fervor, she plans to volunteer as a Red Cross nurse to "do her part." But in her newspaper office, all the talk is of the unusual and deadly epidemic sweeping the country. Very little is known of the sickness, but a fellow reporter says, "They say it is really caused by germs brought by a German ship to Boston."

In reality, it was the flu, a historically lethal virus whose precise origin is still unknown. But wartime rumors swirled about the disease. When Miranda falls ill, her landlady threatens to put her out of her room. The hospitals turn away patients, but Adam helps her find an open bed. As Adam leaves Miranda's bedside with a promise to return, she sinks into fevered hallucinations and lies near death.

Does the "Pale Rider" come for her? Will her lover come back?

ABOUT THE AUTHOR: KATHERINE ANNE PORTER

A member of a select group of authors honored with a U.S. postage stamp, Katherine Anne Porter was one of the most admired American writers of the mid-twentieth century. She was born on May 15, 1890, in Indian Creek, Texas, as Callie Russell Porter. When she was two, Porter's mother died, and she was sent to be raised by a paternal grandmother, Catherine (or Catharine) Ann Porter, whose name she later adopted as her own.

Moving around after her grandmother died meant that Porter never finished high school. At age sixteen, she ran away and married the first of four husbands; they were divorced by the time she was nineteen.

Porter spent her early twenties shifting from Texas to Chicago and back, working as an actress, a singer, and, later, a secretary. In 1917, she took a job as a society columnist for a Fort Worth newspaper. She next moved to Denver and wrote up local events for the *Rocky Mountain News*. Like her fictional Miranda, Porter contemplated joining the Red Cross but fell ill before she could put on the nurse's whites, even as the final offensive against the Germans was splashed across the front pages in October 1918.

For days, Porter lay in bed, hallucinating with a dangerously high fever. As she drifted in and out of consciousness, family members in Texas were informed that she might not survive and fellow reporters prepared her obituary. A group of young doctors tried an experimental dose of strychnine. Porter survived, although she lost all her hair, which turned white when it grew back.

Having endured the pandemic, Porter set off on the itinerant life of a struggling writer. For a time, she lived in Greenwich Village, New York's bohemian literary center, and then Mexico, where she began writing short stories. Her first, "Maria Concepción," was sold to *Century* magazine in 1923. While her stories won critical praise, a first collection, *Flowering Judas* (1930), sold modestly.

Porter struggled through the 1930s with what she called hack work—public relations and ghostwriting—fellowships and grants, and as an uncredited screenwriter in Hollywood. Three more marriages were unhappy, childless, and ended in divorce, as her first had. Between 1933 and 1936, she traveled to Europe on a Guggenheim Fellowship, living in Berlin, Basel, and Paris.

In 1939, three novellas were published under the title *Pale Horse, Pale Rider*. The other two stories are *Old Mortality*, which introduced Miranda, the strong-willed reporter of the title story, and *Noon Wine*. It was followed in 1944 by another collection, *The Leaning Tower and Other Stories*.

Literary academia took note. By the 1940s, Porter was invited to teach writing at a string of universities—having never attended one herself. She was also working on a novel based on her 1931 voyage from Mexico to Germany. More than twenty years after the journey, the long-awaited book was published as *Ship of Fools* (1962). A sprawling novel with a literal shipload of characters, it told of a group of passengers, many Germans, sailing from Veracruz to their homeland as Hitler rose to power. A Book-of-the-Month Club selection, it was the best-selling novel of 1962.

In 1965, Porter's *Collected Short Stories*—which included *Pale Horse, Pale Rider*—won the National Book Award and a Pulitzer Prize. In 1977, after she suffered a disabling stroke, her last work was published. *The Never-Ending Wrong* was an account of the case of Sacco and Vanzetti, two Italian immigrants executed as anarchists in 1927 for taking part in a bank robbery. In the 1920s, Porter had joined the worldwide protests over their controversial trial and eventual execution.

Katherine Anne Porter died in a Maryland nursing home on September 18, 1980, at the age of ninety. She was featured in "Katherine Anne Porter: The Eye of Memory" in the PBS series *American Masters*.

WHY YOU SHOULD READ IT

This is a short novel that called out to be included, first, for its obvious timeliness. In the midst of the Covid pandemic, I thought that this fictional depiction of the world's last, worst pandemic was of immediate interest. Arriving in the United States in the spring of 1918, the influenza spread around the world in the closing months of World War I and carried over well into 1919 and perhaps beyond.

Known widely as the Spanish flu, it was responsible for an estimated 675,000 American deaths in a little more than a year.*

The global toll was more than 50 million people worldwide—the worst pandemic in history since the Black Death of medieval times. The title of Porter's story referred to a line in the apocalyptic New Testament Book of Revelation: "So I looked, and behold, a pale horse. And the name of him who sat on it was Death . . ." (Revelation 6:8). The story refers to an old spiritual based on the verse.

Porter's novel will be of interest to all of us who lived through the Covid pandemic. But it is also a very worthy piece of fiction, vividly capturing the fevered, hallucinatory visions suffered by many victims of the influenza.

Overwhelmed by fear and propaganda, most Americans did not understand what they were experiencing during the 1918 influenza. Two decades later, Porter crafted this highly accurate depiction of American society in the fall of 1918, describing the twin crises of war and influenza, which often led to crushing depression in survivors.

Certainly, read it for its insight as a piece of history. But also read it because Porter was a gifted writer.

Bells screamed all off key, wrangling together as they collided in midair, horns and whistles mingled shrilly with cries of human distress; sulphur-colored light exploded through the black windowpane and flashed away in darkness. Miranda waking from a dreamless sleep asked without expecting an answer, "What is happening?" for there was a bustle of voices and footsteps in the corridor, and a sharpness in the air; the far clamor went on, a furious exasperated shrieking like a mob in revolt.

The war was over. But the flu kept killing.

---

* The 1918 pandemic is the subject of my book *More Deadly than War: The Hidden History of the Spanish Flu and the First World War* (2018).

Once known as "the grand dame of American fiction," Porter is best remembered today for her short works. *The Leaning Tower and Other Stories* includes six stories featuring Miranda, the semiautobiographical character in *Pale Horse*. The two other novellas collected in *Pale Horse, Pale Rider* hold up well. *Old Mortality* introduces the young Miranda, growing up in Texas. *Noon Wine* is a story of building violence, set on a Texas dairy farm in the 1890s, that has a mood and crescendo to tragedy that is reminiscent of Wharton's *Ethan Frome*.

While Porter's *Ship of Fools* became her most successful and well-known work, the critical reception at the time was mixed. More recently, critic Harold Bloom called the novel "an interesting failure" while greatly admiring her shorter work. Completed when Porter was in her seventies, the novel provided the financial success she lacked during her life, but not universal acclaim. Writing after Porter's death, critic Elizabeth Hardwick commented of the book:

> There is something a little musty, like old yellowing notes: The flawless execution of the single scenes impresses and yet the novel remains too snug and shipshape for the waters of history.

A Pale View of Hills

— 1982 —

Kazuo Ishiguro

New York: Vintage International, 1990; 183 pages

FIRST LINES

Niki, the name we finally gave my younger daughter, is not an abbreviation; it was a compromise I reached with her father. For paradoxically it was he who wanted to give her a Japanese name, and I—perhaps out of some selfish desire not to be reminded of the past—insisted on an English one. He finally agreed to Niki, thinking it had some vague echo of the East about it.

PLOT SUMMARY

There is some irony here. Though Ishiguro's narrator, Etsuko, says she wants "not to be reminded of the past," the Nobel laureate's complex and haunting novel is entirely a remembrance of things past.

The novel opens as Etsuko, a widowed Japanese woman, is being visited in contemporary England by Niki, her somewhat estranged adult daughter—the child of an unnamed British father. The two are tiptoeing around the recent suicide of Etsuko's first child, a daughter named Keiko. In a narrative that shifts abruptly in time and place, we are carried back to Nagasaki, Japan, Etsuko's home, in the early 1950s. Still occupied by American troops, Nagasaki has begun to rebuild in the aftermath of the dropping of the second atomic bomb and the end of the war.

"The worst days were over by then," Etsuko recalls. "American soldiers were as numerous as ever—for there was fighting in Korea—but in Nagasaki, after what had gone before, those were days of calm and relief."

The worst days might be over. But the shadow of the bombing inescapably hangs over the city and the novel, like a shroud. Etsuko describes life in Nagasaki with her first husband, Jiro, as they await the birth of their first child. In great detail, Etsuko retraces days spent with her husband and her visiting father-in-law—symbol of Japan's fading traditions.

She is also focused on her relationship with a friend named Sachiko and her daughter; Sachiko speaks constantly of plans of taking her daughter to the United States with an American named Frank. Etsuko's relationship with Sachiko and the child, Mariko, who is prone to disappearing ominously, forms the anxious emotional core of the novel. These memories parallel Etsuko's own life in England, her troubled relationship with her living daughter, and the suicide of her firstborn.

Ishiguro never explains that suicide. Other facets of Etsuko's life also go unexplained. But those events are secondary to the relentless pull of memory and the deep sense of loss that pervades the book, a remarkable first novel. In the book's elegiac atmosphere, what is left unsaid often seems to carry more significance.

ABOUT THE AUTHOR: KAZUO ISHIGURO

Winner of the Nobel Prize in Literature (2017), Kazuo Ishiguro was born on November 8, 1954, in Nagasaki, a little more than nine years after it was the target of the second atomic bomb. While his father was in China at the time of the bombing, his mother survived the attack.

When Ishiguro was five, his family left Japan and moved to England, where his father, an oceanographer, took a job with the British government. Kazuo Ishiguro grew up and was schooled in England, but with a Japanese perspective. "I've always had a faith that it should be possible," he told the BBC when he learned of his Nobel award, "if you tell stories in a certain way, to transcend barriers of race, class and ethnicity."

Ishiguro's first love was music and he set out to write songs, hitchhiking around America with a guitar in 1973. His idols were Joni Mitchell and Bob Dylan—winner of the Nobel Prize the year before Ishiguro. "I was trying to be the singer-songwriter," he once told an interviewer. "I don't know why I thought that, but in those days, like a lot of English people, we thought San Francisco was where, you know, all these wonderful things happened."

Returning to university in England, Ishiguro wrote a master's thesis in creative writing in 1980 that became *A Pale View of Hills*. The book was published during the time Ishiguro was working in a homeless center in London, where he met his future wife, social worker Lorna MacDougall. He followed with *An Artist of the Floating World* (1986), a second novel set in postwar Japan. It tells of the reflections of an aging painter looking back at his life and the changes brought by the war. However, Ishiguro did not return to Japan until 1989, after both novels had been published.

That was also the year in which his celebrated *The Remains of the Day* was published. The story of an English butler who has dedicated his life to serving a man who would prove to be a Nazi sympathizer, the book received the prestigious Man Booker Prize, became an international best seller, and was the basis for an acclaimed 1993 film.

Ishiguro had plainly arrived. And he kept going. Two more novels, *The Unconsoled* (1995) and *When We Were Orphans* (2000), were followed by his next major success, *Never Let Me Go* (2005), a dystopian novel about children raised in an exclusive boarding school whose purpose shall go unspoiled here. A fantasy novel set in post-Arthurian Britain, *The Buried Giant* appeared in 2015, and Ishiguro received his Nobel Prize in 2017.

In accepting his prize, Ishiguro said:

> Firstly, we must widen our common literary world to include many more voices from beyond our comfort zones of the elite first world cultures. We must search more energetically to discover the gems from what remain today unknown literary cultures, whether the writers live in far away countries or within our own communities. Second: we must take great care not to set too narrowly or conservatively our definitions of what constitutes good literature. The next generation will come with all sorts of new, sometimes bewildering ways to tell important and wonderful stories. We must keep our minds open to them.

Published in 2021, his eighth novel, *Klara and the Sun*, is set in a near-future America. Focusing on the theme of artificial intelligence and its impact, it won wide acclaim, was long-listed for the Booker Prize, and became an immediate best seller

WHY YOU SHOULD READ IT

As the first work of one of the finest novelists of our time, *A Pale View of Hills* can be read simply as an appetizer to his other works. But on its own, the book is delicate, ironic, and most of all haunting. It is vividly etched with images of death and destruction set against the memory of the ultimate destruction, the bomb—mentioned fleetingly but ever present.

"Its characters, whose bursts of self-knowledge and honesty erase their inspired self-deceptions only briefly, are remarkably convincing," novelist Edith Milton wrote in a *New York Times* review. "But what one remembers is its balance, halfway between elegy and irony."

WHAT TO READ NEXT

You could move on to Ishiguro's dystopian vision in *Never Let Me Go*. It is an understated yet remarkably chilling view of emerging adolescence, with spooky overtones of cloning. But like *A Pale View of Hills*, and much of Ishiguro's work, it is also about memory of a dark past.

But perhaps that should be a second choice. Memories and loss are also at the center of Ishiguro's masterwork, *The Remains of the Day*. The story of a reserved butler and his unspoken love for the housekeeper in the grand home in which he serves is, without reservation, one of the best novels I have ever read. And yes, it also made a wonderful film, memorably starring Anthony Hopkins as the "gentleman's gentleman" and Emma Thompson as the dignified housekeeper.

If you haven't yet read it, don't delay.

Passing

— 1929 —

Nella Larsen

*New York: Modern Library, 2019; with an introduction by Kaitlyn
Greenidge and explanatory notes by Thadious M. Davis; 147 pages; other
available versions include a Penguin Classic and Norton Critical edition*

FIRST LINES

It was the last letter in Irene Redfield's little pile of morning mail. After her
other ordinary and clearly directed letters the long envelope of thin Italian
paper with its almost illegible scrawl seemed out of place and alien. And
there was, too, something mysterious and slightly furtive about it. A thin sly
thing which bore no return address to betray the sender.

PLOT SUMMARY

Irene Redfield and Clare Kendry are biracial women who grew up
together in turn-of-the-century Chicago but separated as teenagers.

Years later, in the late 1920s, they have a chance encounter in a posh Chicago hotel where both women are able to "pass" as white, free to enter the hotel's strictly segregated bounds.

"Passing" was neither a benign social convenience nor an intriguing plot device. It was a practice connected to America's ugly conventions of racial exclusion, discrimination, and violence, and, in particular, the "one-drop rule." As an editorial note in the novel explains, "Nearly every State in the union had some version of the one-drop rule, conceived during slavery, that held an individual legally black at the presence of a single drop of Negro blood." That classification carried all the dreadful weight of discrimination, exclusion, and racial violence in Jim Crow America.

The meeting is their first reunion since Clare was a teenager and her violent father, who was also biracial, died in a saloon fight. Clare disappeared from the neighborhood shortly afterward, which inspired gossip but no news. Now, over an elegant tea twelve years later, Irene learns a secret: blond and fair-skinned Clare has been "passing" as white for her entire adult life. Irene then meets Clare's wealthy white husband, Jack Bellew, a hateful racist who freely tosses off racial slurs. Nella Larsen uses these slurs here to disturbing effect, as Bellew professes that he has never known any "Negroes" even as he speaks to women, including his wife, who would all be legally considered "Negro."

Irene lives in Harlem with her husband, a Black physician, where they are pillars of the community's upper-middle-class elite. For her, "passing" at the segregated hotel was a momentary decision, not the way she conducts her life. After returning home from Chicago, Irene is unsettled by the beguiling Clare—"selfish, and cold, and hard," yet possessing "a strange capacity of transforming warmth and passion."

When Clare visits New York two years later, Irene's comfortable world explodes. As her alluring friend insinuates herself into her orderly household, Irene grows certain that Clare has seduced her husband. She also fears that Clare, drawn like a moth to the flame of Harlem's enticing Black society, is doomed if the malevolent Jack Bellew discovers Clare's true identity. Irene also knows that, if she chooses, she can make sure that he does.

ABOUT THE AUTHOR: NELLA LARSEN

The biracial daughter of immigrants, Nella Larsen was born in Chicago on April 13, 1891. Her mother was a white woman from Denmark and her father a biracial man from the Dutch West Indies. When Nella was two, her father disappeared and her mother married Peter Larsen, another Dane, whose last name Nella took.

While her birth certificate classified her as "colored," Nella Larsen was raised in a mostly white world of her European immigrant Chicago neighborhood. But in 1907, she enrolled in a teacher-training program at Fisk Normal School—affiliated with Nashville's historically Black Fisk University—and was immersed in Black society for the first time. Before finishing school—a biographer suggests she was expelled over a dress code—she went to Copenhagen and lived for a time with Danish relatives and returned to Chicago. In 1912, Larsen went to New York's Lincoln Hospital school for nurses, established to recruit Black women into the field. Graduating in 1915, she worked as superintendent of nurses at Alabama's Tuskegee Institute, the historic Black school shaped by Booker T. Washington.

A year later, Larsen returned to New York and worked at Lincoln Hospital, which served a largely Black community. She met Elmer Imes, the second Black American to receive a Ph.D. in physics, and they married in May 1919. In the blossoming Harlem Renaissance, the couple moved among the circle of intellectuals and artists that included writers and civil rights pioneers James Weldon Johnson and W. E. B. Du Bois, founder of the NAACP. Nella Larsen hosted a party for his daughter, Yolande Du Bois, before her 1928 marriage to poet and novelist Countee Cullen, a wedding widely described as Harlem's social event of the decade.

Enrolling in the New York Public Library's teaching program, Larsen became its first female graduate identified as Black. She spent five years as a librarian in the 135th Street Branch, which is now known as the Countee Cullen Library.

Under a pseudonym, Larsen had by 1926 begun writing stories and become friends with Carl Van Vechten, a prominent critic, novelist, and photographer who helped bridge the worlds of white publishing and the Black writers of the Harlem Renaissance. Van Vechten recommended Larsen's work to Blanche Knopf, wife of publisher Alfred Knopf. In 1928, Larsen's autobiographical first novel, *Quicksand*, was published by Knopf, winning a prestigious Harmon Award prize, soon followed in 1929 by *Passing*.

While living and working in Harlem, Larsen never attempted to "pass" by her own account. But in a 1932 letter to Van Vechten, she wrote, "You will be amused that I who have never tried this much discussed 'passing' stunt have waited until I reached the deep South to put it over." In the letter, she described having lunch without incident in an all-white Tennessee restaurant with her friend Grace Nail Johnson, a civil rights and feminist activist married to James Weldon Johnson.

The episode mirrors the hotel scene in *Passing*, which by then had appeared to modest success. But her life was about to collapse. Her next novel, *Mirage*, was rejected by Knopf. In 1930, Larsen was accused of plagiarism over a short story she had written that drew upon an earlier work by a British writer. In spite of this controversy, she won a Guggenheim Fellowship—she was recognized as "the first African American woman" to receive the honor—and used the grant to travel to Spain.

By then, Larsen had learned that her husband was having an affair with a professor at Fisk, where he had taken a position. After she returned to New York, they divorced in 1933. Supported by alimony payments, Larsen continued to write, completing a novel and several short stories that went unpublished. Although exonerated of the plagiarism charge, Larsen never published again.

After Elmer Imes died in 1942, Larsen moved out of Harlem, returned to nursing to support herself, and eventually fell into literary obscurity. Nella Larsen spent the rest of her life as a nurse before dying of a heart attack on March 30, 1964, at the age of seventy-two. Her death did not receive an obituary in the *New York Times*. The oversight was corrected in 2018 in the series "Overlooked No More" highlighting the lives of significant women whose achievements had been ignored by the paper.

Larsen was among four writers of the Harlem Renaissance honored by the U.S. Postal Service with a stamp in May 2020. Attention to Larsen, and *Passing*, was further heightened by a film adaptation, which won praise after its debut at the Sundance Film Festival in 2021 and was a *New York Times* "Critic's Pick" when it opened in November 2021. While the film is excellent, I still say "Read the book."

WHY YOU SHOULD READ IT

There are crucial clues to be found in this provocative novel's opening lines: "out of place," "alien," "mysterious," "furtive," "sly," and "betray."

All of these words speak to the powerful themes at the heart of this elegant tale of race, class privilege, personal identity, and female friendship—the last a subject also central to Toni Morrison's *Sula* (see entry).

In Irene's eyes, Clare is sly, mysterious, and furtive. Choosing to pass as white, she is out of place in Irene's Harlem world but longs to rejoin the company of Black people. Many critics and scholars also hint at Irene's possible attraction to the bewitching Clare, even as she resents her. And the notion of betrayal—of one's race, true identity, marriage, or friend—drives the novel forward even as it peels back the burdens of "passing."

In America's racial history, passing occupies a tortured place. As Allyson Hobbs wrote in *A Chosen Exile*, a history of the practice:

> Once one circumvented the law, fooled coworkers, deceived neighbors, tricked friends, and sometimes even duped children and spouses, there were enormous costs to pay. . . . Each era determined not only how racially ambiguous men and women lived, but also what they lost.

Exploring those costs, *Passing* examines 1920s Jazz Age Harlem in much the way its contemporaries *The Age of Innocence* (1920) and *The Great Gatsby* (1925) reveal their very distinctive visions of New York: Wharton's Knickerbocker society and Fitzgerald's Prohibition-era new wealth. And, much like *Gatsby* (see entry), Larsen's novel was rescued from obscurity. Rediscovered by Black and feminist scholars in the 1970s, Larsen's work is now read and studied in academic circles.

But *Passing* has not enjoyed the wider readership it richly deserves. Perhaps it is because Nella Larsen never produced the large body of work of a Wharton or Fitzgerald, or perhaps the book was simply forgotten after its author left the literary scene. But the fact that her novel and name are so little known may serve as another reflection of race and privilege.

Reviewing the reissued novel in 2001, *New York Times* critic Richard Bernstein wrote:

> But the genius of this book is that its protagonists, especially its Anna Karenina–like central figure, Irene Redfield, are complex and fully realized and individually responsible as well. Larsen's treatment of race in this sense was both candid and tough-minded. She understood the power of its impact, but she never let her characters escape from the weight of their choices.

He concluded that Larsen was "an original and hugely insightful writer whose literary talent developed no further."

Differing markedly in tone, style, and setting from the more widely read *Their Eyes Were Watching God* (see entry) by Zora Neale Hurston, another Harlem Renaissance figure rescued from literary oblivion, *Passing* deserves much greater recognition.

WHAT TO READ NEXT

Nella Larsen's first novel, *Quicksand,* tracks closely with Larsen's own life. It follows Helga Crane, a biracial teacher at a boarding school for Black girls in the South, modeled somewhat on the Tuskegee Institute. Discontented, Helga eventually leaves the school in search of her true identity, caught like Nella Larsen was between white and Black worlds, at home in neither. This pilgrimage eventually takes her to Harlem and then Denmark in search of a connection to a past and a self that she will struggle to uncover.

Larsen's short stories, including "The Wrong Man," "Freedom," and "Sanctuary"—the 1930 story that created the plagiarism controversy— are what first brought her literary attention. They also explore the themes that play out in her novels and are still critically admired and available in collections.

The Perfect Nanny

— 2016 —

Leïla Slimani

New York: Penguin Books, 2018; translated from the French by Sam Taylor; 228 pages; originally published in 2016 as Chanson douce

* Winner of the Prix Goncourt, 2016 *

FIRST LINES

The baby is dead. It took only a few seconds. The doctor said he didn't suffer. The broken body, surrounded by toys, was put inside a gray bag, which they zipped shut. The little girl was still alive when the ambulance arrived. She'd fought like a wild animal. They found signs of a struggle, bits of skin under her soft fingernails.

There is no spoiler here. The ghastly opening scene is blunt-force trauma for the reader, ending with two young children dead. We know who did it: their "perfect nanny," Louise. The rest of Slimani's unnerving, prizewinning second novel tries to get to the "why."

Music producer Paul Massé and his wife, Myriam, a French-Moroccan attorney at home with two small children, want more from life. Crowded into a smallish Paris apartment with toddlers Mila and Adam, they are suffocating. Myriam feels it most. "The bills piled up. Myriam became gloomy. She began to hate going to the park. The winter days seemed endless."

When a former law school classmate offers her a job, Myriam leaps at the chance. It means spending much of what she earns on childcare. But the trade-off seems desirable. Especially when they hire Louise, a Frenchwoman. Quiet, polite, she cleans, she cooks, she plays endless games with the children. Myriam can announce to friends, "My nanny is a miracle-worker."

As Myriam's legal career flourishes and Paul scores a major client, their world opens up. Louise is so wonderful that they take her to Greece for a family vacation.

But as their lives entwine, there are signs of trouble. The Massés and Louise grow more dependent upon each other. Completely hidden to her employers, Louise's private life is filled with difficulties: a dead husband who left her debt-ridden; a grown daughter who has run away. It is a devastating psychological thriller that tracks Louise's world as it unravels and ultimately spirals out of control.

ABOUT THE AUTHOR: LEÏLA SLIMANI

Born on October 3, 1981, in Rabat, Morocco, Leïla Slimani made a provocative entrance on the French literary scene when her first novel, *Dans le jardin de l'ogre* ("In the garden of the ogre," published in the United States as *Adèle*), appeared in 2014. Set in chic Paris neighborhoods, this erotically charged account of a woman journalist with an insatiable need for risky sex was a critical and popular success.

Leïla Slimani possessed a literary pedigree, as her maternal grandmother had written an autobiographical novel. Raised in a liberal-minded, French-speaking household—with a nanny—Slimani attended French schools in Morocco. Her parents were successful professionals, but her father was accused of bank fraud in 2002 and only acquitted posthumously eight years later.

By then, Slimani had left Morocco at seventeen to enroll at Sciences Po in Paris, one of France's most prestigious universities. After graduation came a brief foray into acting and she appeared in two films. Slimani married her husband, a Parisian banker, in 2008 and then worked as a journalist with *Jeune Afrique*, a French-language newsweekly covering Pan-African news.

Following the birth of a son in 2011, Slimani was arrested while covering the Arab Spring uprisings in Tunisia. Leaving *Jeune Afrique*, she wrote freelance and concentrated on a novel, which went unsold. After taking a writing workshop with a prominent French editor, she published *Adèle* to instant celebrity.

Its success was followed in 2016 by *Chanson douce* (literally "sweet song"), published as *Lullaby* in the U.K. and *The Perfect Nanny* in the United States. Inspired by the true story of a nanny in Manhattan who in 2012 had killed two children in her care, Slimani wrote what a headline in the *New Yorker* called "The Killer-Nanny Novel That Conquered France." The central character was named after Louise Woodward, a British au pair involved in the notorious 1977 case of a caregiver charged with killing a child.

The novel became a major best seller, further boosted when Slimani won France's most prestigious literary award, the Prix Goncourt. She is the first Moroccan-born woman to win the award, which in the past has gone to such eminent French writers as Marcel Proust (1919), Simone de Beauvoir (1954), and Marguerite Duras

(1984) for *The Lover* (see entry). When published in the United States, it was named one of the "Best Books of 2018" by the *New York Times*.

"The subject came from the fact that I myself had nannies growing up in Morocco," Slimani said after receiving the Prix Goncourt, which came while she was pregnant with a second child. "At 7 or 8, I was already very sensitive to the very strange position they had in the house; they were both women we loved as mothers, and strangers. I was always touched by their difficult position, sometimes by the humiliations they might go through."

In 2017, French president Emmanuel Macron appointed Slimani as an unpaid Francophone Affairs Minister to promote the French language and culture around the world. That year, she also published her first work of nonfiction, *Sexe et mensonges: La vie sexuelle au Maroc* (*Sex and Lies: True Stories of Women's Intimate Lives in the Arab World* in English), based on interviews with Moroccan women "about sex, men, family, women, religion and dress codes."

Slimani's third novel, *Le pays des autres*, was published in 2020, appearing in English in 2021 as *In the Country of Others*. Based on the life of Slimani's maternal grandmother, it is the first of a planned trilogy based on the author's family history.

At this writing, Leïla Slimani resides in Paris with her husband and two children.

WHY YOU SHOULD READ IT

It must be said: "The baby is dead" as a book's opening line may turn off some readers.

"It is hard to think of a more primal sentence. It out-Hemingways Hemingway, shearing sentimentality from the dread," commented Lauren Collins, in the *New Yorker*. Collins continued:

I read "Chanson Douce" as though I were running away from those four words, with the sense that they could cause me real harm, that the only way to master the fear was to outread it. The book felt less like an entertainment, or even a work of art, than like a compulsion. I found it extraordinary.

Setting aside its shock first line, the novel plays out as investigation of the mind and heart. It is not a gory plunge into the mind of a serial killer. It is a page-turning exploration of the psychology of its central character, Louise, while at the same time peeling back the attitudes of Paul and Myriam. Slimani is raising important, nuanced questions about the power of class, sex, desire, status, marriage, and motherhood—themes explored elsewhere in this collection by such writers as Kate Chopin, Jenny Offill, Doris Lessing, and Elena Ferrante and in the story of another nanny, *Lucy* by Jamaica Kincaid.

WHAT TO READ NEXT

The book that announced Slimani's arrival, *Adèle* is a suspenseful and sexually frank character study of a young wife and mother—a journalist—who organizes her life around illicit affairs. Discussing the book, Slimani said:

> Actually, when I began to write, I was very much inspired by classical characters: Anna Karenina, Emma Bovary, and Thérèse Desqueyroux [the title character in a 1927 François Mauriac novel]. They are all married women, mothers, and they are all disappointed by their lives and their marriages. For a very long time, women didn't have choices. If they wanted to belong to society and not be considered as outcasts or losers, they had to marry and to become mothers. But of course, they continued to have desires and secret dreams.

Adèle acts out those desires and dreams until betrayed by her phone.

Published in the United States in August 2021, *In the Country of Others*, Slimani's third novel, has won admiring notices, with a *New York Times* reviewer writing, "In the first installment of a planned trilogy loosely based on the lives of Slimani's grandparents, the character of Mathilde lays bare women's intimate, lacerating experience of war and its consequent trauma."

A Portrait of the Artist as a Young Man

— 1916 —

James Joyce

New York: Vintage International, 1993; 244 pages

* Number 3 on the Modern Library list of 100 Best Novels *

FIRST LINES

Once upon a time and a very good time it was there was a moocow coming down along the road and this moocow that was coming down along the road met a nicens little boy named baby tuckoo . . .

His father told him that story: his father looked at him through a glass: he had a hairy face.

PLOT SUMMARY

James Joyce's first novel, a telling of the artistic emergence of Stephen Dedalus, his literary alter ego, breaks my arbitrary page limit for "short novels." But it is a monumental piece of writing that helped transform literature in the twentieth century. It is filled with the intricate playfulness of language that is at the heart of Joyce's work, as well as the intense focus on religion and myth, which are among Joyce's fundamental interests. It also introduces the character who will reappear in *Ulysses*, widely considered one of the greatest novels of the twentieth century.

Of these, *A Portrait* is the far more accessible. And it is prerequisite before the challenge of taking on Joyce's later masterwork.

The outlines of this story are simple. From the opening lines, Joyce brings the reader into the emerging consciousness of Stephen Dedalus, from early childhood, through his years at school, taught by priests. Stephen is seen bullied by older boys; at a family meal where politics and religion boil over in an angry argument; punished unfairly by a priest with his "pandybat"; and then, in an act of rebellion, protesting this treatment to the headmaster. From the beginning, it becomes clear that Stephen will become a person set apart.

Stephen is named for Christianity's first martyr. The name Dedalus is derived from the character in Greek mythology who was the mythical architect, sculptor, and inventor who built the famed Labyrinth of the Minotaur and later crafted wings of wax and feathers with which to fly. In that mythical account, Dedalus's son, Icarus, ignores his father's warning and flies too close to the sun.

Stephen's story is set against the core influences of family, Ireland and its politics, and the overwhelming impact of Irish Catholicism. As Stephen passes through adolescence, he eventually emerges as a writer who says, "Welcome, O life! I go to encounter for the millionth time the reality of experience and to forge in the smithy of my soul the uncreated conscience of my race."

ABOUT THE AUTHOR: JAMES JOYCE

James Augustus Aloysius Joyce was born in Dublin on February 2, 1882. The eldest of ten children to survive infancy, he was sent at age six to Clongowes Wood College, a Jesuit boarding school. He was forced to leave the school in 1892 when his dissolute father bankrupted the family and could no longer pay the fees. As Louis Menand put it:

> After he started school, his family changed houses nine times in eleven years, an itinerancy not always undertaken by choice. They sometimes moved, with their shrinking stock of possessions, at night, in order to escape the attention of creditors. They did not leave a forwarding address.

A gifted student and lover of language, Joyce wrote his first poem at age nine, under the title "Et Tu, Healy," attacking an Irish politician his father disliked. Joyce attended a Christian Brothers School and then the Jesuit Belvedere College (a secondary school) before attending University College Dublin, where he studied English, French, and Italian and began to write theatrical reviews.

A brief foray to study medicine in Paris was followed with a return to Dublin to attend his dying mother. After her death in 1903, Joyce remained in Ireland, scraping together a meager living by teaching, writing literary reviews, and singing in what was described as a fine Irish tenor voice.

The following year, in 1904, he wrote *Stephen Hero*, a preliminary version of *A Portrait* that went unpublished. Joyce also began writing stories set in Dublin that appeared under the name of Stephen Dedalus in an Irish farmer's magazine. Later that year, Joyce met a chambermaid named Nora Barnacle. On their first date, they strolled around Dublin. Then, as Louis Menand describes the encounter:

She put her hand inside his trousers and masturbated him. It was June 16, 1904, the day on which Joyce set "Ulysses." When people celebrate Bloomsday, that is what they are celebrating.

With Nora at his side, Joyce left Ireland in late 1904, spending the rest of his life in near poverty as he struggled to find publishers for his work, a task made difficult by its literary complexity and later by the fact that it was deemed "obscene." He lived for much of the time in Trieste, working as an English teacher, with later stretches in Paris. In 1914, the earlier published stories were collected as *Dubliners*.

Joyce's financial difficulties were complicated by eye problems. Between 1917 and 1930 he underwent twenty-five operations for a variety of eye ailments. He survived with financial support from wealthy patrons including Harriet Shaw Weaver, publisher of a magazine called *The Egoist*, where *A Portrait* first appeared in serialized form.

The acclaim given *A Portrait* led to the serialization of episodes from *Ulysses* in the magazine *Little Review*. After World War I, Joyce had moved to Paris at the invitation of poet Ezra Pound. In 1922, *Ulysses* was published there by Sylvia Beach, owner of Shakespeare and Company, the famed Left Bank bookshop that was also home to the artistic and literary community of 1920s Paris, including American expatriates such as Hemingway, Fitzgerald, and Gertrude Stein.

In 1922, the *Little Review*, along with a New York City bookshop, was charged with obscenity for having published one of the book's episodes, known as "Nausicäa," which contains a scene of masturbation. The book was prohibited from entering the United States. To test the ban, American publisher Random House imported a copy, forcing the Customs Service to seize it, and then sued. The landmark 1933 court decision in *United States v. One Book Called Ulysses* ruled that it was not obscene and Random House could publish its edition, which appeared in January 1934.

In Paris, Joyce completed his final novel, *Finnegans Wake*, a work of even greater complexity than *Ulysses*. It was published in its entirety in 1939. When Paris fell to the Nazis in 1940, Joyce and his family—wife, Nora, and two children, Giorgio and Lucia—moved to Zurich, Switzerland. After undergoing surgery for a perforated ulcer, James Joyce died on January 13, 1941, a few weeks before his fifty-ninth birthday.

WHY YOU SHOULD READ IT

The answer is simple. For anyone who wants a literary education, *A Portrait* is a required text. As a *Bildungsroman*—the German word meaning "novel of education" or "novel of formation"—it is among the finest in English. If Joyce did not actually invent the literary technique of "stream of consciousness," in which the characters' thoughts and mind processes carry the narrative, he elevated it to high art.

Innovative and evocative, the novel's interplay of language and ideas is genius. It is poetry when Stephen describes a priest unfairly punishing him and he describes "the swish of the sleeve of the soutane as the pandybat was lifted to strike."

Two passages in particular remain with me vividly more than forty years after first reading them: the "Hellfire" sermon delivered to Stephen and his schoolmates by a priest and the "Bird Girl" scene in which Stephen receives a vision or his epiphany:

> A girl stood before him in midstream: alone and still, gazing out to sea. She seemed like one whom magic had changed into the likeness of a strange and beautiful seabird.

WHAT TO READ NEXT

Depicting a day in Dublin and the eventual encounter between Stephen Dedalus and Leopold Bloom, *Ulysses* it is widely considered among the twentieth century's greatest works of literature. It is first on the Modern Library list of 100 Best Novels. And around the world, Bloomsday (June 16) is celebrated with marathon public readings.

But before attempting the considerable challenge of *Ulysses*, start with *Dubliners*. Acclaimed as one of the greatest collections of short fiction of modern literature, the stories bring alive Joyce's native city with its sights, sounds, peculiar personalities, and the often-tragic outcomes of unfulfilled lives. In their minute actions, Joyce forged that "reality of experience" that Stephen Dedalus yearns to create.

Through the rich and real detail Joyce brought to the page, combined with the religious, historical, and political myths and symbols that fed his genius, Joyce created a masterpiece not limited to his city.

"It is a work that . . . compels attention by the power of its unique vision of the world, its controlling sense of the truths of human experience as its author discerned them in a defeated, colonial city," writes Terence Brown of Trinity College, Dublin. The concluding story, "The Dead," the longest piece in the collection, is by itself a masterpiece describing a single night's Christmas party.

To take on *Ulysses*—unless guided in a seminar—I would suggest turning to the annotated editions and reader's guides for Joyce's masterwork. These provide context for the many often-obscure artistic, religious, mythological, and linguistic allusions—as well as laying out Dublin's geography—that enriches a reading of one of the twentieth century's literary giants.

The Postman Always Rings Twice

— 1934 —

James M. Cain

New York: Vintage Crime/Black Lizard, 1992; 116 pages

* Number 98 on the Modern Library list of 100 Best Novels *

FIRST LINES

They threw me off the hay truck about noon. I had swung on the night before, down at the border, and as soon as I got up there under the canvas, I went to sleep. I needed plenty of that, after three weeks in Tia Juana, and I was still getting it when they pulled off to one side to let the engine cool. Then they saw a foot sticking out and threw me off. I tried some comical stuff, but all I got was a dead pan, so that gag was out. They gave me a cigarette, though, and I hiked down the road to find something to eat.

Can you say "noir"? How about "hard-boiled"?

Along with contemporaries Dashiell Hammett and Raymond Chandler, James M. Cain embodied the genre in a first novel that helped define a category in fiction and film. The staccato dialogue of cynical characters, the dark mood, sexual tension, and sudden violence Cain employed, are hallmarks of the "hard-boiled" or "noir" style.

Set in Depression-era California, Cain's highly compact story of adultery and murder wastes no time on preliminaries or a slow buildup. Frank Chambers is one of those Depression-era drifters, tramping from city to city, always on the verge of trouble. One day, he stops at the filling station and roadside diner owned by Nick Papadakis. Then he sets eyes on Cora, Nick's wife. One look and Frank takes up Nick's offer of a job.

"From now on, it would be business between her and me," Frank says. "She might not say yes, but she wouldn't stall me. She knew what I meant, and she knew I had her number." And it is not long before the two of them are plotting to be rid of Nick.

Cain's book crackles with erotic electricity. When Cora tells Frank, "Rip me! Rip me!" it was sensational enough to help earn the book an obscenity trial in Boston. But in those days, publishers knew "Banned in Boston" made good promotional copy.

Does Frank love Cora enough to do what she wants? When he kisses her, "it was like being in church." Just how far will the lovers go?

James Mallahan Cain was born on July 1, 1892, in Annapolis, Maryland. His father was president of Washington College, from which

Cain graduated in 1910. His mother was a singer and Cain also had ambitions to sing. "My mother told me I didn't have the voice," he said. "She was right, but she could have kept her flap shut and let me find out for myself." Singers gone astray would later figure in some of his books.

Cain started as a newspaperman and, during World War I, wrote for a U.S. Army newspaper in France. He would eventually work under three legendary editors: H. L. Mencken in Baltimore, Walter Lippman of the *New York World*, and briefly Harold Ross of the *New Yorker*.

After his first short story was published in the *American Mercury*, Cain set out for Hollywood. He "stayed there for 17 years," John Leonard wrote in Cain's obituary, "marrying four women and divorcing three, 'trying to drink up Hollywood,' and writing the four novels on which his reputation rests."

The first of these was *The Postman Always Rings Twice*, published when he was forty-two years old. Considered obscene in 1934, it was a commercial sensation. Cain followed with *Double Indemnity* (first serialized in 1936), *Serenade* (1937), and *Mildred Pierce* (1941). Hollywood later turned both *Double Indemnity* and *Mildred Pierce* into film classics, but *The Postman* was untouchable under Hollywood's rigid morals code. Only after the first two successes did *The Postman Always Rings Twice* make it to the big screen in 1946 with Lana Turner and John Garfield as the torrid murderous couple. It was remade in 1981 with Jack Nicholson and Jessica Lange as the leads.

Cain's later work does not rival his earlier triumphs. But in 1969, the three books considered his best—*The Postman Always Rings Twice*, *Double Indemnity*, and *Mildred Pierce*—were reissued in a single volume, spawning a major revival of interest in his work. James M. Cain died of a heart attack at age eighty-five on October 27, 1977, in University Park, Maryland.

WHY YOU SHOULD READ IT

I confess, I am a sucker for this genre and cut my teeth by reading—or watching—a great many of the classic stories by Dashiell Hammett, Raymond Chandler, and Cain. The clipped pacing, amoral intrigues, gritty settings, and tough-guy dialogue are all hallmarks of a deeply influential style.

Even if now slightly dated, and perhaps diminished because Cain's writing has been mimicked by generations of imitators, *The Postman Always Rings Twice* remains a classic. In its quick tempo, high sexual tension, and violence—although fairly demure by modern standards—Cain's first novel deals with themes that fascinate many great fiction writers: lust, ambition, greed, and murder. But the author once argued, "There's more violence in 'Hamlet' than in all my books. I write love stories, and about the wish that terrifies."

Cain does it in hard-hitting, no-nonsense prose that has no pretense of literary high-mindedness. He once commented:

> I make no conscious effort to be tough, or hard-boiled, or grim, or any of the things I am usually called. I merely try to write as the character would write, and I never forget that the average man . . . has acquired a vividness of speech that goes beyond anything I could invent.

There is no literal "Postman" in the novel. The message is that you may miss the Postman—fate, bad news, or worse—the first time. But there is no escaping the second. *The Stranger* by Albert Camus (see entry) is said to have been inspired by *The Postman*. The novel also provided the unattributed source of Luchino Visconti's film *Ossessione* (1943), an early Italian neorealist classic.

WHAT TO READ NEXT

Cain's two other best works fit into the *Great Short Books* category, so it's easy to try them both. *Double Indemnity*, first serialized as a Depression-era tale of adultery and murder for insurance money, was based on a true story Cain had covered as a reporter in New York. *Mildred Pierce* is also a Depression-era story, of a woman who uses her wiles—and pie-baking skills—to escape poverty and an unemployed husband. But she can't escape her relationship with a scheming and somewhat monstrous daughter, Veda, an aspiring opera singer. The 1945 film version departed from Cain's original story, while a recent HBO miniseries starring Kate Winslet is more faithful to Cain's plot.

The Prime of Miss Jean Brodie

— 1961 —

Muriel Spark

New York: HarperPerennial Modern Classics, 2018; 137 pages

* Number 76 on the Modern Library list of 100 Best Novels *
* TIME: "All-TIME 100 Novels" *

FIRST LINES

The boys, as they talked to the girls from Marcia Blaine School, stood on the far side of their bicycles holding the handlebars, which established a protective fence of bicycle between the sexes, and the impression that at any moment the boys were likely to be away.

PLOT SUMMARY

It is the 1930s, in Edinburgh, Scotland, and Miss Jean Brodie is an unorthodox teacher at an elite school for girls. She tosses aside the prescribed textbooks to instruct her students about "Goodness, Truth, and Beauty." And Giotto, and Einstein, and the proper care of the skin and hands—and Hugh, her "felled fiancé" who died in World War I. Her six chosen acolytes are the "Brodie set." Each wears her hat in a particular style. Each is destined for a unique fate.

But their fates and devotion to Miss Brodie will be tested. As they move through school and into their teenage years, the girls observe Miss Brodie's somewhat scandalous notions of life and love. And they speculate about her relationship with the unmarried music teacher, Mr. Lowther, and the married art teacher, Mr. Lloyd. They also learn of her admiration for all things Italian, including, most disquietingly, Mussolini.

"Give me a girl at an impressionable age and she is mine for life," Miss Brodie likes to say. "The gang who oppose me shall not succeed."

But that opposition comes in the form of the headmistress, who hatches a plot to dislodge Miss Brodie from the school. Ultimately, one of Miss Brodie's six girls, the "crème de la crème," will betray her.

ABOUT THE AUTHOR: MURIEL SPARK

Yet again, a complicated, confounding author's life.

Muriel Spark was born on February 1, 1918, as Muriel Camberg to an engineer father and a music-teacher mother, in an Edinburgh suburb. From the age of five, she attended James Gillespie's High School for Girls, where one of her teachers would become the model for Miss Jean Brodie. Demonstrating a gift for poetry and language from a young age, but lacking funds, Muriel Camberg took secretarial classes and worked in a department store instead of attending university.

In 1937, at nineteen, she married Sydney Oswald Spark, an older man, and left Scotland with him when he took a teaching post in Rhodesia. Spark later commented, "I was attracted to a man who brought me bunches of flowers when I had flu. (From my experience of life I believe my personal motto should be 'beware of men bringing flowers.')" They had a son, Robin, but after seven years of marriage she divorced the increasingly violent Spark. As she later wrote, "He became a borderline case, and I didn't like what I found on either side of the border."

Retaining the name Spark, she moved to wartime London, leaving behind her son in a convent due to restrictions on children traveling during the war; later Robin was sent to live with Spark's parents in Edinburgh. She spent the last year of the war working for British intelligence, writing propaganda that was broadcast in Germany. After the war, Spark edited a poetry journal but was fired when her tastes were deemed too modern. By then, she was writing her own poetry, publishing a collection of verse in 1952.

In the 1950s, Spark converted to Catholicism around the same time she entered a dark period of drugs and despair. In poverty, she used amphetamines to ward off hunger, bringing on hallucinations. "The words she had once manipulated turned on her," noted her *New York Times* obituary, "trapping her in a fog of anagrams and crosswords and convincing her that a code ran through the literature she read."

The experience led to her first novel, *The Comforters* (1957), in which a young woman imagines that she is a character in a novel being written on a typewriter only she can hear. A more lucid Spark soon began turning out a new book every year, with her novels receiving considerable acclaim, including *Memento Mori* (1959), *The Ballad of Peckham Rye* (1960), and *The Bachelors* (1960).

Then in 1961, the *New Yorker* devoted almost an entire issue to *The Prime of Miss Jean Brodie*. Later published in hardcover, it became a best seller, and Spark moved to New York in 1963 to work at the *New Yorker*. A later stage adaptation of *The Prime of Miss Jean Brodie* by Jay Presson Allen became a hit in London and New York and was filmed in 1969. The book became what Spark called her "milch cow," providing the reliable income that had previously eluded her.

In 1967, Spark moved to Italy, where she lived for the rest of her life, first in Rome and later in Tuscany. She continued to write novels that were often critically praised. But none of her later work achieved the widespread popularity of her "milch cow."

In Rome in 1968, she met Penelope Jardine, a sculptor, who became her secretary and companion. The two women lived and traveled together for the rest of Spark's life, although both denied a romantic relationship. Spark was made a Dame of the British Empire in 1993. Estranged from her son, Spark left her entire estate to Jardine when she died in Florence in April 2006, at the age of eighty-eight.

WHY YOU SHOULD READ IT

First, if your notion of Miss Jean Brodie derives from Maggie Smith's Oscar-winning performance in the 1969 film, read the book. The film—and the stage adaption on which the film was based—departs from the novel in several crucial plot points.

But more significantly, read it for its vivid characters, sparkling dialogue, and profound moral dilemmas. The novel's focus might seem to be on the iconoclastic and iron-willed Jean Brodie, with her reservoir of witty aphorisms and high-minded approach to the education of her "little girls."

But a closer read is that this is a coming-of-age story about the girls, and particularly Sandy, the Brodie girl who—and this is no spoiler—becomes a nun. It is Sandy, in particular, who is the focus of the novel's moral quandary. Sandy is a girl with insight. That insight includes watching Miss Brodie perversely manipulate the "Brodie set," even encouraging one of the girls to become involved with Mr. Lloyd, the married art teacher–painter. Mr. Lloyd, for his part, seems quite open to the possibility—a theme that has acquired a different connotation in our "Me Too" era. When one of the girls does become Lloyd's lover, she is no longer a student. But these are the moral hazards that Muriel Spark forces us to examine.

Miss Jean Brodie is, of course, an extraordinary and iconic fictional creation. And Spark's depiction of her battling the traditionalists looking to remove her is worth the price of admission. But the book is about a dilemma larger than an alluringly charming schoolteacher and the undue power she exerts over her charges. At its heart, it examines the uses of authority—and how dangerous a magnetic personality can be. As Lev Grossman of *Time* observed, "The archly, tartly narrated adventures of these young girls and their eccentric, autocratic leader form a delightful group portrait and something more: an immortal parable of the temptations of charisma and the dangers of power."

WHAT TO READ NEXT

Ranked among the greatest postwar British writers by *The Times* of London, Spark left a catalog of more than twenty novels. Among them is *The Girls of Slender Means* (1963), the immediate successor to *The Prime of Miss Jean Brodie*. It describes a group of young women living together in a London women's residence in the aftermath of World War II. Alan Taylor, who later wrote of his friendship with Spark, says of it:

> I always think of *The Girls of Slender Means* as a sequel of sorts to *The Prime of Miss Jean Brodie*. . . . They've moved away from their upbringing and school and now they're making their way in the big world.

Having lived through the Watergate era and the downfall of Richard Nixon, I am intrigued by *The Abbess of Crewe*, Spark's 1974 tale of Machiavellian political machinations. Inspired by Nixon's bugging of his political opponents and subtitled *A Modern Morality Tale*, it is set in a convent and revolves around the election of a new abbess. One of the nuns monitors her rivals with video and audio surveillance. Reviewing it in 1974, critic George Stade wrote, "Muriel Spark is the first writer to demonstrate that Watergate and its attendant immoralities are materials not of tragedy, but of farce."

It is a delightful conceit, but Spark takes it beyond the confines of a single notorious moment in American political history to a larger tale of morality, the central concern coursing through her body of work.

The Red Badge of Courage

— 1895 —

Stephen Crane

New York: Bantam Classics, 2004; with an introduction by Alfred Kazin; 128 pages

FIRST LINES

The cold passed reluctantly from the earth, and the retiring fogs revealed an army stretched out on the hills, resting. As the landscape changed from brown to green, the army awakened, and began to tremble with eagerness at the noise of rumors. It cast its eyes upon the roads, which were growing from long troughs of liquid mud to proper thoroughfares. A river, amber-tinted in the shadow of its banks, purled at the army's feet; and at night, when the stream had become of a sorrowful blackness, one could see across it the red, eyelike gleam of hostile camp fires set in the low brows of distant hills.

Written by a twenty-one-year-old who had not set foot on a battle-field, Stephen Crane's *The Red Badge of Courage* is still considered the greatest novel of the American Civil War.

Simply put, it recounts the story of young Henry Fleming, seen in a Union camp as an army masses for an expected battle. Untested, Henry is worried about how he will respond in combat. "It had suddenly appeared to him that perhaps in a battle he might run," writes Crane. "He was forced to admit that as far as war was concerned he knew nothing of himself."

Like other young men, Henry had read and heard accounts of the war. And, like many young men, he holds grandiose visions of an epic Homeric contest where he would rise as a hero. In a brilliant section of the novel's opening, we hear him announce, against his mother's protests, "Ma, I'm going to enlist."

She then packs eight pairs of socks, clean shirts, and his favorite blackberry jam and sends him off saying: ". . . yeh must never do no shirking, child, on my account. If so be a time comes when yeh have to be kilt or do a mean thing, why, Henry, don't think of anything 'cept what's right."

Knowing something of himself and doing "what's right" will become the great issues that "the youth"—as Stephen Crane often calls Henry—must ultimately confront.

ABOUT THE AUTHOR: STEPHEN CRANE

First fact: Stephen Crane was born six years after the Civil War ended. He wouldn't see an actual battlefield until after his greatest work was published.

Born in Newark, New Jersey, on November 1, 1871, Stephen Crane was the youngest of fourteen children, whose father, a Methodist minister and prominent abolitionist, died when he was eight. Raised by his mother, a member of the Woman's Christian Temperance Union, and his older siblings, Crane was sent to a preparatory school, Claverack Academy, a quasi-military school where he excelled in history and literature and was greatly interested in the soldierly drills he received—later put to use in writing *The Red Badge of Courage*.

Intent on writing and journalism from an early age, he briefly attended Syracuse University. Quickly deciding that a college education was useless, he embarked on a writing career in 1891. As a freelance journalist, he wrote for local newspapers in upstate New York and New Jersey.

But Crane was drawn to New York City and its sprawling slums, especially around the Bowery. Intrigued by the saloons, brothels, flophouses, and dance halls that filled that notorious neighborhood, Crane used it as the setting for his first novel. His gritty account of Rum Alley and Devil's Row and a young girl who descends into prostitution was rejected by publishers. Using inherited money and under a pseudonym, Crane self-published the book, later called *Maggie: A Girl of the Streets* (1893). It was not a success.

Fascinated by accounts of the Civil War he read in popular magazines, Crane envisioned a novel told from the point of view of a young soldier with boyish dreams of glory who then quickly becomes disenchanted by the reality of war. *The Red Badge of Courage* was first serialized in *McClure's Magazine*, famed for its "muckraking" journalism in the late nineteenth and early twentieth centuries. In 1895, *The Red Badge of Courage* was published in book form to wide acclaim in both the United States and England. Many readers could not believe that Crane had not been in the war himself.

Despite the book's success, Crane struggled financially. In 1897, he was given an advance of seven hundred dollars by a newspaper syndicate to go to Cuba, still a Spanish colony, to cover an insurrection that eventually boiled over into the Spanish-American War. A capsized boat off Florida left Crane and other crew members floundering in the water for nearly two days before coming ashore.

To avoid drowning, Crane abandoned a money belt carrying his advance in gold. He fictionalized the episode in "The Open Boat," considered one of the world's finest short stories.

Plagued by financial difficulties, Crane traveled to Greece during its war with Turkey in 1897 as a war correspondent for the Hearst papers, accompanied by Cora Taylor, owner of a Florida brothel. Although they were not married, they later settled in England as a couple, running up debt while entertaining the literary likes of friends Henry James, H. G. Wells, and Joseph Conrad. In 1898, Crane was dispatched as correspondent to cover the Spanish-American War in Cuba, where he contracted yellow fever.

Returning to England deeply in debt, Crane was in worsening health. In 1900, he traveled to Germany's Black Forest, hoping to improve his lungs. He died there, on June 5, of tuberculosis and related problems. He was twenty-eight.

WHY YOU SHOULD READ IT

As a reader and historian, over many years, I have studied a great deal of "war literature," both fiction and nonfiction. Men at war has been a central theme in Western literature since Homer's *Iliad*. For me, such books as *Johnny Tremain*, *The Killer Angels*, *All Quiet on the Western Front*, and *The Things They Carried* have always held a special lure. Many of them follow the path set by Stephen Crane.

Like many people, I was assigned to read *The Red Badge of Courage* in school. It was, and still may be, required reading for many students. I don't remember what grade it was assigned. But I do remember reading it. And it was an unforgettable novel.

Unlike many war novelists before and since, Crane did not concern himself with grand schemes, tactics, the strategies of generals, or even the epic violence of war—although there is plenty of that in Crane's novella. Crane was much more interested in what Henry thought and felt than in merely describing what he had witnessed on the battlefield.

The distinguished literary critic Alfred Kazin called *The Red Badge of Courage* "the first great 'modern' novel of war by an American—the first novel of literary distinction to present war without heroics and this in a spirit of total irony and skepticism."

What makes the novel modern is, first, its literary realism, which Crane certainly pioneered, a reflection of his roots in journalism. It is a path in American fiction that led to, among many others, Theodore Dreiser, Upton Sinclair, Edith Wharton, Ernest Hemingway, and John Steinbeck.

But it is also modern in Crane's attempt to portray the inner experience—the psychology—of his character. These stylistic distinctions are achieved with a sense of language that is often sublime. Crane was also a poet, and it shows in this novel.

In the end, he accomplishes something else of great consequence. As Herbert Mitgang put it in the *New York Times*, "He proves that any authentic war novel—in any country's literature—is perforce an antiwar novel."

WHAT TO READ NEXT

Because he died so young, Stephen Crane did not leave a large library of work. While he did write poetry, his fiction is still what marks his essential genius. Crane's first novel, *Maggie: A Girl of the Streets*, was deemed unpublishable in its day because of its plot—the descent of a young woman into prostitution—and its realistic style. Today these are considered hallmarks of Crane's accomplishments. *Maggie* is worth reading for its significance in moving American letters toward realism and a sense of social conscience.

His short stories are also considered among his most notable works and the best of these are "The Open Boat" and "A Dark Brown

Dog," an allegory about the South during Reconstruction. Crane's short stories are widely anthologized and collected.

An expansive biography of Crane, *Burning Boy: The Life and Work of Stephen Crane*, was written by novelist Paul Auster and published to considerable acclaim in 2021.

Rita Hayworth and Shawshank Redemption

— 1982 —

Stephen King

New York: Scribner, 2020; 111 pages

FIRST LINES

There's a guy like me in every state and federal prison in America, I guess—
I'm the guy who can get it for you. Tailor-made cigarettes, a bag of reefer if
you're partial to that, a bottle of brandy to celebrate your son or daughter's
high school graduation, or almost anything else . . . within reason, that is.
It wasn't always that way.

PLOT SUMMARY

Andy Dufresne, a once-respectable young banker, is serving a life
sentence in Maine's notorious Shawshank prison for killing his wife

and her lover. Like most convicts, he maintains his innocence while trying to negotiate an unforgiving world of brutal prison violence, corrupt guards, and malevolent wardens.

When Andy befriends Red, the veteran prisoner who narrates this story, trust slowly develops between the two men. Over decades in jail, Red will come to hold Andy in special regard among the rest of the inmates. "In all my years at Shawshank," says Red, "there have been less than ten men whom I believed when they told me they were innocent. Andy Dufresne was one of them."

A prison fixer, Red smuggles in all the things that the other prisoners want—for Andy, a small rock hammer, an occasional whiskey bottle, and a movie poster of Rita Hayworth. A money man, Andy gains the confidence of guards and prison officials with investment and tax advice. Yet while Andy's prison life gets easier over the years, he is still behind bars. And there is no way out.

Then comes a game changer. A new prison inmate may have the evidence that will set Andy free. But the warden is going to make sure Andy remains exactly where he is. The story becomes a classic of the prison-breakout genre.

ABOUT THE AUTHOR: STEPHEN KING

If any writer in this collection needs no introduction, it might be Stephen King. Unless, perhaps, you are from another planet. Or have lived in a cave since the 1970s.

One of the most prolific and successful novelists in recent publishing history, King has written more than sixty books, many of them international best sellers. You may have seen a movie or television miniseries—even a Broadway play—based on one. *Carrie? The Shining? Stand by Me? Misery? It?*

Ring a bell?

Now some facts. First of all, Stephen King informs visitors to his website, he is not dead. Nor is he going blind. Or retired. "Not yet," he says.

Born in Portland, Maine, on September 21, 1947, Stephen King is the second son of Donald and Nellie King. When Stephen was two, his father left the family. Stephen and his older brother, David, were raised by their mother, moving in with various relatives around the country.

When King was eleven, the family returned to Maine to live with King's aging grandparents. Attending public schools, King graduated from high school in 1966 and from there went to the University of Maine in Orono, where he wrote a weekly column for the campus newspaper.

He met his future wife, Tabitha, on campus and, after graduating in 1970, they married in 1971. With plans to teach, King had to take a job at an industrial laundry until he was eventually hired to teach high school in Hampden, Maine. By then he had already published some short stories in magazines, like *Startling Mystery Stories*, and he continued to write as he taught classes.

His breakthrough came when he received a modest advance for *Carrie*, which was published in 1974. A six-figure paperback reprint sale allowed King to quit teaching for full-time writing. *'Salem's Lot* followed, and on its heels came a long succession of enormously successful horror novels and thrillers. King describes his early life in entertaining style in *On Writing* (2000).

The Kings lived for a time in Boulder, Colorado, during which King wrote *The Shining* (1977), the story of a writer struggling with alcoholism who is hired as a caretaker for a hotel during the off-season. King recalls being inspired by a visit to the Stanley Hotel in Estes Park, Colorado, near the end of the season. "They asked me if I could pay cash because they were taking the credit card receipts back down to Denver," King told the *Paris Review*. "I went past the first sign that said, Roads may be closed after November 1, and I said, Jeez, there's a story up here."

A best seller, the book became the basis for Stanley Kubrick's 1980 film of the same title, an adaptation that King told an interviewer did not please him. "So where is the tragedy if the guy shows up for his job interview and he's already bonkers? No, I hated what Kubrick did with that."

Returning to Maine, King completed *The Stand*, a postapocalyptic novel that describes a world decimated by an influenza pandemic. Initially published in 1978, it had been edited down by some five hundred pages. In 1990, *The Stand* was reissued with the editorial cuts restored and other changes in the chronology. At 1,153 pages, the revised edition is his longest book, and considered by many his best—although, of course, not a candidate for this collection.

Space does not allow a full tally of all his works, including those written under pen name Richard Bachman. It was an identity he used because he believed he could write more than one book per year, but his publisher balked at the risk of saturating the market. In one of those books, *Thinner*, a man is cursed to uncontrollably lose weight. Based on the book's style, an astute fan figured out that Bachman was King and blew his cover.

The recipient of the 2003 National Book Foundation Medal for Distinguished Contribution to American Letters and the 2014 National Medal of Arts, King has demonstrated convincingly, with sales of more than 300 million books worldwide, that "popular fiction" and "serious fiction" can coexist. King lives in Bangor, Maine, and Florida.

WHY YOU SHOULD READ IT

Unlike many of King's books, this one may not keep you awake, listening for things that go bump in the night. No ghouls, vampires, scary cemeteries, or little girls with the power to set fires. It is about something even scarier—reality. *Rita Hayworth and Shawshank Redemption* is a taut, riveting story of an unjust world in which innocence is no defense.

Let me first point out that this King novella has been made into one of my favorite films, *The Shawshank Redemption*, a Best Picture nominee in 1994. With some plot and character deviations, the movie is a largely faithful adaptation that has become a popular modern classic. If you have never seen the movie, see it.

But don't skip the novel. Read it for its sharp characters, intriguing plot, and small, brilliant scenes, such as Andy getting the guards to provide a prison work gang with some "suds"—bottles of beer—on a hot day. The book spotlights Stephen King as a master storyteller with larger ambitions than creating page-turners.

Part of King's appeal, and his genius, is to take the ordinary or commonplace and make it extraordinary. Teen angst becomes a story of telekinesis (*Carrie*). A junkyard dog becomes a satanic beast (*Cujo*). A cell phone becomes an object of dread (*The Cell*).

But here, with prison as his metaphor, King addresses innocence and guilt, justice and injustice, in a muscular, inventive story, rich in character despite the short narrative. Ultimately, Stephen King is interested in morality—good and evil. He often investigates commonplace malevolence in his fiction, whether on a grand scale, as in *The Stand*, or in the compact gem of *Rita Hayworth*.

"So whether you talk about ghosts or vampires or Nazi war criminals living down the block, we're still talking about the same thing, which is an intrusion of the extraordinary into ordinary life and how we deal with it," he told an interviewer for the *Paris Review*. "What that shows about our character and our interactions with others and the society we live in interests me a lot more than monsters and vampires and ghouls and ghosts."

The theme of imprisonment is at the core of several other selections in this book—*One Day in the Life of Ivan Denisovich, If This Is a Man, The Nickel Boys, The Postman Always Rings Twice, The Stranger*. All of these examine, in some respect, the plight of the falsely accused and the possibility of justice. And as settings, the prison camp provides a backdrop for a visceral exploration of the human condition and the potential for depravity in the world. King's tightly packed and captivating story joins that august company.

WHAT TO READ NEXT

Where to begin? If you are new to Stephen King, maybe at the beginning. Start with his first published novel, *Carrie* (1974), the story of bullied teenager Carrie White who exacts revenge on her schoolmates and fanatically religious mother. King's second published novel, *'Salem's Lot* (1975) is also vintage King, offering his take on the classic vampire genre.

His memoir and advice on the craft of writing, *On Writing*, is enlightening and a lot of fun to read.

Two of my other top choices from the King catalog are *The Dead Zone*, about a high school teacher who can see the future and confronts the threat of a politician who may become a dangerous autocrat; and *Firestarter*, the story of a young girl with remarkable destructive powers and the attempt by the government to weaponize those powers.

And then there is *The Stand*, all 1,153 pages of it. I suppose after a year of short books in a time of pandemic, maybe it will be time for a very long one about another plague.

The Sailor Who Fell from Grace with the Sea

— 1963 —

Yukio Mishima

New York: Vintage International, 1994; translated from the Japanese by John Nathan; 181 pages; originally published in Japan in 1963 as Gogo no eiko

FIRST LINES

"Sleep well, dear."

Noboru's mother closed his bedroom door and locked it. What would she do if there were a fire? Let him out first thing—she had promised herself that. But what if the wooden door warped in the heat or paint clogged the keyhole? The window? There was a gravel path below; besides, the second floor of this gangling house was hopelessly high.

In postwar Yokohama, Japan, a thirteen-year-old boy named Noboru makes a discovery. Behind a chest of drawers in his room, he finds a small hole in the wall that allows him to secretly look into his widowed mother's bedroom. He begins spying on her at night, particularly when she had nagged or scolded him and is preparing for bed.

Noboru is locked in because he had been caught sneaking out to join his friends, a gang of precocious teenage boys led by a "chief" who has formidable notions about the imperfections and hypocrisy of adults. Noboru decides that his mother, who owns a shop selling fashionable Western luxury goods, is imperfect.

When he meets Ryuji, his mother's new romantic interest, Noboru is in awe. In this merchant marine officer, with his manly reserve and tales of the sea, Noboru sees the sailor as a heroic figure. One night, as the boy spies through the peephole, he sees his mother and the sailor make love. Noboru is "certain he had watched a tangle of thread unravel to trace a hallowed figure."

Noboru's admiration quickly fades when he learns that the sailor will leave his ship and marry his mother. All reverence for Ryuji is shattered. Why is the sailor ready to sacrifice his honor? Disgusted, Noboru and his gang plot to make "the sailor who fell from grace" pure and heroic once more, with dreadful consequences.

ABOUT THE AUTHOR: YUKIO MISHIMA

Recognized in the literary world as one of Japan's most significant writers in the years after World War II, Yukio Mishima was once a candidate for the Nobel Prize. He failed to win the award but rather reached a new level of notoriety on November 25, 1970, when he committed ritual suicide—known as seppuku. Disemboweling himself, he was decapitated by a loyal follower in a public display that made international headlines.

Born Hiraoka Kimitake in Tokyo on January 14, 1925, the author of *The Sailor* was the son of a high-ranking civil servant. Kimitake's mother's family came from Japan's traditional aristocracy and he was educated at Peers' School, established as an academy for Japan's royal family and members of Japan's feudal nobility. Fascinated from an early age by classical Japanese theater, he began writing poetry for the school's literary magazine.

In 1941, at the age of sixteen, he published a short story in a prestigious literary magazine. Its editors coined his pen name, Yukio Mishima, combining the Japanese word for snow and the name of a railway station in the city of Mishima.

Mishima graduated at the top of his class in 1944 in a ceremony attended by the Japanese Emperor. Japan was then at war and he received his draft notice. But he failed his physical examination and was spared fighting in the war's final year when many young men, willing to die for the Emperor, embarked on suicide missions.

While working in Japan's Ministry of Finance, he began pursuing writing professionally, encouraged by novelist Yasunari Kawabata, later the first Japanese winner of the Nobel Prize. Drawing heavily on Japanese literature and cultural traditions, Mishima wrote short stories that explored violence and sexuality in many forms.

Though Yukio Mishima married and had two children, gay themes reverberated throughout his work. His 1949 novel, *Kamen no kokuhaku* (*Confessions of a Mask* in English), was a semiautobiographical story of a closeted gay man. The book established twenty-four-year-old Yukio Mishima as a leading voice among postwar Japanese writers.

He followed with a series of novels whose main characters are tormented by physical or psychological problems. The most acclaimed of these was *Kinkaku-ji* (1956), published in English as *The Temple of the Golden Pavilion*, the story of monk, obsessed with beauty, who burns down a famous Buddhist temple.

In 1955, Mishima began an intense period of body building and martial arts training. As his celebrity grew, Mishima took to modeling in body-building magazines and acting. He played a soldier in the film of his story "Patriotism" in which an army officer and his wife commit ritual suicide to demonstrate loyalty to the Emperor.

"A sickly, scholarly schoolboy, he transformed himself into a muscular man, expert at Japanese fencing and swordsmanship and a proficient student of karate," wrote Philip Shabecoff of the *New York Times*, who interviewed Mishima shortly before his death. "Mr. Mishima said that he worked so hard on body building because he intended to die before he was 50 and wanted to have a good looking corpse. He laughed, but then added, 'I am half-serious, you know.'"

With his reputation set, he emerged as a candidate for the Nobel Prize, but the award went instead to his mentor Yasunari Kawabata in 1968. Mishima then published a cycle of novels collectively called *The Sea of Fertility* that are considered his masterwork: *Spring Snow* (1969), *Runaway Horses* (1969), and *The Temple of Dawn* (1970) were all published before his death.

By the time they were released, Mishima had become a fanatical nationalist, devoted to restoring Japanese traditional values, which he saw being overrun by American influences, even though he privately maintained an essentially Western lifestyle. He formed a right-wing militia group called the Tate No Kai, or Shield Society, whose uniformed members regularly drilled together.

But it was no drill on November 25, 1970, when Mishima and four members of the Shield Society seized a Japanese general at an army compound. From a rooftop, Mishima urged the troops assembled below to rebel and throw off Japan's postwar constitution, which restricted the country's rearmament. When his call for a coup was ignored, the forty-five-year-old novelist took his own life in the manner of the traditional samurai warrior.

The Decay of the Angel, the final book in the *Sea of Fertility* cycle, was published posthumously in 1971.

WHY YOU SHOULD READ IT

The Sailor's prose is at times violent—describing, for instance, the gang killing a kitten. But Mishima can also be delicately sensual, with a Matisse-like eye for the interplay of color:

> Fusako was wearing a black-lace kimono over a crimson under-robe, and her obi was white brocade. Her milky face floated coolly in the dusk. Crimson peeped seductively through the black lace. She was a presence suffusing the air around them with the softness of being a woman; an extravagant, elegant woman—Ryuji had never seen anything like her.

Tightly constructed, skillfully written, *The Sailor* builds toward its dark conclusion. Does Mishima admire Noboru and his friends as representatives of traditional Japanese values? Or is he mocking their adolescent philosophy as pretentious posturing?

In my reading, it is difficult not to see this gang of boys as representatives of the heart of darkness that lies within.

Before getting very far into this novel, I recalled *Agostino* (see entry), a tale of another thirteen-year-old enthralled by his mother and caught up with a gang of boys. But Noboru's fascination goes far beyond Agostino's. And Noboru's gang is ready to do far worse. By the end of the novel, we are in *Lord of the Flies* territory, as Noboru's gang descends to dark depths.

Read it. You decide.

WHAT TO READ NEXT

The Temple of the Golden Pavilion is based on an actual event in which a Buddhist temple was burned by a monk in 1950. In Mishima's fictional version, a traumatized boy with a hopeless stutter becomes an acolyte in a famous temple and becomes obsessed with its beauty.

It was widely viewed as his masterpiece, before the publication of the four novels in the *Sea of Fertility* cycle.

The four books in this series follow the reincarnation of a character in four different time periods. Nobel laureate Kawabata, who died in 1972, said of the cycle:

> It used to be said that "Kinka-kuji"—"The Temple of the Golden Pavilion"—was his masterpiece. But this new one is greater. Mishima is really going at it with his whole heart now. He has a tremendous gift of words, and it has never been richer than in this new book. . . . Before I received the Nobel Prize I said that Mishima would get it. . . . I regard the prize as having been awarded not so much to me as to Japan. As far as talent goes, Mishima is far superior to me.

Finally, also consider Kawabata's *Snow Country* (1956), chronicling the romance of a wealthy man and a geisha; it was a candidate for inclusion in this collection.

The Stranger

— 1942 —

Albert Camus

New York: Vintage International, 1989; translated from the French by Matthew Ward; 123 pages; originally published in French as L'Étranger *in 1942*

FIRST LINES

Maman died today. Or yesterday maybe, I don't know. I got a telegram from the home: "Mother deceased. Funeral tomorrow. Faithfully yours." That doesn't mean anything. Maybe it was yesterday.

PLOT SUMMARY

A Frenchman living in Algiers receives news that his mother has died. Given two days off to attend her funeral, Monsieur Meursault arrives at his mother's nursing home, sits a vigil, and then goes through the motions at her funeral service. Distant, unmoved, even apathetic, Meursault shows little outward grief to the home's director and staff.

As a small group proceeds to the cemetery, a nurse warns him not to walk too fast or too slow. "She was right," Meursault says, telling his own story. "There was no way out."

Those words carry great meaning.

In this classic work of absurdist literature, Meursault returns home and renews a relationship with a former lover, but he still feels numb. "It occurred to me that anyway one more Sunday was over, that Maman was buried now, that I was going back to work, and that, really, nothing had changed."

But soon, everything changes. During an otherwise beautiful day at the beach, Meursault is caught up in an act of sudden violence.

An arrest, imprisonment, and ultimately a trial follow in the novella's second half. A parade of witnesses will scrutinize all of the seemingly innocent events in Meursault's day-to-day life. His lack of grief and his apathetic nature weigh heavily against him. Was that nurse right? Was there no way out?

ABOUT THE AUTHOR: ALBERT CAMUS

One of the most influential writers of the twentieth century, Albert Camus was born on November 7, 1913, to French parents in Algeria, a French colony at the time. His father, a farmworker, died in the First Battle of the Marne, one of the first massive battles of World War I, fought outside Paris in 1914. His mother took up housecleaning and the family moved to a small apartment with grandparents and an uncle.

Raised in relative poverty, Camus was able to attend a prestigious secondary school near Algiers. At seventeen, he was diagnosed with tuberculosis and had to abandon his love of swimming and playing goalkeeper for his soccer club. Camus began to study philosophy and, with a scholarship, attended the University of Algiers part-time while working odd jobs to earn money.

As Fascism spread in Europe in the 1930s, Camus moved to France to edit the *Paris-soir* newspaper. When World War II began in 1939, he tried to enlist in the French army but was rejected due to his poor health. After the Nazis invaded France, he left Paris and married Francine Faure, a mathematician and pianist, and they returned to Algeria, where Camus taught school in the city of Oran.

Advised to move to improve his health, he returned to France, eventually landing in Nazi-occupied Paris. Living on the Left Bank near the headquarters of the German military police, Camus worked as a manuscript reader for French publisher Gallimard, which had been permitted to continue publishing by the Nazis. At the same time, Camus was working with the French Resistance, taking great risk to secretly write and edit *Combat*, a banned anti-Fascist newspaper, while simultaneously writing a novel, a play, and a philosophical essay.

In 1942, Gallimard published his novel *The Stranger* to a strong reception in Paris literary circles. It was the same year that Camus published *The Myth of Sisyphus*, a book-length essay in which he used the ancient Greek tale of a man condemned to endlessly roll a boulder up a hill as a symbol of the absurdity of human effort. In this Paris of the 1940s, Camus became part of the extraordinary circle of French writers and intellectuals that included Jean-Paul Sartre and Simone de Beauvoir.

Lecturing widely after the war, Camus then published two more of his most consequential books, the novel *La Peste* (1947, *The Plague*) and another book-length essay, *L'Homme révolté* (1951, *The Rebel*). Rejecting communism as another form of totalitarianism, Camus split from Sartre and other contemporaries.

A surprise came in 1957, when Camus received news of his Nobel Prize. At age forty-four, he was the second-youngest recipient, after

Rudyard Kipling, forty-two when he won. The Nobel Committee cited Camus "for his important literary production, which with clear-sighted earnestness illuminates the problems of the human conscience in our times."

Accepting the award, Camus said, "By the same token, the writer's role is not free from difficult duties. By definition he cannot put himself today in the service of those who make history; he is at the service of those who suffer it."

On January 4, 1960, at the age of forty-six, Camus died in a car crash with his publisher, Michael Gallimard.

WHY YOU SHOULD READ IT

The Stranger is one of the most widely read French novels of the twentieth century. It is also, according to critic Claire Messud, "the exemplary existentialist novel," despite the author's rejection of the label.

And here is why it should be read: *The Stranger* allows you to ponder a philosophy by living in a man's head and hearing his thoughts. Listen to Meursault as he realizes:

> Nothing, nothing mattered, and I knew why. . . . Throughout the whole absurd life I'd lived, a dark wind had been rising toward me from somewhere deep in my future, across years that were still to come, and as it passed, the wind leveled whatever was offered to me at the time.

If you've read it before, read it for a new translation. Until 1988, readers opened the 1946 English translation of *The Stranger* and encountered these famous three words: "Mother died today."

But a revised English translation published that year—beginning with "Maman died today"—was meant to better capture a sense of the author's original, and less formal, sensibility. "Camus admitted using an 'American method,' particularly in the first half of the book," Matthew Ward, translator of the 1988 edition, told the *New York Times*. "He mentioned Hemingway, Dos Passos, Faulkner and James M. Cain as influences. My feeling is that 'The Stranger' is more like Cain's 'The Postman Always Rings Twice' [see entry] than Camus cared to admit."

In his highly compressed but haunting narrative, Camus explored the very meaning of existence. Meursault's story represents what Camus called "the nakedness of a man faced with the absurd." Tight, short sentences—the staccato style of the great "hard-boiled" novels—build to the abrupt and unexpected violence that changes Meursault's life.

WHAT TO READ NEXT

Apart from his fiction, Camus was best known for his philosophical works. Perhaps the most famous of these, written at about the same time as *The Stranger*, was *The Myth of Sisyphus*, published in 1942. In it, Camus addressed what he saw as the crucial issue: "Judging whether life is or is not worth living amounts to answering the fundamental question of philosophy. All the rest . . . comes afterwards."

While begun earlier in his life, the book-length essay was completed as people fled from the advance of the Nazis. It is admittedly a more challenging read than *The Stranger*. In it, Camus argued that human existence in an absurd universe is similar to the Greek story of Sisyphus, the "absurd hero," who has been condemned to eternally roll a boulder up a hill, only to have it roll down again.

As for his other fiction, another masterpiece that has gained new relevance and attracted much attention during the Covid pandemic is *The Plague*. This 1947 novel begins as a pestilence is sweeping the Algerian city of Oran during World War II. As rats die and the whole town is sickened by a deadly fever, Camus examines the response of the people to the outbreak.

"The plague is, of course, the virus of Fascism," historian Jill Lepore wrote in the midst of the Covid pandemic. "No one in the town gives much thought to the rats until it's too late—even though the plague 'rules out any future, cancels journeys, silences the exchange of views'—and few pay sufficient attention to the rats even after it's too late."

Sula

— 1973 —

Toni Morrison

New York: Vintage International, 2004; with a foreword by the author;
174 pages

FIRST LINES

In that place, where they tore the nightshade and blackberry patches from
their roots to make room for the Medallion City Golf Course, there was once
a neighborhood. It stood in the hills above the valley town of Medallion and
spread all the way to the river. It is called the suburbs now, but when black
people lived there it was called the Bottom. One road, shaded by beeches,
oaks, maples and chestnuts, connected it to the valley. The beeches are gone
now, and so are the pear trees where children sat and yelled down through
the blossoms to passersby.

PLOT SUMMARY

Commencing after the end of World War I and carrying through to 1969, *Sula* covers a great deal of territory—in both time and human passions. Largely set in "the Bottom," a Black enclave near the fictional town of Medallion, Ohio, the story entwines myth and history, key components of Toni Morrison's work. But at its heart, Morrison's novel focuses on the friendship of two women, Nel Wright and Sula Peace, who meet as children and become instant soul mates.

> So when they met, first in those chocolate halls and next through the ropes of the swing, they felt the ease and comfort of old friends. Because each had discovered years before that they were neither white nor male, and that all freedom and triumph was forbidden to them, they had set about creating something else to be.

Against a distant but still dominant white world, the story unfolds as the two girls grow up and their families endure tragedies and traumas—including one in which a woman allows a train to run over her leg for insurance money. As children, the girls share a dreadful secret. Then a stunning act of betrayal reshapes their lives, which remain inseparably connected in this compact, often-poetic, and tragic narrative.

ABOUT THE AUTHOR: TONI MORRISON

Born in the working-class town of Lorain, Ohio, on February 18, 1931, Toni Morrison grew up Chloe Anthony Wofford. Her father was a ship welder and her mother a homemaker. "Young Chloe grew up in a house suffused with narrative and superstition," wrote Margalit Fox in the *New York Times*. "She adored listening to ghost stories; her grandmother ritually consulted a book on dream interpretation, from which she divined the day's selections when she played the numbers."

At twelve, Chloe joined the Roman Catholic Church, choosing the baptismal name Anthony—the name from which her familiar nickname, Toni, emerged while at Howard University, where she did undergraduate work in English.

After earning a master's in English literature at Cornell in 1955, Morrison taught at Houston's Texas Southern University and then at Howard, where she joined a writing workshop and began writing fiction. In 1958, she married Harold Morrison, an architect from Jamaica, with whom she had two sons, Harold Ford and Slade. The marriage ended in divorce in 1964, and Morrison moved to Syracuse, New York, where she worked as a textbook editor. She later moved with her sons to New York, where she supported the family as a book editor at Random House for two decades, while continuing to pursue her own writing.

Her first novel, *The Bluest Eye*, was published in 1970 under her college nickname. Clearly, it stuck.

While continuing as an editor, she next published *Sula*, followed by a breakthrough work, *Song of Solomon* (1977), which became a Main Selection of the Book-of-the-Month Club, the first novel by a Black author to be so honored since Richard Wright's *Native Son* in 1940.

Following her fourth novel, *Tar Baby* (1981), Morrison came across the true story of a fugitive enslaved woman who had killed her infant daughter. This slice of history became the seed of her masterwork, *Beloved* (1987), which won the Pulitzer Prize for Fiction. After its publication, she joined the faculty of Princeton University in 1989.

In 1993, Toni Morrison was awarded the Nobel Prize in Literature, the first African American woman so honored. Her Nobel Prize citation read, in part, that Toni Morrison's work, "characterized by visionary force and poetic import, gives life to an essential aspect of American reality."

Morrison continued teaching and wrote several more novels, children's books, essay collections, and a libretto for an opera. In 2000, she was awarded the National Humanities Medal; and in 2012, the Presidential Medal of Freedom, presented by President Barack Obama. A Morrison short story, originally published in 1983, was published in book form in 2022 as *Recitatif: A Story*.

Toni Morrison died of pneumonia in a Bronx hospital at the age of eighty-eight on August 5, 2019.

WHY YOU SHOULD READ IT

If you have never read Morrison, the first answer is for the pure pleasure of Morrison's rich, poetic voice. From passages like the following, we immediately know we are in the hands of a master storyteller, gifted literary artist, and distinctive and compelling writer:

> Her flirting was sweet, low and guileless. Without ever a pat of the hair, a rush to change clothes or a quick application of paint, with no gesture whatsoever, she rippled with sex. In her same old print wraparound, barefoot in the summer, in the winter her feet in a man's leather slippers with the backs flattened under her heels, she made men aware of her behind, her slim ankles, the dew-smooth skin and the incredible length of neck.

Sula is a riveting narrative, touching upon the enormous weight of being Black and a woman. As Toni Morrison wrote in a foreword to a later edition of *Sula*:

> Outlaw women are fascinating—not always for their behavior, but because historically women are seen as naturally disruptive and their status is an illegal one from birth if it is not under the rule of men. In much literature a woman's escape from male rule led to regret, misery, if not complete disaster. In *Sula*, I wanted to explore the consequences of what that escape might be, on not only a conventional black society, but on female friendship.

WHAT TO READ NEXT

The body of Morrison's work is broad and deep and there are many treasures to mine. Her first novel, *The Bluest Eye* (1970), could have just as easily been included in this collection. Another great short book, it is the story of a young Black girl who yearns for the blond hair and blue eyes she thinks confer beauty. *Song of Solomon* and *Tar Baby*, the works that followed *Sula*, are longer novels that solidified Morrison's stature as one of the most consequential American novelists.

Ultimately, one must come to what is widely acknowledged as Morrison's masterwork, *Beloved* (1987), which opens in the immediate aftermath of the Civil War. Inspired by the actual incident in which a fugitive enslaved woman kills her child, the novel is about Sethe, also a fugitive, forced to make a dreadful decision about what to do when her own baby is at risk of being taken by a slave catcher. In 2006, *Beloved* was selected by the *New York Times* as "the Best Work of American Fiction of the Last 25 Years."

Critic A. O. Scott wrote at the time:

> With remarkable speed, "Beloved" has, less than 20 years after its publication, become a staple of the college literary curriculum, which is to say a classic. This triumph is commensurate with its ambition, since it was Morrison's intention in writing it precisely to expand the range of classic American literature, to enter, as a living black woman, the company of dead white males like Faulkner, Melville, Hawthorne and Twain.

Surfacing

— 1972 —

Margaret Atwood

New York: Anchor Books, 1998; 199 pages

FIRST LINES

I can't believe I'm on this road again, twisting along past the lake where the white birches are dying, the disease is spreading up from the south, and I notice they now have seaplanes for hire. But this is still near the city limits; we didn't go through, it's swelled enough to have a bypass, that's success.

PLOT SUMMARY

The unnamed woman artist who narrates this compelling, discomforting story is on a quest. With her boyfriend Joe and a married couple, David and Anna, she is traveling back to her family's island cabin on a remote Canadian lake in search of her missing father. Seeking clues to his disappearance in the abandoned cabin and the surrounding woods, she is moving back through time and memory as well.

Although not precisely specified, the setting is the late 1960s or the cusp of the 1970s, and the encroachment of Vietnam War-era American culture—"the disease is spreading up from the south"—is ever present. The threat is also environmental, as the artist/narrator sees the lake's natural state despoiled by trash, motorboats, and tourists arriving by seaplane.

What starts out as the mystery of her vanished father becomes a much more complex psychological detective story and spiritual journey. As the artist observes David and Anna's uncomfortable banter heading toward a marital meltdown, she ponders her own future with Joe. Questions of men and sex and power plague her, coming together with the assault on nature she is watching.

Eventually, these personal and political conflicts crash and shake her to the core. Thinking about the men she has "leafed through," she says, "But then I realized it wasn't the men I hated, it was the Americans, the human beings, men and women both. They'd had their chance but they had turned against the gods, and it was time for me to choose sides."

ABOUT THE AUTHOR: MARGARET ATWOOD

There is much more to poet, novelist, and essayist Margaret Atwood than "Blessed be the fruit," one of the signature catchphrases from her 1985 dystopian novel, *The Handmaid's Tale*. The American political atmosphere after the 2016 presidential election, and the debut of a television miniseries based on that novel, have elevated both book and author to cultural icon status. Politically and environmentally outspoken, Atwood also has more than 2 million followers on her Twitter account.

But her fame and success were a long time in the making. Margaret Atwood has written more than fifty books of poetry, essays, and fiction, including graphic novels, published in more than forty-five countries.

Atwood was born November 18, 1939, in Ottawa, the daughter of an entomologist father and mother who was a dietitian and nutritionist. Her father's work in forest entomology gives some context to *Surfacing*, as Atwood spent considerable time in the woods while her father did research. She told an interviewer, "I grew up in and out of the bush." This kept her out of regular school until she reached eighth grade.

Like her parents, she was a voracious reader. "They didn't encourage me to become a writer, exactly, but they gave me a more important kind of support," she told writer Joyce Carol Oates in a *New York Times* interview, "that is, they expected me to make use of my intelligence and abilities and they did not pressure me into getting married."

After high school in Toronto, she graduated in 1961 from Victoria College at the University of Toronto and then gained her master's degree in literature at Radcliffe in 1962. She published a series of poetry collections and also began teaching at the university level. She married Jim Polk, an American writer, in 1968. And in 1969, her first novel, *The Edible Woman*, was published. Divorced in 1973, she began a long relationship with Canadian novelist Graeme Gibson. Their daughter was born in 1976. In the meantime, *Surfacing*, her second novel, appeared in 1972.

Atwood continued teaching and publishing poetry and fiction through the 1970s in work that explored identity, gender, and sexual politics. The publication of *The Handmaid's Tale* (1985) brought a Booker Prize nomination, as did *Cat's Eye* (1988), the story of a painter reflecting on her childhood and teen years. In 2000, her tenth novel, *The Blind Assassin*, was published to great acclaim and won the coveted Booker Prize.

Writing what she called "speculative fiction," she followed with *Oryx and Crake* (2003), the first of a dystopian trilogy in a world struggling with overpopulation that continued with *The Year of the Flood* (2009) and *MaddAddam* (2013). In 2019 *The Testaments*, a sequel to *The Handmaid's Tale*, was published, becoming an international best seller and sharing the Booker Prize.

Her longtime partner, Graeme Gibson, died, suffering dementia, in 2019; he was eighty-five. At this writing, Margaret Atwood resides in Toronto.

WHY YOU SHOULD READ IT

Surfacing was clearly addressing Canadian identity and the French-Canadian separatist movement, which was at its peak when the novel was published. Half a century later, these political concerns are no longer at the forefront. But the novel is not stuck in a time warp.

Atwood's artist/narrator is a woman who is searching for more than just her missing father. "Atwood's best novels bring to bear a psychologist's grasp of deep, interior forces and a mad scientist's knack for conceptual experiments that can draw these forces out into the open," wrote Jia Tolentino appraising Atwood in the *New Yorker*. And that is very much the case here.

Surfacing is vivid and deeply felt. For example, in a vibrant passage, she describes the general store in the lakeside village she had visited as a child:

> Madame sold khaki-colored penny candies which we were forbidden to eat, but her main source of power was that she had only one hand. Her other arm ended in a soft pink snout like an elephant's trunk and she broke the parcel string by wrapping it around her stump and pulling. This arm devoid of a hand was for me a great mystery, almost as puzzling as Jesus.

Atwood's descriptive powers are often dazzling, which makes the book a pleasure to read. Then, the mood shifts—somewhat abruptly—as Atwood works in a more complex style toward the novel's climax. As the reader is taken more deeply into the consciousness of the woman artist, we are caught by those "interior forces" that make this such a deeply provocative work.

WHAT TO READ NEXT

If you have not read Atwood's most famous work, it is time to take in *The Handmaid's Tale*. In case you haven't heard, it takes place in a near-future American theocracy in which some women are captive breeding concubines, ritually raped each month by a "Commander" who controls them and every aspect of their lives.

Published in 1985, during the ascendence of the "Moral Majority" and the Reagan years, it acquired new timeliness in our recent era of political turmoil, the rise of evangelism, and growing American authoritarianism. It is without question a chilling view of a dictatorial, patriarchal state, governed by religious fanaticism. While I found the writing stilted at times and the final section presented as an academic's research somewhat contrived, it is certainly a contemporary cultural marker.

Written in part to answer questions Atwood had received from readers over the years, *The Testaments*, its sequel, has been both a critical and commercial success. If dystopian Atwood is what you want, look to *Oryx and Crake*—on the BBC list of "100 Novels That Shaped Our World"—the first of the MaddAddam trilogy, followed by *The Year of the Flood* (2009) and *MaddAddam* (2013). Of Atwood's earlier works, *Cat's Eye* and *The Blind Assassin* are considered among her best.

Their Eyes Were Watching God

— 1937 —

Zora Neale Hurston

New York: HarperPerennial Modern Classics, 2013; with a foreword by
Edwidge Danticat and an afterword by Henry Louis Gates Jr.; 193 pages

* BBC: "100 Novels That Shaped Our World" *

FIRST LINES

Ships at a distance have every man's wish on board. For some they come in with the tide. For others they sail forever on the horizon, never out of sight, never landing until the Watcher turns his eyes away in resignation, his dreams mocked to death by Time. That is the life of men.

PLOT SUMMARY

Raised by her grandmother, who was born enslaved, Janie Crawford is a little girl who spends her time with a white family. Janie is around six when she realizes that she "wuzn't white." That revelation marks the beginning of this remarkable story, set in the early twentieth century, of a Black woman in search of identity—much of it recounted in dialect—and now a landmark in American literature.

At sixteen, after Nanny, her grandmother, sees her kissing a boy, Janie is turned over to be married to her first husband, Logan Killicks, an older man with sixty acres and a mule. Realizing that Logan treats her as little more than a beast of burden, Janie runs off with Joe Starks, "a cityfied, stylish dressed man with his hat set an angle that didn't belong in these parts."

They settle in Eatonville, Florida, a Black township where Joe becomes mayor and owner of a general store. Her lot improved, Janie is still restless, feeling more possession than person. After Joe's death, into Janie's life walks Tea Cake, a younger man. "She looked him over and got little thrills from every one of his good points. Those full, lazy eyes with the lashes curling sharply away like drawn scimitars."

Now forty, Janie is wary but thinks, "Tea Cake wasn't strange. Seemed as if she had known him all her life." Leaving town together, Janie and Tea Cake land in the Everglades, where a hurricane will tragically alter their fates.

ABOUT THE AUTHOR: ZORA NEALE HURSTON

The fifth of eight children, Zora Neale Hurston was born on January 7, 1891, into a family of sharecroppers in Notasulga, Alabama. Hurston's family then moved to Eatonville, Florida, the first Black town incorporated in the United States, where her father became a Baptist preacher and mayor. Zora's mother, a teacher, taught Zora to read before she went to school.

After her mother's death in 1904, Hurston began a nomadic period, passing herself off as a teenager to attend a Baltimore high school while in her twenties; working as a waitress and a manicurist;

attending Washington, D.C.'s Howard Prep and then Howard University, where her first short story appeared in a campus magazine.

Encouraged by a professor, Hurston made her way to New York in 1925, landing in the center of the Harlem Renaissance, a cultural explosion of Black music, art, literature, and theater, the dynamic era in which contemporaries Nella Larsen and Richard Wright (see entries) began their careers. She knew and worked with poet Langston Hughes and white writer Carl Van Vechten and then published a story in *Opportunity*, a magazine that featured the "New Negro" writing.

A scholarship to Barnard College brought Hurston into the classroom of influential anthropologist Franz Boas, who dispatched Hurston on fieldwork in the South to collect "Negro folklore." During her travels, she met a man whom she wrote about in 1927 in the *Journal of Negro History*, a survivor of the last slave ship to reach America. During this period, Hurston also married and divorced, the first of three short-lived marriages.

Her first novel, *Jonah's Gourd Vine*, came next. Published in 1934, it told the story of a married preacher with a penchant for other women—like her own father. It was an alternate selection of the Book-of-the-Month Club, a considerable distinction, especially for a Black woman at the time. (Richard Wright's *Native Son* became the first Main Selection by a Black author, in 1940.) The sharecropper's daughter had arrived.

The following year, *Mules and Men*, a nonfiction book based on her fieldwork on Black folklore, led to a Guggenheim Fellowship to study folk religions in Jamaica and Haiti. While in Haiti, Hurston wrote *Their Eyes Were Watching God* in seven weeks, according to her account. Published in 1937, it was not well received. In fact, it was heavily criticized by other Black writers, including novelist Richard Wright, who viewed Hurston's use of dialect as demeaning.

But this highly productive period continued with Hurston's study of Voodoo, *Tell My Horse*, published in 1938. By then, she had attracted national literary attention. Another novel, *Moses, Man of the Mountain* was released in 1939, to little success. In 1942, Hurston's memoir, *Dust Tracks on a Road*, was published. And in 1948, *Seraph on the Suwanee*, her final published novel, was also poorly received as a controversy roiled her life.

Shortly after its publication, Hurston was falsely accused of molestation by an emotionally disturbed boy. "Although the case was eventually thrown out," wrote Claudia Roth Pierpont in a *New Yorker* profile, "a court employee spilled the news to one of the city's black newspapers . . . and the lurid story made headlines. Hurston contemplated suicide, but slowly came back to herself on a long sailing trip."

With her reputation shattered, Hurston returned to Florida and wrote occasional articles and several books that were deemed unpublishable. A Republican and anti-communist, she was seen as out of step with the times, especially in the Black community. Hurston and her work slipped into obscurity. And there was no bottom, as she fell on hard times.

During the 1950s, Hurston worked as a librarian, a substitute teacher, and eventually a maid in Miami. In early 1959, she suffered a stroke and was placed in a county welfare home, where she died on January 28, 1960. She was buried in an unmarked grave in a segregated cemetery in Fort Pierce, Florida.

Her literary resurrection came in the early 1970s. Intrigued by her work, writer Alice Walker set out in 1973 to track down Hurston's burial place and, in March 1975, published "In Search of Zora Neale Hurston" in *Ms.* magazine. The article catapulted Hurston and her long-neglected works into a major revival. *Their Eyes Were Watching God* became required campus reading and Hurston's work later added her to the ranks of writers published by the Library of America.

"Hurston herself was refreshingly free of all the ideologies that currently obscure the reception of her best book," wrote critic Harold

Bloom in assessing the author of *Their Eyes Were Watching God*. "With [Walt] Whitman, Hurston herself is now an image of American literary vitality."

WHY YOU SHOULD READ IT

Hurston's use of dialect—controversial at its publication and challenging today—makes it a unique cultural benchmark. (I would also note that Stephen Crane's use of dialect in *The Red Badge of Courage* does not elicit similar criticism.) But that element of this novel is only one part of the indelibly lasting impact of *Their Eyes Were Watching God*. Since its revival, the novel is the wellspring from which flow, among others, Alice Walker's *The Color Purple* and Toni Morrison's *Beloved*: two of the most honored works in modern American fiction.

"In *Their Eyes Were Watching God*, Hurston ransacked the language—the King's English as well as Eatonville's Ebonics—to achieve a precision of expression that was stunning," wrote Valerie Boyd, the late professor at the University of Georgia and biographer of Hurston. "For more than fifteen years . . . the author had been working to capture in words the beauty and the complexity of her Eatonville experience—and of the rural, self-educated black folks who'd been her neighbors there. In *Their Eyes Were Watching God*, she finally achieved this elusive goal."

A vivid re-creation of life in early-twentieth-century Florida, the novel pulses with the unique rhythms of its place and time. But it is no museum piece to be studied for its social significance.

It endures as a soulful and exciting story. Fiercely independent, Janie Crawford is a character who stands beside other memorable fictional heroines who face down adversity. At its heart, *Their Eyes Were Watching God* is a compelling love story and testament to a woman's resolve to make her way in the world.

Accomplishing this, Claudia Roth Pierpont asserts in the *New Yorker*, required a rare and potentially treacherous combination of gifts: a delicate ear and a generous sympathy, a hellbent humor and a determined imperviousness to shame. All this Hurston brought to "Their Eyes Were Watching God"—a book that, despite its slender, private grace, aspires to the force of a national epic, akin to works by Mark Twain . . . offering a people their own language freshly caught on paper and raised to the heights of poetry.

WHAT TO READ NEXT

Hurston's first novel, *Jonah's Gourd Vine* (1934), is generally considered her next-best piece of fiction. Loosely autobiographical, it is based on her parents and her early life in Eatonville and tells of a young minister who, as the publisher describes it, "loves too many women for his own good."

If you are interested in her nonfiction, *Mules and Men* (1935) reflects her work as a folklorist/anthropologist and explores Black American folklore. *Tell My Horse* (1938) based on her travel to Jamaica and Haiti, is an account of her experiences with Voodoo. *Dust Tracks on a Road*, published in 1942, is a memoir that goes through early life in Eatonville to her education and accomplishments as a key figure in the Harlem Renaissance.

Rediscovered in an archive and published in 2018, *Barracoon* is a nonfiction account of one of the last-known survivors of the Atlantic slave trade, the last "Black Cargo" ship to arrive in the United States. Expanding on the article she wrote in 1927, Hurston turned her interviews with the survivor into a book in the 1930s. But it was rejected at that time by publishers who objected to Hurston's use of dialect to tell his story. The material sat for nearly ninety years before it was finally edited and published.

Things Fall Apart

— 1958 —

Chinua Achebe

New York: Penguin, 2017; with glossary of Igbo words and phrases; 209 pages

* BBC: "100 Novels That Shaped Our World" *
* TIME: "All-TIME 100 Novels" *

FIRST LINES

Okonkwo was well known throughout the nine villages and even beyond. His fame rested on solid personal achievements. As a young man of eighteen he had brought honor to his village by throwing Amalinze the Cat. Amalinze was the great wrestler who for seven years was unbeaten, from Umuofia to Mbaino. He was called the Cat because his back would never touch the earth. It was this man that Okonkwo threw in a fight which the old men agreed was one of the fiercest since the founder of their town engaged a spirit of the wild for seven days and seven nights.

PLOT SUMMARY

The title of this landmark work in contemporary literature comes from the W. B. Yeats poem "The Second Coming," whose lines are used as the book's epigraph:

> *Things fall apart; the centre cannot hold;*
> *Mere anarchy is loosed upon the world, . . .*

For untold years, the center has held for the people of Umuofia, home of the novel's central character, Okonkwo. Fierce wrestler, fearless warrior, proud farmer, formidable man in his clan, Okonkwo resides in a place of unchanging traditions. Through time-honored seasons of planting and harvest, it is a world largely untouched by European contact.

All that will soon fall apart. Set in the late 1800s in what is now Nigeria, the story is told in three parts. The first richly describes the circumscribed universe of Okonkwo's village and how he has strived mightily to distance himself from his lazy, drunken father. With hard work Okonkwo has acquired a degree of wealth, and he is admired as a village leader, with his three wives and large family as symbols of his station. Hidebound by tradition, Okonkwo's world is no pastoral paradise. It is an often-unforgiving society with demanding rules. Okonkwo is unwilling to break those rules, even if it means he must sacrifice a young boy when the village oracle demands it.

The book's second and third parts are about that world invaded by white men. First come missionaries, bringing Christianity, which divides Okonkwo's family and people. The missionaries are followed by a British colonial administration with its own set of rules. This clash of cultures moves the novel toward its dramatic climax and stature as a tragedy of classical proportion. "The white man is very clever . . . ," says Okonkwo. "He has put a knife on the things that held us together and we have fallen apart."

ABOUT THE AUTHOR: CHINUA ACHEBE

Born on November 16, 1930, in what was then British colonial Nigeria, Chinua Achebe has been called the "father of modern African literature" by South African Nobel laureate Nadine Gordimer (see entry).

He came into a world straddling two cultures. Achebe's parents were Christian converts and evangelists who traveled widely to spread their faith. Achebe went to Nigeria's first university, University College (now the University of Ibadan), studying English, literature, and religion, both Christian and African. The conflict between African traditions and European Christian colonizers would inform his work from the outset.

His acclaimed first novel almost never was. While in London in 1957, Achebe had shown the book in draft to another writer who was enthusiastic. After returning home, Achebe mailed the manuscript to a London typing service. He never heard back—the parcel from Nigeria had apparently been tossed aside. A British colleague then demanded that the service produce the typescript, which was then sent off to British publisher Heinemann. According to Achebe, Heinemann's editors had never seen a novel by an African writer and sent it to an outside reader. The reaction: *"The best first novel since the war."*

Even after publication, the novel might have been stillborn. "They had no idea if anybody would want to read it. It went out of print very quickly," Achebe told the *Paris Review* in 1994. "It would have stayed that way if [publisher] Alan Hill hadn't decided that he was going to gamble even more and launch a paperback edition of this book. . . . But that was how the African Writers Series came in to existence. . . . So it was a very small beginning, but it caught fire."

Published when Achebe was twenty-eight, *Things Fall Apart* may have started slowly but became a classic of world literature. "It would be impossible to say how 'Things Fall Apart' influenced African writing," scholar Kwame Anthony Appiah wrote. "It would be like asking how Shakespeare influenced English writers or Pushkin influenced Russians." The book has since been translated into fifty-seven languages and is required reading for students, with more than 20 million copies sold, according to the publisher.

Achebe joined the Nigerian Broadcasting Company, working there until 1966. During that time, he completed two more novels, *No Longer at Ease* (1960)—featuring the grandson of the character Okonkwo in *Things Fall Apart*—and *Arrow of God* (1964), which together with *Things Fall Apart* form the African Trilogy.

A fourth novel, *A Man of the People* (1966), would be his last for two decades. When the region of Biafra attempted to break away from Nigeria in 1967, it marked the beginning of a dreadful civil war, rooted in religious differences and tribalism, known as the Biafran War. Aligned with the Biafran cause, Achebe was forced to leave the country, settling in England with his wife, Christiana, and their four children. With brutal civilian massacres and horrific images of starving children broadcast to the world—part of the estimated 2 million who perished from famine caused by a Nigerian blockade—the conflict lasted to 1970.

Achebe returned to Nigeria after the war. But he later moved to the United States to take a series of teaching posts, first with the University of Massachusetts at Amherst. It was there that he gave a lecture, later published in a 1977 essay, that stirred considerable controversy by attacking one of the giants of English literature, Joseph Conrad.

"The point of my observations should be quite clear by now, namely that Joseph Conrad was a thoroughgoing racist," Achebe said. "That this simple truth is glossed over in criticisms of his work is due to the fact that white racism against Africa is such a normal way of thinking that its manifestations go completely unremarked." It is worthy of note that the Modern Library's famous list of 100 Best Novels included four by Conrad, *Heart of Darkness* among them, but none of Achebe's fiction.

While producing essays and nonfiction, Achebe did not publish another novel for twenty-one years. "For more than 20 years a case of writer's block kept him from producing another novel," Jonathan Kandell explained in Achebe's 2013 obituary. "He attributed the dry spell to emotional trauma that had lingered after the civil war."

In 1987, his fifth novel, *Anthills of the Savannah*, was named a finalist for the Booker Prize. Reviewing the book, novelist Nadine Gordimer wrote, "It is a work in which 22 years of harsh experience, intellectual growth, self-criticism, deepening understanding and mustered discipline of skill open wide a subject to which Mr. Achebe is now magnificently equal."

During a stay in Nigeria to teach in 1990, Achebe was seriously injured in a car accident that left him wheelchair bound, paralyzed from the waist down. He returned to the United States to teach at Bard College in New York, remaining there until 2009.

In 2007, Chinua Achebe was awarded the Man Booker International Prize, a lifetime achievement award. He died in Boston after a brief illness on March 21, 2013, at the age of eighty-two.

WHY YOU SHOULD READ IT

You could listen to the late Nobel laureate Toni Morrison, who wrote, "African literature is incomplete and unthinkable without the works of Chinua Achebe. For passion, intellect and crystalline prose, he is unsurpassed."

In placing *Things Fall Apart* on *Time* magazine's list of "All-TIME 100 Novels," Richard Lacayo wrote:

> Achebe guides us through the intricacies of Igbo culture, its profound sense of justice, its sometimes murderous rules, its noble and harmful machismo. By the time the British colonial administrator arrives towards the end of the book to dismiss the natives as savages, we know how profoundly mistaken that word is.

Richly told, with its lush sense of Okonkwo's world, *Things Fall Apart* is firmly rooted in its place—in wet and dry seasons, in deep connections to the earth, and in ever-present spirits of past generations—and with dialogue sparkling with Igbo aphorisms and wisdom. But this book is more than a moment in history or an indictment of colonialism's heavy weight.

In Okonkwo, novelist Achebe created a figure in the mold of classic Greek tragedy—a noble character with ideals of honor who is brought down by both the fates and his prideful arrogance, his own fatal flaw.

WHAT TO READ NEXT

I plan to move on to the succeeding two novels in Achebe's African Trilogy: *No Longer at Ease*, in which Okonkwo's grandson has become a Christian; and *Arrow of God*, set in the 1920s, in which Ezeulu, the traditional chief priest of several Nigerian villages, confronts the forces of Christianity and the colonial British overlords. These three novels have been bound together in several editions.

Tokyo Ueno Station

— 2014 —

Yu Miri

New York: Riverhead Books, 2020; translated from the Japanese by Morgan Giles; 180 pages

FIRST LINES

There's that sound again.
>That sound—
>I hear it.
>But I don't know if it's in my ears or in my mind.
>I don't know if it's inside me or outside.
>I don't know when it was or who it was either.
>Is that important?
>Was it?
>Who was it?

PLOT SUMMARY

Living in Ueno Park—a major tourist attraction near a metro station in modern Tokyo—narrator Kazu is witness to the painful existence of people, like himself, who live in makeshift shelters, collect cans, and eat food left outside restaurants to survive. As the global economic meltdown upends Japanese society and the ranks of the homeless grow, Kazu observes the widening chasm between Japan's rich and poor. His sometimes-dreamlike musings are mingled with recollections of his troubled life, which intersect with significant moments in the life of Japan's imperial family.

Through Kazu's reveries, we learn that he was born in 1933, the same year that Japan's future Emperor was born. After the Second World War ended in 1945, Kazu spent his boyhood struggling to make ends meet—fishing, farming, harvesting kelp. But later, after his son is born—in 1960, on the same day the Emperor's son is born—Kazu reluctantly leaves his family for Tokyo to work on the construction of the 1964 Olympics site. For much of the next twenty years, Kazu sends home most of his pay but is largely absent from his family's life.

After years of separation, bad luck, and loss, Kazu eventually joins the homeless in the park, where they are occasionally rousted from their tarp-covered tents to prepare for the possibility of a member of the imperial family driving past. One day, Kazu sees the imperial couple wave from their car, another moment when Kazu crosses paths with the Emperor. "The pair gave us a look that could only be described as gentle," he observes, "and smiles came across their innocent faces, ones that had never known sin or shame. . . . A life that had never known struggle, envy, or aimlessness, one that had lived the same seventy-three years as I had."

In Kazu's tale of sharp contrasts—of privilege versus deprivation, of rich versus poor—he offers snippets of overheard conversations and railway announcements ending in "FOR YOUR SAFETY PLEASE STAND BEHIND THE YELLOW LINE."

Where is the yellow line? Where does one stand to be safe in this divided society? These questions and memories eventually carry Kazu forward to the novel's ultimate disaster.

A word to the wise: the publisher's descriptive copy reveals a detail of the novel that readers may want to avoid as a spoiler.

ABOUT THE AUTHOR: YU MIRI

Little-known in the United States before *Tokyo Ueno Station* won a National Book Award for Translated Literature in 2020, Yu Miri is among Japan's best-known writers, having produced award-winning plays, poetry, essays, and fiction.

Born in Japan on June 22, 1968, Yu Miri is the eldest of four children of Korean descent—known in Japan as Zainichi, many of whom came to Japan during its wartime occupation of Korea. Growing up in Yokohama, she confronted a tradition of harsh Japanese discrimination against Koreans. "My father fixed pachinko machines.* My mother was a cabaret hostess," she once told an interviewer. "These were the lowest occupations in Japan. But they were the only ones open to Koreans."

Following her parents' divorce when she was five, she lived with her mother and faced difficult times in school. Bullied by classmates and singled out by teachers because of her background, Yu Miri started to skip classes and was expelled after one year of high school. "Books were the escape room for my soul," Yu Miri once told a *New York Times* interviewer, who noted that Yu Miri "often used them to conceal her face from classmates."

After several suicide attempts as a teenager, Yu Miri left home and at sixteen joined a theater troupe, the Tokyo Kid Brothers, later

---

* Pachinko machines are arcade games, like slot machines, widely used in Japan for gambling.

moving in with one of its directors, a much older man. She also began to write plays, formed her own theater group, and then turned to fiction. Her first novel (title translated as *The Fish Swimming in the Stone* but never published in English) won a literary prize in 1994. It also created a controversy when a friend who claimed to be portrayed in the book sued to stop its publication; a court allowed a revised version to be issued in 2002.

A breakthrough came in 1997 when her book *Kazoku shinema* (*Family Cinema*) won the Akutagawa Prize, one of Japan's most prestigious literary awards. And in 2002, *Gold Rush*, a story set in the gritty neighborhood of Yokohama's pachinko parlors and bars where Yu Miri was raised, became the first of her novels to appear in English.

After the 2011 earthquake and deadly tsunami triggered a nuclear meltdown in Fukushima, she began to visit the badly damaged area to do radio interviews with survivors. These conversations, along with hundreds she had earlier conducted with homeless people she had met in the Tokyo park, gave her the details and inspiration to write *Tokyo Ueno Station*, first published in Japan in 2014.

Later moving to Minami-Sōma, a village near Fukushima, Yu Miri opened a bookstore and a theater there in 2018, both founded to provide a space for those affected by the disaster. At this writing, she resides there.

WHY YOU SHOULD READ IT

How Kazu comes to be homeless, his ultimate fate, and the dream-like quality of his memories all propel this exquisite, almost hypnotic novel. As it moves toward a final disaster, Yu Miri has adroitly merged the social realism and naturalism of such writers as Stephen Crane, Upton Sinclair, and early John Steinbeck with the more transcendent qualities of *Mrs. Dalloway*'s (see entry) remarkable London day.

But her novel is more than just a socially responsible work that exposes the underside of contemporary Japanese society hidden to many Westerners. Yu Miri has composed an almost confessional novel about the great costs of a modern world in which family and human connections are sacrificed for survival. *Tokyo Ueno Station* explores the heavy price of memory and regret—themes also prominent in Kazuo Ishiguro's *A Pale View of Hills* (see entry). The writing is sensitive and poignant, but never mawkishly sentimental.

In one of his reveries, Kazu recalls taking his children to an amusement park on a rare visit home from his distant Tokyo workplace. His son pleads for an expensive helicopter ride. Kazu instead buys his children ice cream:

> That day the sky was as blue as a strip of cloth. I wanted to give him that helicopter ride, but I couldn't afford it, and so I didn't—I still regret it. And ten years later, on that awful day, that regret again stabbed at my heart, it is still with me now, it never leaves—

WHAT TO READ NEXT

The only other novel by Yu Miri translated into English to date is *Gold Rush*. The book offers an account of a violent teenager, based on the true story of a boy who killed several people in the pachinko machine world much like the one in which Yu Miri was raised. "It is a passionate 'J'accuse' against a society where parenting has been virtually abandoned," commented Jonathan Napack in the *International Herald Tribune*, continuing, "money trumps all and any sense of human possibility is stunted by self-fulfilling despair."

Waiting for the Barbarians

— 1980 —

J. M. Coetzee

New York: Penguin Books, 2010; 180 pages

FIRST LINES

I have never seen anything like it: two little discs of glass suspended in front of his eyes in loops of wire. Is he blind? I could understand it if he wanted to hide blind eyes. But he is not blind. The discs are dark, they look opaque from the outside, but he can see through them. He tells me they are a new invention.

PLOT SUMMARY

In a barren outpost of an imaginary Empire, set in an unspecified place and time, this fable-like political thriller is related by the Magistrate, the unnamed central character. Living on the edges of "civilization," the Magistrate is comfortable, modestly corrupt, and far from brutal. The small farming and trading settlement he oversees has its drawbacks, but the Magistrate is content and complacent.

As the book opens, he is confronted by Colonel Joll, a heartless military bureaucrat, a member of "the Third Bureau"—think the Gestapo, Stalinist secret police, or Orwell's "Thought Police."

Joll's arrival comes as there are rumors of an impending attack by the "Barbarians," a nomadic people living on the fringes of the Empire. Joll has a group of these supposed rebels captured and brought back to the settlement. As they are tortured, the Magistrate weakly objects.

But Colonel Joll has his methods. "First I get lies, you see—this is what happens—first lies, then pressure, then more lies, then more pressure, then the break, then more pressure, then the truth. That is how you get the truth."

Among the prisoners is a young woman with whom the Magistrate begins a complex relationship—he bathes her feet, broken during an interrogation. Eventually, she moves into his room. But when the Magistrate decides to return the woman to her people, he comes under suspicion and will ultimately fall victim himself to Colonel Joll's interrogation techniques.

ABOUT THE AUTHOR: J. M. COETZEE

Like his fellow Nobel laureates Nadine Gordimer and Doris Lessing (see entries), J. M. Coetzee writes of a life lived under the era of apartheid. But the scope of his work is larger than a single moment in history.

Born in Cape Town, South Africa, on February 9, 1940, John Maxwell Coetzee was educated at a university in Cape Town with a degree in mathematics. He traveled to Britain in 1962 and worked for IBM as a computer programmer, later doing graduate work at the University of Texas under the Fulbright Program. He subsequently taught literature at the State University of New York at Buffalo, where he wrote his first novel, *Dusklands*. It was comprised of two separate stories, one of which tells of a man who works for a U.S. government agency that creates psychological warfare during the war in Vietnam. This was followed by an experimental work, *In the Heart of the Country* (1977).

In 1980, *Waiting for the Barbarians* brought Coetzee wide international acclaim. He returned to Cape Town as a professor of English in 1972 and soon published *Life & Times of Michael K*, set in South Africa torn by civil war, which won the 1983 Booker Prize. After publishing several other novels, he wrote *Disgrace* (1999), about the struggle of a discredited university teacher after the collapse of white supremacy. The book garnered a second Booker Prize, and Coetzee became the first writer to win this prestigious British fiction award twice. In 2003, he was awarded the Nobel Prize. In announcing his Nobel award in 2003, the committee commented:

> J. M. Coetzee's novels are characterised by their well-crafted composition, pregnant dialogue and analytical brilliance. But at the same time he is a scrupulous doubter, ruthless in his criticism of the cruel rationalism and cosmetic morality of western civilisation.

Coetzee moved to Australia in 2002 and became an Australian citizen in 2006.

WHY YOU SHOULD READ IT

I first read this novel more than forty years ago. I knew at the time it was an extraordinary piece of fiction. But I also looked at it through the lens—like Colonel Joll's "little discs of glass" in the opening lines—of the moment when apartheid still ruled South Africa. It was difficult to see Coetzee's brilliant fable as more than an assault on the repressive, wicked white colonial regime then in control. It is the same historical and geographic context Nadine Gordimer wrote of a year later in *July's People* (see entry).

But now, many years later, with apartheid on history's ash heap, this book must be read in the wider context of the ways authoritarian regimes wield power. As democracy is increasingly under assault around the globe and in the United States, Coetzee's chilling fable is as timelessly significant as ever.

WHAT TO READ NEXT

With a long and distinguished career, highlighted by his award-winning works, the Coetzee catalog is extensive and highly regarded. But to pare down the list, perhaps the most significant are his two Booker Prize winners: *Life & Times of Michael K*, the 1983 novel about a fictitious civil war in South Africa during the apartheid era; and *Disgrace* (1999), which is—if anything—even more timely. It recounts the story of a professor who loses everything over a sexual affair that ruins him. In 2019, the BBC included this novel on a list of "100 Novels That Shaped Our World."

We Have Always Lived in the Castle

— 1962 —

Shirley Jackson

New York: Penguin Books, 2006; with an afterword by Jonathan Lethem;
146 pages

FIRST LINES

My name is Mary Katherine Blackwood. I am eighteen years old, and I live
with my sister Constance. I have often thought that with any luck at all I
could have been born a werewolf, because the two middle fingers on both
my hands are the same length, but I have had to be content with what I had.
I dislike washing myself, and dogs, and noise. I like my sister Constance, and
Richard Plantagenet,* and *Amanita phalloides*, the death-cup mushroom.
Everyone else in my family is dead.

---

* I looked it up so you don't have to. The Richard Plantagenet referred to was a
reclusive bricklayer reputed to be the son of England's Richard III.

PLOT SUMMARY

With that intriguing introduction, we meet the first of two sisters, Mary Katherine, called Merricat but assuredly not a werewolf. Mary Katherine and her older sister, Constance, live with their wheelchair-bound uncle Julian as outcasts in their small village, presumably but not specifically in New England. This trio lives reclusively, cut off from almost all contact with neighbors and the townspeople. The suspicious villagers believe the sisters harbor a secret about a deadly event that took place years earlier in the Blackwood house. That occurrence is why, as Merricat reveals in this opening, "Everyone else in my family is dead."

One day, an estranged cousin named Charles turns up. Somewhat surprisingly, Constance welcomes him into the household. But Merricat is deeply suspicious of Charles and his motives. Why has he come and moved into her dead father's room? She uses all her powers, real and imagined, to be rid of him, in this harrowing gothic tale of psychological suspense.

ABOUT THE AUTHOR: SHIRLEY JACKSON

There is a good chance that you know Shirley Jackson's name because of her most famous piece of writing. Her short story "The Lottery" was published in the *New Yorker* in 1948 and has since become required reading for many American students. The plot, in case you don't know it, involves a small town in which a member of the community is chosen by lot in a yearly ritual. What happens to the chosen one is not revealed until the end—and no spoilers here.

Suffice it to say that the reaction from readers to the story's initial appearance included a cascade of hate mail and many cancelled subscriptions. According to Jackson's biographer Ruth Franklin, it was at the time "the most mail the magazine had ever received in response to a work of fiction."

Jackson was born in San Francisco on December 4, 1916, and grew up an outsider. She was a bookish, somewhat overweight teenager, who disappointed her hectoring mother; according to one biographer, Jackson's mother told her she was the product of a failed abortion.

After her family moved to New York, Jackson made her way to Syracuse University. A journalism student, Jackson also worked on the school's literary magazine, where she met her future husband, Stanley Edgar Hyman, later a prominent literary critic. They married in 1940, and Hyman, a Jewish Brooklynite, joined the faculty at Bennington College. The couple settled in North Bennington, Vermont, where Shirley would give birth to four children. She found the insular small town repressive, anti-intellectual, and anti-Semitic. The hostility she felt would fuel "The Lottery" and We Have Always Lived in the Castle.

In 1948, the same year that "The Lottery" appeared in the New Yorker, Jackson published a first novel, a semiautobiographical account of growing up in California called The Road Through the Wall with characteristic gothic elements. A second novel, Hangsaman (1951), was based on the actual disappearance—still unsolved—of a Bennington College student. Two more novels, The Bird's Nest (1954), about a woman with multiple personalities, and The Sundial (1958), about a group who believe that they will survive the end of the world, cemented her place as a serious writer of psychological stories.

But in 1959, The Haunting of Hill House, her fifth novel, reached new heights. Mixing the psychological and the supernatural, it has been cited as one of the most influential horror stories of the twentieth century. It became the source of two film versions, both called The Haunting, and the inspiration for a 2018 Netflix anthology series. It was followed in 1962 by We Have Always Lived in the Castle, which reached even greater critical success, with Time calling it one of the best novels of the year.

By then, Jackson was in poor health. A smoker, she was asthmatic and overweight. Plagued by her husband's open infidelities, often with Bennington students, she began drinking and used both barbiturates and amphetamines, commonly prescribed at the time. Though her mental health improved with therapy, Shirley Jackson died in her sleep in her North Bennington home in August 1965. She was forty-eight years old.

WHY YOU SHOULD READ IT

This was, for me, a one-sitting read. Yes, it is that compelling a story. As the mystery of the deaths of the Blackwell family slowly unravels, the arrival of Charles upsets the carefully ordered and delicate balance that Constance has created in the house.

Disturbing yet comic, the novel gathers momentum and intensity, working toward a conflagration that threatens the Blackwood women's strange but perfectly arranged lives.

Writing in *The Atlantic* in 2016, columnist Heather Havrilesky commented:

> Reading her work today sometimes feels like discovering a detailed prophecy not just of rape culture but of the vitriolic thugs who seem to rule the internet and have somehow invaded politics lately. . . . Jackson unveiled the brutality and contempt that lurk beneath the surface of neighborly human interactions.

WHAT TO READ NEXT

If you never read "The Lottery," do so right away. If you read it long ago in school, reread it. Widely anthologized, it is one of the most famous American short stories of the twentieth century. The story begins on a bucolic summer day in a New England village. Everything seems perfect: the children are out of school and the landscape has turned green. Jackson abruptly turns this idyllic scene into an examination of human superstition and cruelty.

In 1988, Shirley Jackson's biographer wrote:

"The Lottery" came out in the June 26, 1948, issue of *The New Yorker*, and its effect was instant and cataclysmic. Nothing in the magazine before or since would provoke such a huge outpouring of fury, horror, rage, disgust and intense fascination. . . . This story was incendiary; readers acted as if a bomb had blown up in their faces, as indeed in a sense it had. Shirley struck a nerve in mid-20th-century America the way few writers have ever succeeded in doing, at any time.

Shirley Jackson was a genius practitioner of gothic horror, and *The Haunting of Hill House* is a masterpiece of the genre and still sets a standard for tales of spooky houses. But it is not a "comfort read." Curl up in bed with it. But be sure to leave the lights on.

Wide Sargasso Sea

— 1966 —

Jean Rhys

*New York: W. W. Norton, 2016, with introduction by Edwidge Danticat;
171 pages; a Norton Critical Edition, edited by Judith L. Raiskin with notes,
essays, and criticism, is also available (New York: W. W. Norton, 1999)*

* Number 94 on the Modern Library list of 100 Best Novels *
* BBC: "100 Novels That Shaped Our World" *
* TIME: "All-TIME 100 Novels" *

FIRST LINES

They say when trouble comes close ranks, and so the white people did. But
we were not in their ranks. The Jamaican ladies had never approved of my
mother, "because she pretty like pretty self" Christophine said.

She was my father's second wife, far too young for him they thought,
and, worse still, a Martinique girl.

PLOT SUMMARY

To get to the plot of *Wide Sargasso Sea*, understand that this novel was born from another—like *The Hours* with its debt to *Mrs. Dalloway*. In this case, Jean Rhys illuminated a shadowy character from Charlotte Brontë's much beloved *Jane Eyre*. In that 1847 classic, Bertha Mason is the madwoman, the first wife of Mr. Rochester locked in the attic of Thornfield Hall.

In fact, *Wide Sargasso Sea* is a "prequel" to *Jane Eyre*. Bertha Mason's story is envisioned by Rhys using hints from Brontë, who described Bertha as a Creole, or a white native of the West Indies. Jean Rhys imagines her as Antoinette Cosway, first seen as a young girl growing up on a Jamaican sugar plantation.

Told in three parts, the story opens shortly after the enslaved people of Jamaica were freed, a prolonged process that began with British passage of the Slavery Abolition Act in 1833. Once a slave owner, Antoinette's English father is dead; the plantation is in shambles. Nearly destitute, Antoinette, her widowed mother, and Antoinette's sickly brother, Pierre, live among the formerly enslaved Black islanders, many of whom despise the white family.

As Creoles, Antoinette and her family are outsiders, part of neither the island's English world nor its Black community. After Antoinette's mother marries a wealthy Englishman, Antoinette is sent to a convent school.

With a leap in time and a sharp shift of narrator, the next part of the story is mostly told by an unnamed Englishman whose account begins after he has married Antoinette and the couple arrives on the nearby island of Dominica.

But their honeymoon is no paradise. The newlyweds' relationship quickly disintegrates in a landscape that is beautiful, but filled with threats. When her husband starts to call her Bertha—a name he claims he is fond of but is symbolic of his power over her—and leaves her bed, Antoinette turns to an old and loyal servant to try traditional West Indies magic to restore her husband's affections.

The novel's brief coda is voiced by Antoinette. She is in England, now confined to a room, and tended constantly by a woman named Grace Poole, who dares not turn her back on her charge.

Gentle Reader, you may know how Bertha Mason ends up in Brontë's version. In this imagining of Antoinette's life, Rhys offers a very different picture.

ABOUT THE AUTHOR: JEAN RHYS

It is remarkable that a writer described in 1974 as "the best living English novelist" had disappeared for decades without a trace and was even thought dead in the 1950s.

Jean Rhys, a pen name, was born Ella Gwendolyn Rees Williams on the Caribbean island of Dominica on August 24, 1890, the daughter of a Welsh doctor and a Creole mother of Scots ancestry. At sixteen, Ella was sent to a girls' school in Cambridge, England, where she was mocked for her accent and being island born. Attempting to study at London's Royal Academy of Dramatic Art, Ella was dismissed for her inability to speak "proper English."

Refusing to return to Dominica after her father's death, she used adopted names to work as a chorus girl. An affair with a wealthy older man followed. Then, in 1919, she married the first of three husbands, a Dutch journalist who was jailed in France for embezzlement. Destitute and alone in Paris, she met prominent novelist Ford Madox Ford there in 1924. He introduced her to the literary world of Fitzgerald, Joyce, and Hemingway and encouraged her writing. Ford also suggested her pen name and provided an introduction to a collection of Rhys's stories, *The Left Bank and Other Stories*, released in 1927 by Ford's publisher.

Rhys had an affair with Ford, who became the model for a character in her first novel. The famed novelist was clearly identifiable and Ford's publisher rejected the book. In 1928, *Postures* (*Quartet* in the United States) was picked up by another house.

After divorcing her first husband, Rhys married her literary agent, Leslie Tilden-Smith, in 1934 and within the decade published three more novels—*After Leaving Mr. Mackenzie* (1931), *Voyage in the Dark* (1934), and *Good Morning, Midnight* (1939)—all acclaimed books about rootless, mistreated women. But with the outbreak of World War II, Rhys's sales faded. She was left poor and obscure and began to drink heavily. In 1949 she was arrested for assaulting neighbors and police and sent to a prison hospital for psychiatric evaluation.

And then good fortune intervened. An actress with the BBC, Selma Vaz Dias, wanted to adapt *Good Morning, Midnight* for a dramatic presentation. Told by a book publisher that Rhys had probably died after the war, Dias advertised for news of her in 1949. Rhys saw the ad and replied. The radio version of *Good Morning, Midnight* aired on the BBC in 1957 and Rhys got a boost. Still married, but living in desperate straits, Rhys was encouraged to resume work on a book idea she had begun in 1945. A publisher then offered a contract for what would become *Wide Sargasso Sea*. Published in 1966, the book won literary awards, reestablished Rhys's reputation, and revived interest in her work. In 1968, a collection of her stories, *Tigers Are Better Looking*, was also released.

Jean Rhys died on May 14, 1979, aged eighty-eight, while working on an autobiography, which was published posthumously in 1979 as *Smile Please: An Unfinished Autobiography*.

WHY YOU SHOULD READ IT

A masterful piece of literary imagination, Rhys's novel takes something familiar to millions of readers who admire *Jane Eyre* and weaves a magical story around it. Many of those readers may have also wondered: What made Bertha Mason go mad?

In transforming a few strands from Brontë's novel into the tragic account of Antoinette Conway, Rhys produces a triumph of fiction in its own right. As novelist Edwidge Danticat remarks:

In spite of its connections to Charlotte Brontë's novel, *Wide Sargasso Sea* is more than, to use a contemporary term, fan fiction. It is its own jewel of a novel, which can be read with or without its original inspiration in mind.

What makes it a jewel is its vivid island setting and remarkable characters, especially Antoinette and Christophine, the aging nurse-maid with seemingly magical powers. "It is a hallucinatory novel, as detailed, abrupt and undeniable as a dream, and with a dream's weird and irresistible logic," critic A. Alvarez wrote in the *New York Times*. "Despite the exotic setting and the famous, abused heroine, there is no melodrama. Her prose is reticent, unemphatic, precise, and yet supple, alive with feeling, as though the whole world she so coolly describes were shimmering with foreboding, with a lifetime's knowledge of unease and pain."

Finally, the book explores two significant thematic streams that are as timely as ever. The first is the place of women in society and their lack of "agency," to use a modern term—the seeming inability to choose or act. In discussing Rhys's work—and her alcoholism—writer Olivia Laing wrote in *The Guardian*, "She shows how power works and how cruel people can be to those who are beneath them, revealing, too, how poverty and social mores pinion women." Antoinette's powerlessness is heightened as she is both a woman and an "Outsider," not belonging to any group.

The second theme coursing below Rhys's narrative is the weight of slavery and colonialism. These are formidable historical forces, and their profound costs, combined with patriarchy, can drive people mad. It is this weight of history that is also explored by Jamaica Kincaid's *Lucy* as well as Nella Larsen's *Passing* (see entries).

While *Wide Sargasso Sea* rescued Rhys from obscurity and has become a modern classic, her first four novels remain widely admired. The books are *Quartet, After Leaving Mr. Mackenzie, Voyage in the Dark,* and *Good Morning, Midnight.* Editor Francis Wyndham, who worked with Rhys on *Wide Sargasso Sea,* wrote of these books, "The elegant surface and the paranoid content, the brutal honesty of the feminine psychology and the muted nostalgia for lost beauty, all create an effect which is peculiarly modern."

All four novels depict women confronting a world with little concern for those without power, class status, or money. Long after they were published and fell into obscurity along with Jean Rhys, the books were brought back to print and secured her reputation as a stylist and truth teller. As critic A. Alvarez put it, the books are "peculiarly timeless."

What's Not Here

"So many books, so little time."

You have, no doubt, heard the expression. In my case, I chose to carve out time for books, as explained in my introduction. But still, there was neither time nor space for all the world's great short books.

Sorry: Alvarez, Bellow, Cather, Dos Passos. Sorry, Ellison, Forster, Gide, Himes, James—Henry and P.D.—Kafka, Wilde, and Wilder.

These are but a few of the worthy authors whose books were long-listed for this compendium. I could easily go through the alphabet more than once: Austen, Brönte (all three), Cheever, et alia. You get the picture. Extraordinary writers were left out. Many remain stacked high on my desk's "TBR" (To-Be-Read) pile.

There is an entire galaxy of great short books still to be explored. Aren't you lucky?

To reduce this compendium to fifty-eight great short books, I read—or, in some cases, started—many others. But rules are rules. First, I honored my page-length standard, which knocked out a large number of great novels. Short story collections also did not count. Next, I was guided by my ambition to read work that was new to me rather than just sticking with the familiar canon.

But that meant forgoing some of my most-admired writers: Louise Erdrich, Patricia Highsmith, Jhumpa Lahiri, Salman Rushdie,

José Saramago, and John Steinbeck among them. I also left out *The Spy Who Came In from the Cold*, whose author, John le Carré, passed away late in 2020. Another favorite, he was by no means just a "spy novelist."

Also omitted were short works by important writers that I felt don't quite measure up. That was the case with William Faulkner, perhaps the most obvious absence in this collection. Initially, I planned to include *The Bear*, a coming-of-age tale told through a hunt for a legendary bear—a landlocked version of *Moby-Dick*. But *The Bear* is more appropriately read with the stories comprising the novel *Go Down, Moses*. By all means, read Faulkner.

In fact, don't stop here. This guide is about inspiring more reading. So, to playfully paraphrase the old saying about voting in Chicago, "read early and often!"

I had also pledged that I would not read out of duty. This project emerged from arguing the indispensable, intrinsic value of the *pleasure of reading*. So, in my search for great reading, there were a few false starts. I must confess I did set aside, among others, Thornton Wilder's *The Bridge of San Luis Rey* and Philip K. Dick's *Do Androids Dream of Electric Sheep?* I plan to revisit them.

Perhaps the thorniest question I faced surrounds the debate over reckoning with writers whose work has fallen from favor in light of changing conventions, a question raised in the entry on Kate Chopin's *Awakening*. Racism, anti-Semitism, sexism, and other "isms" represent views no longer acceptable, thanks to decades of social progress. How, then, do we deal with writers—many of them dead and unable to respond—whose attitudes about race, gender, and sexual identity are no longer deemed tolerable?

Some modern readers and critics have applied such a judgment to Ernest Hemingway, whose racism and anti-Semitism were explored in the Hemingway entry. Joseph Conrad is a writer of elegance and insight. But his novels are now viewed by many critics and scholars as unacceptably racist, as discussed in the entry on Chinua Achebe. In a later essay Achebe wrote, "The writer cannot expect to be excused from the task of reeducation and regeneration that must be done." But do we relegate Hemingway and Conrad to the literary dustbin? Or do we still read them with new critical eyes?

From Voltaire to Kate Chopin, James Joyce, and James M. Cain—and Toni Morrison in our time—writers considered "offensive" have been suppressed by civil and religious authorities. Throughout my career as a writer and as an individual, I have argued forcefully for intellectual freedom, literary license, and the right to expression. I am loath to tell anyone what *not to read.*

That said, I will single out one title that I initially thought was a shoo-in for this collection, *Breakfast at Tiffany's.* But first, another confession. I had never read Truman Capote's novella that made an icon of Holly Golightly. Nor, like George Costanza of *Seinfeld,* had I ever seen the movie in which Audrey Hepburn was immortalized as Capote's beloved courtesan. I was taken aback, then, by Holly Golightly's vulgar racism and homophobic utterances. By all means read it if you choose. But it is not on my list of great short books.

Nor are any works by Georges Simenon, whose detective novels feature Inspector Maigret. Among the most prolific novelists of the twentieth century, Simenon has been celebrated as a singular writer of mysteries. But I was unimpressed by my choice of *Maigret at Picratt's.* Neither psychologically insightful nor intriguing, it also suffered from dated, derogatory references to gay men in the Parisian demimonde. That book crossed a line for me. It is a line that each of us must draw for ourselves based on what we may deem ugly and gratuitous. I may try another of Simenon's hundreds of novels.

While these works of Capote and Simenon were regrettable surprises, most of my reading experiences were far more satisfying. Certainly, to re-encounter a familiar book from many years ago—*The Red Badge of Courage* and *Waiting for the Barbarians* come to mind—provided the pleasurable surprise of reading something old and wonderful with different eyes.

I first read Crane's Civil War masterpiece before my own attitudes about war were reshaped by Vietnam (and, since then, by a great many other senseless, unnecessary wars). The notions of duty, honor, bravery, and service I may have felt as the young son of a World War II veteran read very differently now.

Many years ago, Coetzee's fantastical tale of the Magistrate confronting Colonel Joll and his remarkable eyeglasses had to be viewed in light of South Africa's apartheid policies. Returning to this brilliant work now, I see it in much broader strokes as an indictment of soulless authoritarianism that carries a warning that is both timely and timeless.

The point is we grow up, changing as people and readers, bringing new perspectives to old ideas. We may have experienced some of the crises faced by characters in these novels—becoming parents, losing a lover, indulging in an affair, or catching a very large fish. As we view these stories from altered vantage points, our sympathies may shift. Our insights may deepen. It is the natural process of becoming older—hopefully wiser—and questioning some of the assumptions and values we once held. Revisiting a familiar book permits us to see something we may have missed the first time. And, of course, the times change, so books that held some specific meaning fifty years ago may resonate very differently today.

But for me, the best surprise by far in compiling this book was the delight of discovering extraordinary writers for the first time and knowing there is more of their exceptional work still to be read. In this category, I would place Edna O'Brien, Colson Whitehead, and Nella Larsen. With O'Brien and Whitehead, I enjoyed becoming familiar with novelists whose fiction has garnered richly deserved praise and attention. In Larsen's case, it was the wonder of encountering a writer whose work was woefully lost to the literary world for too long but whose historical and social relevance is completely of the moment.

In my year of reading briefly, I also learned something that bears mention—something rather astonishing. Reading can help you live longer. Yes, you read that right. According to a report on a 2016 Yale study, "Bookworms live longer." How much longer? The Yale researchers reported, "Book readers averaged a two-year longer life span than those who did not read at all." So, in addition to providing you with a year of great reading, I may be helping give you two more years to read.

Additional longevity or not, this seems to confirm what I suspected all along. But it is worth repeating. Reading is its own best reward, both psychologically and spiritually. The lifelong learner may find a richer, deeper sense of fulfillment in life, especially in a moment when it feels in such short supply.

Happily, I can report that has been true for me. In a year of remarkable stress over health, disconnection from family, and political upheaval, my year of reading briefly provided some of what one of the Yale researchers called the "survival advantage." It taught me that being absorbed in a book does provide a balm to the soul and psyche. And it helps create empathy. These novels allowed me to examine anew the world and my life, as well as exploring those of others. And if the world needs anything now, it is empathy and understanding. But something more as well.

Although fallen from favor, Joseph Conrad wrote compellingly of the role of the writer as artist in an 1897 essay:

> My task which I am trying to achieve is, by the power of the written word, to make you hear, to make you feel—it is, before all, to make you *see*. That—and no more, and it is everything. If I succeed, you shall find there according to your desserts: encouragement, consolation, fear, charm—all you demand; and perhaps also that glimpse of truth for which you have forgotten to ask.

So, I hope, Gentle Reader, that you have found in this collection all these things: encouragement, consolation, fear, and charm—and, most important, a glimpse of truth.

Of course, these are the views of one "Common Reader." I am certain that someone else might propose a different canon. But that brings me back to my starting point. Yes, there are so many books—great short books. But you can choose your own adventure.

Make time to read them all.

My Favorite Fifteen
Great Short Books

This was a challenging list to compile. Just as it was not easy to narrow down to the fifty-eight books chosen for this collection, it was even more difficult to single out my favorites among these great books. And once again, I was forced to make an arbitrary exception. My fifteen favorites are really sixteen. I argue that *Mrs. Dalloway* and *The Hours* by Michael Cunningham are a "two-fer." So here is my Best of List, again in alphabetical order by title:

Agostino Alberto Moravia

Animal Farm: A Fairy Story
   George Orwell

Candide, or Optimism Voltaire

The Country Girls Edna O'Brien

The Dry Heart Natalia Ginzburg

If This Is a Man [*Survival in*
   Auschwitz] Primo Levi

Lord of the Flies William Golding

The Lost Daughter Elena Ferrante

Lucy Jamaica Kincaid

Mrs. Dalloway Virginia Woolf

The Hours Michael Cunningham

The Nickel Boys Colson Whitehead

A Portrait of the Artist as a Young Man
   James Joyce

The Stranger Albert Camus

Sula Toni Morrison

We Have Always Lived in the Castle
   Shirley Jackson

Index of Entries by Date of Publication

1961 *The Prime of Miss Jean Brodie*
Muriel Spark

1962 *A Clockwork Orange*
Anthony Burgess

1962 *One Day in the Life of Ivan Denisovich*
Aleksandr Solzhenitsyn

1962 *We Have Always Lived in the Castle* Shirley Jackson

1963 *The Sailor Who Fell from Grace with the Sea* Yukio Mishima

1966 *Wide Sargasso Sea* Jean Rhys

1971 *The Lathe of Heaven*
Ursula K. Le Guin

1972 *Surfacing* Margaret Atwood

1973 *Sula* Toni Morrison

1974 *If Beale Street Could Talk*
James Baldwin

1979 *The Ghost Writer* Philip Roth

1980 *Waiting for the Barbarians*
J. M. Coetzee

1981 *July's People* Nadine Gordimer

1982 *A Pale View of Hills*
Kazuo Ishiguro

1982 *Rita Hayworth and Shawshank Redemption* Stephen King

1984 *The House on Mango Street*
Sandra Cisneros

1984 *The Lover* Marguerite Duras

1985 *Oranges Are Not the Only Fruit*
Jeanette Winterson

1986 *Maus I: A Survivor's Tale: My Father Bleeds History*
Art Spiegelman

1988 *The Fifth Child* Doris Lessing

1990 *Lucy* Jamaica Kincaid

1990 *Middle Passage*
Charles Johnson

1998 *The Hours*
Michael Cunningham

2006 *The Lost Daughter*
Elena Ferrante

2007 *On Chesil Beach* Ian McEwan

2014 *Dept. of Speculation*
Jenny Offill

2014 *Tokyo Ueno Station* Yu Miri

2016 *Another Brooklyn*
Jacqueline Woodson

2016 *The Perfect Nanny*
Leïla Slimani

2019 *The Nickel Boys*
Colson Whitehead

Index of Entries by Author's Last Name

Mann, Thomas *Death in Venice*

Márquez, Gabriel García *No One Writes to the Colonel*

McCullers, Carson *The Ballad of the Sad Café*

McEwan, Ian *On Chesil Beach*

Miri, Yu *Tokyo Ueno Station*

Mishima, Yukio *The Sailor Who Fell from Grace with the Sea*

Moravia, Alberto *Agostino*

Morrison, Toni *Sula*

O'Brien, Edna *The Country Girls*

Offill, Jenny *Dept. of Speculation*

Orwell, George *Animal Farm: A Fairy Story*

Porter, Katherine Anne *Pale Horse, Pale Rider*

Rhys, Jean *Wide Sargasso Sea*

Roth, Philip *The Ghost Writer*

Sagan, Françoise *Bonjour Tristesse*

Slimani, Leïla *The Perfect Nanny*

Solzhenitsyn, Aleksandr *One Day in the Life of Ivan Denisovich*

Spark, Muriel *The Prime of Miss Jean Brodie*

Spiegelman, Art *Maus I: A Survivor's Tale: My Father Bleeds History*

Voltaire *Candide, or Optimism*

Wharton, Edith *Ethan Frome*

White, E. B. *Charlotte's Web*

Whitehead, Colson *The Nickel Boys*

Winterson, Jeanette *Oranges Are Not the Only Fruit*

Woodson, Jacqueline *Another Brooklyn*

Woolf, Virginia *Mrs. Dalloway*

Wright, Richard *Big Boy Leaves Home*

Nobel Prize in Literature Laureates in This Book

Thomas Mann (1929)

Ernest Hemingway (1954)

Albert Camus (1957)

Aleksandr Solzhenitsyn (1970)

Gabriel García Márquez (1982)

William Golding (1983)

Nadine Gordimer (1991)

Toni Morrison (1993)

J. M. Coetzee (2003)

Doris Lessing (2007)

Kazuo Ishiguro (2017)

More Great Short Books

Need some more suggestions? Here goes.

The Abbess of Crewe Muriel Sparks

Accabadora Michela Murgia

The Alchemist Paulo Coelho

Amsterdam Ian McEwan

The Aspern Papers Henry James

Bartleby the Scrivener
    Herman Melville

Before We Were Free Julia Alvarez

Being There Jerzy Kosinski

The Big Sleep Raymond Chandler

Billy Budd, Sailor Herman Melville

Bone Fae Myenne Ng

Cain José Saramago

The Call of the Wild Jack London

Cane Jean Toomer

Cannery Row John Steinbeck

Charlie and the Chocolate Factory
    Roald Dahl

Chéri Colette

Child of God Cormac McCarthy

Chocky John Wyndham

The Chrysalids John Wyndham

The Comfort of Strangers
    Ian McEwan

Corregidora Gayl Jones

The Crying of Lot 49
    Thomas Pynchon

Daisy Miller Henry James

Dawn Octavia E. Butler

The Death of Ivan Ilyich Leo Tolstoy

Fateless Imre Kertész

Fathers and Sons Ivan Turgenev

Frankenstein Mary Shelley

Franny and Zooey J. D. Salinger

A Gathering of Old Men
    Ernest J. Gaines

Giovanni's Room James Baldwin

Housekeeping Marilynne Robinson

The Immoralist André Gide

In the Penal Colony Franz Kafka

Acknowledgments

A s with all of my books, a great many people made this under-taking possible. In this case, I must think of, and first recognize, my parents for cultivating my love of reading. We owned few books, but I had all those regular trips to the public library. As a child of the library, I know this great institution made me a reader and perhaps a writer. If we care about books, literacy, education, and democracy, protecting the library must be a national priority.

As I went through school, I also benefited from the many excellent school librarians and teachers who added to and deepened my love of literature and language. I think of the teacher who read aloud *The Odyssey*, keeping an easily distracted young boy's interest in myths and stories alive. I think of the English teacher who took us to see Zeffirelli's *Romeo and Juliet*, a film that shocked some parental sensibilities—bare breasts and bum!—back then. I think of the teacher who had me memorize the "tomorrow and tomorrow and tomorrow" soliloquy from *Macbeth*. And the lady in the church choir who handed me a copy of *Dubliners* as a teenager—the copy still on my shelf. And the choir director who made sure I took some Steinbeck along with comic books for my summer reading.

This literary education continued through college when I read everything from Chaucer to *The Exorcist*. Performing Shakespeare, *Abelard and Heloise*, and *The Zoo Story* on a college stage sharpened my passion for the sound of the words. So to all my professors and drama teachers, my everlasting appreciation.

As I began this project in the pandemic lockdown's darkest early days, I sought recommendations from colleagues and others for "great short books." I am grateful in particular to the librarians at the Hudson Park branch of the New York Public Library and the admirable staff at Three Lives & Co. bookshop in the West Village for aiding my search.

Among the friends who offered wisdom, I especially want to thank Myfanwy Probyn and Andrew Holden, not only for their suggestions but for their encouragement and valued friendship over many years.

As with all of my books, this project marks a collaboration with my publisher, Scribner. First and foremost, I am grateful to my editor, Sally Howe, for her enthusiasm and encouragement from the beginning and her thorough and thoughtful editorial suggestions through the entire process. I am also grateful to all of the other Scribner team members, including Nan Graham, Rick Horgan, Kyle Kabel, Mark LaFlaur, Jaya Miceli, Elisa Rivlin, Barbara Wild, Lisa Nicholas, and Kristen Strange. I would like to thank Sam Kerr, the artist commissioned by Scribner, for his contribution.

My deepest gratitude always goes to my family, my greatest support and often my most challenging interlocutors. Thanks to Colin Davis for his rigorous mind. And to Jenny Davis, a demanding reader who has taught me much over the years and advised me at every step during the creation of this project.

Finally, as always, my greatest thanks go to my wife, Joann Davis, for her loving support, wisdom, and guidance in so many ways. We have lived a life in books together.

Notes About the Books

INTRODUCTION

xv *"For us, books have turned into fast food"*: Jeanette Winterson, preface in Djuna Barnes, *Nightwood* (New York: New Directions, 2006), x.

xv *"languishing," a term coined by sociologist Corey Keyes*: Adam Grant, "There's a Name for the Blah You're Feeling," *New York Times*, April 19, 2021, https://www.nytimes.com/2021/04/19/well/mind/covid-mental-health-languishing.html.

xv *what psychologist Adam Grant called "Zoom fatigue"*: Adam Grant, "There's a Specific Kind of Joy We've Been Missing," *New York Times*, July 10, 2021, https://www.nytimes.com/2021/07/10/opinion/sunday/covid-group-emotions-happiness.html?searchResultPosition=54.

xix *sniffed at as a mere novella*: Julia White, "Too Short for the Booker Shortlist?" *Express*, September 6, 2007, https://www.express.co.uk/expressyourself/18485/Too-short-for-the-Booker-shortlist.

xx *"the novella is the supreme literary form"*: Katy Guest, "Novella Award Organisers Have Defined a Novel as Being a Piece of Fiction Between 20,000 and 40,000 Words," *Independent*, July 18, 2015, https://www.independent.co.uk/arts-entertainment/books/news/novella-award-organisers-have-defined-a-novel-as-being-a-piece-of-fiction-between-20-000-and-40-000-words-10399161.html.

xxi *"The classics are books that exert a peculiar influence"*: Italo Calvino, "Why Read the Classics?," *New York Review of Books*, October 9, 1986,

https://www.nybooks.com/articles/1986/10/09/why-read-the-classics
/?utm_medium=email&utm_campaign=The%20new%20nybookscom
&utm_content=The%20new%20nybookscom+CID_8d6854dc831566e
65daa890de3fe88df&utm_source=Newsletter&utm_term=Why%20
Read%20the%20Classics.

xxii *"He is worse educated"*: Virginia Woolf, *The Common Reader* (New York: Harcourt, Brace, 1925), 11.

AGOSTINO

1 *"... as if he were a man rather than a thirteen-year-old boy"*: Alberto Moravia, *Agostino*, trans. Michael F. Moore (New York: New York Review Books, 2014), 3.

2 *"All the bathers on the beach"*: Ibid., 3.

2 *At his death in 1990:* Clyde Haberman, "Alberto Moravia, Novelist, Is Dead at 82," *New York Times*, September 27, 1990, https://www.nytimes .com/1990/09/27/obituaries/alberto-moravia-novelist-is-dead-at-82 .html.

3 *"My education, my formal education that is, is practically nil"*: Alberto Moravia, "The Art of Fiction No. 6," interview by Ben Johnson and Anna Maria de Dominicis, *Paris Review*, no. 6 (Summer 1954), https://www .theparisreview.org/interviews/5093/the-art-of-fiction-no-6-alberto -moravia.

3 *he wrote* Agostino *in the space of a month:* Michael F. Moore, "Translator's Note" in Moravia, *Agostino*, 105.

4 *Nominated for the Nobel Prize fifteen times:* "Nomination Archive," Nobel Prize.org, November 24, 2021, https://www.nobelprize.org/nomination /archive/show_people.php?id=6403.

4 *he was found dead, at age eighty-two:* Haberman, "Alberto Moravia, Novelist, Is Dead at 82."

4 *"Like many a forlorn poet"*: Moore, "Translator's Note," 108.

ANIMAL FARM: A FAIRY STORY

7 *Number 31 on the Modern Library list of 100 Best Novels:* Modern Library, "100 Best Novels," https://www.modernlibrary.com/top-100/100-best -novels/.

7 Time:*"All-TIME 100 Novels"*: Lev Grossman and Richard Lacayo, "All-Time 100 Novels," *Time*, January 6, 2010, https://entertainment.time.com/2005/10/16/all-time-100-novels/slide/all/.

7 *"Mr. Jones, of the Manor Farm, had locked the hen-houses for the night"*: George Orwell, *Animal Farm: A Fairy Story* (New York: Berkley, 2020), 3.

8 *"Is it not crystal clear, then, comrades"*: Ibid., 7.

8 *"lower-upper-middle class"*: George Orwell, *The Road to Wigan Pier* (London: Left Books Club, 1937), 1.

10 *"a hard-won conviction, born of his experience with Stalinism"*: Timothy Naftali, "George Orwell's List," *New York Times*, July 29, 1998.

10 *". . . no intention of damaging the 'socialist' cause"*: Russell Baker, afterword to Orwell, *Animal Farm*, 102.

11 *"A fairy story, if you will"*: Téa Obreht, introduction to Orwell, *Animal Farm*, xx.

11 *Modern Library list of the 100 Best Novels of the twentieth century:* Modern Library, "100 Best Novels."

ANOTHER BROOKLYN

13 *"what is tragic isn't the moment"*: Jacqueline Woodson, *Another Brooklyn* (New York: Amistad, 2017), 1.

14 *"the music felt like it had always been playing"*: Ibid., 2.

15 *a position created in 2008 by the Library of Congress:* Alexandra Alter, "Jacqueline Woodson Is Named National Ambassador for Young People's Literature," *New York Times*, January 4, 2018.

15 *a MacArthur Fellow—the so-called genius award:* MacArthur Foundation, "Jacqueline Woodson: Class of 2020," https://www.macfound.org/fellows/class-of-2020/jacqueline-woodson.

15 *"whose complete works have made an important, lasting contribution to children's literature"*: International Board on Books for Young People, "Presentation of Hans Christian Anderson Award for 2020," https://www.ibby.org/subnavigation/archives/hans-christian-andersen-awards/2020.

15 *"folded my hands on the desks"*: Jacqueline Woodson, "My Biography" on personal website, https://www.jacquelinewoodson.com/all-about-me/my-biography/.

15 *"That kind of choice was not an option"*: Jacqueline Woodson, interview by Code Switch, *Fresh Air*, National Public Radio, December 10, 2014, https://www.npr.org/sections/codeswitch/2014/12/10/369736205/jacqueline-woodson-on-growing-up-coming-out-and-saying-hi-to-strangers.

17 *"This is a book full of poems"*: Veronica Chambers, "Where We Enter," *New York Times*, August 22, 2014, https://www.nytimes.com/2014/08/24/books/review/jacqueline-woodsons-brown-girl-dreaming.html.

THE AWAKENING

19 *"A green and yellow parrot"*: Kate Chopin, *The Awakening*, in *The Awakening and Selected Stories of Kate Chopin*, ed. Barbara H. Solomon (New York: Signet Classics, 1976), 1.

20 *"Mrs. Pontellier was not a mother-woman"*: Ibid., 9.

20 *"where no woman had swum before"*: Ibid., 32.

20 *"the touch of the sea is sensuous"*: Ibid., 15.

23 *"treating them as no one else had in American fiction"*: Barbara H. Solomon, introduction to Chopin, *The Awakening and Selected Stories of Kate Chopin*, xxix.

23 *"the hundredth anniversary of the publication of* The Awakening*"*: "Kate Chopin: A Re-Awakening," Public Broadcasting Service, June 23, 1999, https://www.pbs.org/katechopin/.

23 *one of her most widely read pieces*: Editors of KateChopin.org, "Kate Chopin's Short Stories," Kate Chopin International Society, https://www.katechopin.org/kate-chopins-short-stories-composition-publication-dates/.

THE BALLAD OF THE SAD CAFÉ

25 *"The town itself is dreary"*: Carson McCullers, *The Ballad of the Sad Café and Other Stories* (New York: Mariner Books, 2005), 3.

26 *"for the sake of pleasure"*: Ibid., 22.

26 *"I was sure that I was born a man"*: Sarah Schulman, "McCullers: Canon Fodder," *The Nation*, June 8, 2000, https://www.thenation.com/article/archive/mccullers-canon-fodder/.

27 *"an overly self-aware adolescent girl"*: Ibid.

27 *"the marriage was plagued by alcoholism"*: Carlos Dews, "Carson McCullers," *New Georgia Encyclopedia*, last modified October 6, 2019, https://www.georgiaencyclopedia.org/articles/arts-culture/carson-mccullers-1917-1967/.

27 *McCullers was inspired by a dwarf she had seen:* Sherill Tippins, "Genius and High Jinks at 7 Middagh Street," *New York Times*, February 6, 2005, https://www.nytimes.com/2005/02/06/nyregion/thecity/genius-and-high-jinks-at-7-middagh-street.html.

28 *a personal drama partly expressed:* Dews, "Carson McCullers."

28 *Reeves McCullers committed suicide:* Ibid.

28 *she died in Nyack, New York:* Ibid.

29 *"There are the lover and the beloved"*: McCullers, *The Ballad of the Sad Café*, 25.

29 *"This opening has the power of music"*: Hilton Als, "Unhappy Endings," *New Yorker*, November 25, 2001.

29 *"Outsiderness was McCullers's great theme"*: Megan O'Grady, "She Found Carson McCullers's Love Letters. They Taught Her Something About Herself," *New York Times*, February 4, 2020.

30 *on the Modern Library list of 100 Best Novels:* Modern Library, "100 Best Novels," https://www.modernlibrary.com/top-100/100-best-novels/.

30 *"embrace white and black humanity in one sweep"*: Richard Wright, cited in Schulman, "McCullers."

BIG BOY LEAVES HOME

32 *"beating tangled vines and bushes with long sticks"*: Richard Wright, *Big Boy Leaves Home*, in *Uncle Tom's Children* (New York: HarperCollins/Olive Editions, 2021), 21.

33 *"low-down politicians, prehensile town boomers, ignorant hedge preachers"*: "About H. L. Mencken," the Mencken House website, https://menckenhouse.org/aboutmencken/.

33 *"He was using words as a weapon"*: Richard Wright, *Black Boy* (New York: HarperPerennial, 1993), 293.

35 *attacked* Native Son *as confirming racist stereotypes:* Ayana Mathis and Pankaj Mishra, "James Baldwin Denounced Richard Wright's 'Native Son' as a 'Protest Novel.' Was He Right?," *New York Times*, February

24, 2015, https://www.nytimes.com/2015/03/01/books/review/james -baldwin-denounced-richard-wrights-native-son-as-a-protest-novel -was-he-right.html.

36 *"propelled by a fierce determination to break the silence"*: Richard Yarborough, "Introduction to the Perennial Edition" in Wright, *Uncle Tom's Children*, xxxiii.

36 *"It was this that made me get to work in dead earnest"*: Richard Wright, "How 'Bigger' Was Born," in *Native Son* (New York: Harper and Brothers, 1940), 531.

37 *"Wright wanted his words to be weapons"*: Hazel Rowley, "Richard Wright" entry in *Harlem Renaissance Lives*, ed. Henry Louis Gates Jr. and Evelyn Brooks Higginbotham (New York: Oxford University Press, 2009), 556.

BONJOUR TRISTESSE

39 *"A strange melancholy pervades me"*: Françoise Sagan, *Bonjour Tristesse*, trans. Irene Ash (New York: HarperPerennial Modern Classics, 2008), 5.

41 *the youngest author to achieve that distinction*: Eric Pace, "Françoise Sagan, Who Had a Best Seller at 19 with 'Bonjour Tristesse,' Dies at 69," *New York Times*, September 25, 2004.

41 *"It was inconceivable"*: Ibid.

42 *"Sagan is far more of a classicist"*: Rachel Cusk, "Françoise Sagan, the Great Interrogator of Morality," *New Yorker*, August 21, 2019.

43 *"Many found it to be the superior book"*: Diane Johnson, foreword to Françoise Sagan, *A Certain Smile* (Chicago: University of Chicago Press, 2011), 3.

CANDIDE, OR OPTIMISM

45 *"Once upon a time in Westphalia"*: Voltaire, *Candide*, trans. and ed. Theo Cuffe (New York: Penguin Classics, 2005), 3.

46 *"with great kicks to his backside"*: Ibid., 5.

50 *"It is the price we pay for the sugar"*: Ibid., 52.

50 *"and goes on making us laugh"*: Charles Styles, "The Best Voltaire Books," Five Books, https://fivebooks.com/best-books/voltaire-nicholas-cronk/.

51 *"charged with atheism by fanatics and scoundrels"*: Voltaire, *A Pocket Philosophical Dictionary* (New York: Oxford University Press, 2011), 31.

CHARLOTTE'S WEB

53 *"'Where's Papa going with that ax?'"*: E. B. White, *Charlotte's Web* (New York: HarperCollins, 2012), 1.

54 *"'But just call me Charlotte'"*: Ibid., 37.

54 *"Charlotte was both"*: Ibid., 184.

55 *"100 Most Important Nonfiction Books"*: Erin Skarda, "All-TIME 100 Nonfiction Books," *Time*, August 16, 2011.

55 *"E. B. White was a great essayist"*: William Shawn, quoted in Herbert Mitgang, "E.B. White, Essayist and Stylist, Dies," *New York Times*, October 2, 1985, https://www.nytimes.com/1985/10/02/books/eb-white-essayist-and-stylist-dies.html.

56 *"As a piece of work"*: Eudora Welty, "Along Came a Spider," *New York Times*, October 19, 1952, https://archive.nytimes.com/www.nytimes.com/books/98/11/22/specials/welty-charlotte.html.

56 *sixth on the list of books most checked out*: New York Public Library, "Top 10 Checkouts of All Time," New York Public Library, 2021, https://www.nypl.org/125/topcheckouts.

56 *"Omit needless words"*: William Strunk Jr. and E. B. White, *The Elements of Style* (New York: Penguin Press, 2005), 39.

A CLOCKWORK ORANGE

57 *Number 65 on the Modern Library list of 100 Best Novels:* Modern Library, "100 Best Novels," https://www.modernlibrary.com/top-100/100-best-novels/.

57 Time*: "All-TIME 100 Novels"*: Richard Lacayo, "All-TIME 100 Novels: *A Clockwork Orange*," *Time*, January 7, 2010, https://entertainment.time.com/2005/10/16/all-time-100-novels/slide/a-clockwork-orange-1963-by-anthony-burgess/.

57 *"'What's it going to be then, eh?'"*: Anthony Burgess, *A Clockwork Orange* (New York: W. W. Norton, 2019), 3.

58 *could be Leningrad or New York:* Anthony Burgess, "The Clockwork Condition," *New Yorker*, May 28, 2012.

58 *"Does God want goodness"*: Burgess, *A Clockwork Orange*, 106.

59 *the brutality he depicted in* A Clockwork Orange*:* Herbert Mitgang, "Anthony Burgess, 76, Dies; Man of Letters and Music," *New York Times,* November 26, 1993, https://www.nytimes.com/1993/11/26/obituaries /anthony-burgess-76-dies-man-of-letters-and-music.html?search ResultPosition=2.

59 *he had been misdiagnosed:* Harry Ransom Humanities Research Center, University of Texas at Austin, "Anthony Burgess, 1917–1993, Biographical Sketch," http://www.hrc.utexas.edu/research/fa/burgess.bio.html.

59 *"I first heard the expression":* Burgess, "The Clockwork Condition," *New Yorker.*

60 *"I needed money back in 1961":* Anthony Burgess, "A Clockwork Orange Resucked," in *A Clockwork Orange,* xi.

60 *extolled by a* New York Times *reviewer as "brilliant":* Brian O'Doherty, "Books of the Times," *New York Times,* March 19, 1963, https://times machine.nytimes.com/timesmachine/1963/03/19/96968044.pdf?pdf _redirect=true&ip=0.

60 *with Mick Jagger as Alex:* American Film Institute, "A Clockwork Orange (1971)," American Film Institute Catalog, https://catalog.afi.com/Catalog /moviedetails/54041.

60 *"The film has just been a damned nuisance":* Anna Edwards, "The Clock-work Collection: Burgess on Kubrick's 'Damned Nuisance' Movie," blogpost on The International Antony Burgess Foundation, May 27, 2021, https://www.anthonyburgess.org/blog-posts/the-clockwork -collection-burgess-and-kubricks-damned-nuisance-movie/.

61 *"It is not the novelist's job to preach":* Burgess, "A Clockwork Orange Resucked," xiv.

62 *"Like* 1984*, this is a book":* Richard Lacayo, "All-TIME 100 Novels: *A Clockwork Orange,*" *Time,* January 7, 2010.

62 *"Eat this sweetish segment or spit it out.":* Burgess, "A Clockwork Orange Resucked," xv.

THE COUNTRY GIRLS

65 *"100 Novels That Shaped Our World":* BBC Arts, "Explore the List of 100 Novels That Shaped Our World," British Broadcasting Com-pany, November 5, 2019, https://www.bbc.co.uk/programmes/articles

/494P4INCbVYHlY319VwGbxp/explore-the-list-of-100-novels-that
-shaped-our-world.

65 *"I wakened quickly and sat up in bed abruptly"*: Edna O'Brien, *The Country Girls: Three Novels and an Epilogue* (New York: Farrar, Straus and Giroux, 2017), 3.

66 *"We're eighteen and we're bored to death"*: Ibid., 145.

67 *burned by the parish priest in Tuamgraney:* Rachel Cooke, "Edna O'Brien: 'A Writer's Imaginative Life Commences in Childhood,'" *The Observer*, February 5, 2011.

68 *"She was a glory, with her pale white skin"*: Roslyn Sulcas, "Edna O'Brien Is Still Gripped by Dark Moral Questions," *New York Times*, March 25, 2016, https://www.nytimes.com/2016/03/26/books/edna-obrien-is-still -gripped-by-dark-moral-questions.html.

68 *"For her powerful voice and the absolute perfection of her prose"*: PEN America website, "2018 PEN America Lifetime and Career Achievement Honorees," February 20, 2018, https://pen.org/2018-lifetime-career-achievement -honorees/#.

69 *"era-defining symbols of the struggle for Irish women's voices"*: Eimear McBride, introduction to O'Brien, *The Country Girls*, ix.

69 *"among the handful of most accomplished living writers"*: Philip Roth, cited in Sulcas, "Edna O'Brien Is Still Gripped by Dark Moral Questions."

DEATH IN VENICE

72 *"hoping that fresh air and exercise would restore him"*: Thomas Mann, *Death in Venice*, trans. and ed. Clayton Koelb (New York: W. W. Norton, 1994), 3.

72 *"a measure he had to take for his health"*: Ibid., 5.

72 *"that coquettish, dubious beauty of a city"*: Ibid., 47.

72 *"a face reminiscent of Greek statues"*: Ibid., 21.

73 *joined the Library of Congress as a Consultant in German Literature:* Taru Spiegel, "Thomas Mann and the Library of Congress," *4 Corners of the World*, Library of Congress, December 18, 2020, https://blogs.loc.gov /international-collections/2020/12/thomas-mann-and-the-library-of -congress/.

74 *Mann's diaries later revealed his own:* Mark Harman, "Mann to Mann: Thomas Mann's 'furious passion for his own ego,'" *Los Angeles Times*,

June 18, 1995, https://www.latimes.com/archives/la-xpm-1995-06-18-bk
-14252-story.html.

74 *"The description of the young boy Tadzio"*: Elizabeth Hardwick, "Thomas
Mann at 100," *New York Times*, July 20, 1975, https://www.nytimes
.com/1975/07/20/archives/thomas-mann-at-100.html?searchResult
Position=5.

74 *It features the music of composer Gustav Mahler*: Thomas Mann, letter cited
in *Death in Venice*, 99.

75 *this book alone secured his 1929 Nobel Prize*: NobelPrize.org, "The Nobel
Prize in Literature 1929," https://www.nobelprize.org/prizes/literature
/1929/summary/.

DEPT. OF SPECULATION

77 *"Antelopes have 10x vision, you said"*: Jenny Offill, *Dept. of Speculation* (New
York: Vintage Contemporaries, 2014), 3.

78 *"The Buddhists say there are 121 states of consciousness"*: Ibid., 11.

78 *"Women almost never become art monsters"*: Ibid., 8.

79 *"There are many autobiographical things in the book"*: Jenny Offill, interview
by NPR Staff, *Weekend Edition Sunday*, January 26, 2014, https://www
.npr.org/2014/01/26/265674275/in-fragments-of-a-marriage-familiar
-themes-get-experimental.

80 *"'Dept. of Speculation' is all the more powerful"*: James Wood, "Mother
Courage," *New Yorker*, March 24, 2014, https://www.newyorker.com
/magazine/2014/03/31/mother-courage-3.

80 *"Part elegy and part primal scream"*: Editors of *The New York Times Book
Review*, "The 10 Best Books of 2014," *New York Times*, December 4,
2014, https://www.nytimes.com/2014/12/14/books/review/the-10-best
-books-of-2014.html?ref=review&_r=1.

80 *"soscaredsoscaredsoscaredsoscaredsoscared"*: Offill, *Dept. of Speculation*, 94.

80 *"In both novels, Offill's fragmentary structure"*: Leslie Jamison, "Jenny
Offill's 'Weather' Is Emotional, Planetary and Very Turbulent," February 7, 2020, https://www.nytimes.com/2020/02/07/books/review
/weather-jenny-offill.html?searchResultPosition=4.

THE DRY HEART

83 *"'Tell me the truth,' I said"*: Natalia Ginzburg, *The Dry Heart*, trans. Frances
    Frenaye (New York; New Directions, 2019), 3.

84 *"a tiresome and monotonous existence, with worn gloves and very little spending
    money"*: Ibid., 7.

84 *"a very rich but batty old woman who spent her time smoking cigarettes"*: Ibid., 9.

85 *Giuseppe Levi was a nonpracticing Jew:* Patrizia Acobas, "Natalia Ginzburg,"
    in *The Shalvi/Hyman Encyclopedia of Jewish Women*, Jewish Women's
    Archive (Brookline, MA: 2021), https://jwa.org/encyclopedia/article
    /ginzburg-natalia, updated July 1, 2021.

85 *Natalia did not attend elementary school:* Joan Acocella, "Rediscovering
    Natalia Ginzburg," *New Yorker*, July 22, 2019, https://www.newyorker
    .com/magazine/2019/07/29/rediscovering-natalia-ginzburg.

85 *Jews were forbidden to publish under Italian racial laws:* Acobas, "Natalia
    Ginzburg."

86 *"Ms. Ginzburg never raises her voice"*: Michiko Kakutani, "Books of the
    Times: 2 Italian Heroines Torn by Loyalties," *New York Times*, April 17,
    1990, https://www.nytimes.com/1990/04/17/books/books-of-the-times
    -2-italian-heroines-torn-by-loyalties.html?searchResultPosition=3.

87 *"Everything that mattered had happened already"*: Ginzburg, *The Dry Heart*, 39.

87 *"I haven't invented a thing"*: Natalia Ginzburg, *Family Lexicon*, trans. Jenny
    McPhee (New York: New York Review Books, 2017), 3.

ETHAN FROME

89 *"I had the story, bit by bit"*: Edith Wharton, *Ethan Frome* (New York:
    Penguin Books, 2005), 1.

90 *"one of those lonely New England farm-houses"*: Ibid., 9.

91 *"a black art and a form of manual labor"*: Unsigned, "Edith Wharton,
    75, Is Dead in France," *New York Times*, August 13, 1937, https://archive
    .nytimes.com/www.nytimes.com/learning/general/onthisday/bday
    /0124.html.

92 *"cruel, compelling haunting story"*: Unsigned, "Three Lives in Supreme
    Torture," *New York Times*, October 8, 1911, https://timesmachine.nytimes
    .com/timesmachine/1911/10/08/104878602.pdf.

93 *"sublime eloquence"*: Harold Bloom, *The American Canon: Literary Genius from Emerson to Pynchon* (New York: Library of America, 2019), 148.

93 *"They had never before avowed their inclination"*: Wharton, *Ethan Frome*, 85.

EVIL UNDER THE SUN

95 *"When Captain Roger Angmering built himself a house"*: Agatha Christie, *Evil Under the Sun* (New York: William Morrow, 2011), 1.

96 *"resplendent in a white duck suit"*: Ibid., 2.

97 *"Was it revenge, depression or amnesia?"*: Tina Jordan, "When the World's Most Famous Mystery Writer Vanished," *New York Times*, June 11, 2019, https://www.nytimes.com/2019/06/11/books/agatha-christie-vanished -11-days-1926.html.

98 *"Hercule Poirot, a Belgian detective who became internationally famous"*: Thomas Lask, "Hercule Poirot Is Dead; Famed Belgian Detective," *New York Times*, August 6, 1975, https://www.nytimes.com/1975/08/06 /archives/hercule-poirot-is-dead-famed-belgian-detective-hercule -poirot-the.html?searchResultPosition=1.

99 *"They're comfort books"*: Tina Jordan, "The Essential Agatha Christie," *New York Times*, October 25, 2020, https://www.nytimes.com/2020/10/25 /books/best-agatha-christie-books-murder-mystery.html?search ResultPosition=2.

THE FIFTH CHILD

101 *"Harriet and David met each other"*: Doris Lessing, *The Fifth Child* (New York: Vintage International, 1989), 3.

102 *"Harriet indeed became pregnant"*: Ibid., 11.

102 *"That Christmas, Harriet was again enormous"*: Ibid., 19.

103 *They had one son, Peter*: Helen T. Verongos, "Doris Lessing, Author Who Swept Aside Convention, Is Dead at 94," *New York Times*, November 17, 2013, https://www.nytimes.com/2013/11/18/books/doris-lessing-novelist -who-won-2007-nobel-is-dead-at-94.html?_r=0.

103 *Disillusioned with party politics—and having an affair*: Alison Flood, "Doris Lessing Donates Revelatory Letters to University," *The Guardian*, October 22, 2008, https://www.theguardian.com/books/2008/oct/22 /doris-lessing-letters.

103 *"For a long time I felt I had done a very brave thing"*: Julia Baird, "Why Mothers Should Lower the Bar," *Newsweek*, May 5, 2010, https://www .newsweek.com/baird-why-mothers-should-lower-bar-72657.

104 *"It was before widespread birth control"*: Margaret Atwood, "Doris Lessing: A Model for Every Writer Coming from Back of Beyond," *The Guardian*, November 18, 2013, https://www.theguardian.com/books/2013/nov/17 /doris-lessing-death-margaret-atwood-tribute.

104 *"with scepticism, fire and visionary power"*: "Doris Lessing: Facts," Nobel Prize.org, https://www.nobelprize.org/prizes/literature/2007/lessing /facts/.

104 *"Oh, Christ! I couldn't care less"*: Verongos, "Doris Lessing, Author Who Swept Aside Convention."

105 *"It's an absolutely horrible book"*: Carolyn Kizer, "Bad News for the Nice and Well-Meaning," *New York Times*, April 3, 1988, https://archive .nytimes.com/www.nytimes.com/books/99/01/10/specials/lessing-fifth .html.

105 *"a gutting examination of the crucible of motherhood"*: Emily Harnett, "Doris Lessing's 'The Fifth Child' and the Spectre of the Ambivalent Mother," *New Yorker*, May 11, 2019, https://www.newyorker.com/books /second-read/doris-lessings-the-fifth-child-and-the-spectre-of-the -ambivalent-mother.

106 *"At times, Lessing's spare, sharp prose lets you see things"*: Michael Pye, "The Creature Walks Among Us," *New York Times*, August 6, 2000, https://archive.nytimes.com/www.nytimes.com/books/00/08/06 /reviews/000806.06pye.html.

THE GHOST WRITER

107 *"It was the last daylight hour of a December afternoon"*: Philip Roth, *The Ghost Writer* (New York: Vintage International, 1995), 3.

108 *"I loved him! Yes, nothing less than love"*: Ibid., 56.

108 *"Hadn't Joyce, hadn't Flaubert, hadn't Thomas Wolfe"*: Ibid., 110.

109 *"In the course of a very long career"*: Charles McGrath, "Philip Roth, Towering Novelist Who Explored Lust, Jewish Life and America, Dies at 85," *New York Times*, May 22, 2018, https://www.nytimes.com/2018/05/22 /obituaries/philip-roth-dead.html.

109 *"When Roth learned, in 1968"*: David Remnick, "The Secrets Philip Roth Didn't Keep," *New Yorker*, March 22, 2021, https://www.newyorker.com /magazine/2021/03/29/the-secrets-philip-roth-didnt-keep.

109 *his unhappy marriage to Williams*: McGrath, "Philip Roth, Towering Novelist Who Explored Lust, Jewish Life and America."

109 *"filthy and hilarious"*: Ibid.

110 *"made him wealthy, celebrated, and notorious"*: Remnick, "The Secrets Philip Roth Didn't Keep."

111 *"Oh, if only I could have imagined the scene"*: Roth, *The Ghost Writer*, 121.

111 *"The Essential Philip Roth"*: Taffy Brodesser-Akner, "The Essential Philip Roth," *New York Times*, April 19, 2021, https://www.nytimes.com/interactive /2021/books/best-philip-roth-books.html.

111 *"a tragicomedy, and its Shakespearean reverberations"*: Harold Bloom, *The American Canon: Literary Genius from Emerson to Pynchon* (New York: Library of America, 2019), 396.

112 *number 52 on the Modern Library list of 100 Best Novels*: Modern Library, "100 Best Novels," https://www.modernlibrary.com/top-100/100-best-novels/.

112 *"a deliciously funny book"*: Josh Greenfield, "Portnoy's Complaint," *New York Times*, February 23, 1969, https://timesmachine.nytimes.com/times machine/1969/02/23/90674895.pdf?pdf_redirect=true&ip=0.

THE GREAT GATSBY

113 *Number 2 on the Modern Library list of 100 Best Novels*: Modern Library, "100 Best Novels," https://www.modernlibrary.com/top-100/100-best -novels/.

113 *"In my younger and more vulnerable years"*: F. Scott Fitzgerald, *The Great Gatsby* (New York: Scribner, 2018), 1.

114 *"Let me tell you about the very rich"*: Unsigned Letter to the Editor, "The Rich Are Different," *New York Times*, November 13, 1988, https://www .nytimes.com/1988/11/13/books/l-the-rich-are-different-907188.html.

115 *"Fitzgerald received good reviews"*: James L. W. West III, "Note on the Text," in Fitzgerald, *The Great Gatsby*, 182.

116 *"Whenever he was drunk"*: Arthur Mizener, "Gatsby, 35 Years Later," *New York Times*, April 24, 1960, https://archive.nytimes.com/www.nytimes .com/books/00/12/24/specials/fitzgerald-gatsby60.html.

116 *"Roughly, his own career began and ended with the Nineteen Twenties"*: Unsigned, "Scott Fitzgerald, Author, Dies at 44," *New York Times*, December 23, 1940, https://web.archive.org/web/20200622003513/http: /movies2.nytimes.com/books/00/12/24/specials/fitzgerald-obit.html.

116 *"a period piece that had almost entirely disappeared"*: Ibid.

117 *helping create a postwar surge*: Danna Bell, Kathleen McGuigan, and Abby Yochelson, "Challenging Students to Consider the Roles Books Played in Wartime," *Teaching with the Library of Congress* (blog), July 1, 2020, https://blogs.loc.gov/teachers/2020/07/challenging-students-to -consider-the-roles-books-played-during-wartime/.

117 *"With 'The Great Gatsby,' the question is simpler and stranger"*: Parul Seghal, "Nearly a Century Later, We're Still Reading—and Changing Our Minds About—Gatsby," *New York Times*, December 303, 2020, https://www .nytimes.com/2020/12/30/books/great-gatsby-fitzgerald-copyright .html?searchResultPosition=3.

118 *with lyrics and music composed by Florence Welch of Florence + the Machine fame*: Sarah Bahr, "'Great Gatsby' Musical Sets Creative Team," *New York Times*, April 28, 2021, https://www.nytimes.com/2021/04/28/theater /great-gatsby-musical.html?searchResultPosition=1.

118 *"This is a book that endures, generation after generation"*: Jesmyn Ward, introduction to Fitzgerald, *The Great Gatsby*, xi.

118 *"They were careless people, Tom and Daisy"*: Fitzgerald, *The Great Gatsby*, 179.

THE HOUR OF THE STAR

119 *"All the world began with a yes"*: Clarice Lispector, trans. Benjamin Moser, *The Hour of the Star* (New York: New Directions, 2011), 3.

120 *"I've also had to give up sex and soccer"*: Ibid., 14.

120 *"It was a time of chaos, famine"*: Benjamin Moser, "The True Glamor of Clarice Lispector," *New Yorker*, July 10, 2015, https://www.newyorker .com/books/page-turner/the-true-glamor-of-clarice-lispector.

121 *James Joyce, a writer Lispector had not yet read*: Dwight Garner, "Writer's Myth Looms as Large as the Many Novels She Wrote," *New York Times*, August 11, 2009, https://www.nytimes.com/2009/08/12/books/12garner .html?searchResultPosition=8.

122 *"I think she's a 'self-taught' writer"*: Elizabeth Bishop, cited in Colm Tóibín, "A Passion for the Void," in Lispector, *The Hour of the Star*, viii.

122 *a New York Times Notable Book of 2009:* New York Times Book Review, "100 Notable Books," *New York Times*, December 6, 2009, http://web .archive.org/web/20180113213738/http://www.nytimes.com/gift-guide /holiday-2009/100-notable-books-of-2009-gift-guide/list.html?ref= review.

122 *The* Times *corrected its oversight in 2020:* Lucas Iberico Lozada, "Overlooked No More: Clarice Lispector, Novelist Who Captivated Brazil," *New York Times*, December 18, 2020, https://www.nytimes.com/2020/12/18 /obituaries/clarice-lispector-overlooked.html?searchResultPosition=1.

123 *"moves from a deep awareness about the tragedy of being alive"*: Tóibín, "A Passion for the Void," xi.

123 *what one Brazilian colleague at the time called "Hurricane Clarice"*: Lozada, "Overlooked No More."

THE HOUSE ON MANGO STREET

125 *"We didn't always live on Mango Street"*: Sandra Cisneros, *The House on Mango Street* (New York: Vintage Contemporaries, 2009), 3.

126 *"it made me feel like nothing"*: Ibid., 4–5.

126 *"Your little lemon shoes are so beautiful"*: Ibid., 41.

126 *"In English my name means hope"*: Ibid., 10.

126 *named a MacArthur Fellow in 1995:* Unsigned, "MacArthur Fellows Program: Sandra Cisneros," MacArthur Foundation, https://www .macfound.org/fellows/class-of-1995/sandra-cisneros, updated January 1, 2005.

127 *"a self-educated woman who got library cards"*: Bebe Moore Campbell, "Keeping It Short: A Season of Stories; Crossing Borders," *New York Times*, May 26, 1991, https://www.nytimes.com/1991/05/26/books/keeping -it-short-a-season-of-stories-crossing-borders.html.

127 *issued by Arte Público, a nonprofit imprint of the University of Houston:* Arte Público Press, "About Us," https://artepublicopress.com/about/.

127 *"After I published* The House on Mango Street *with a small press"*: Mike Thomas, "Sandra Cisneros," *Chicago*, February 20, 2019, https://www .chicagomag.com/Chicago-Magazine/March-2019/Sandra-Cisneros/.

128 *the book was challenged by parents and school boards:* ALA Office for Intellectual Freedom, "Frequently Challenged Books with Diverse Content," Banned & Challenged Books, undated, https://www.ala.org/advocacy /bbooks/frequentlychallengedbooks/diverse.

128 *"Everybody in our family has different hair":* Cisneros, *The House on Mango Street,* 6.

128 *"Sandra Cisneros has said that she writes":* PEN America, "PEN America to Honor Sandra Cisneros for Achievement in International Literature at February 26 Ceremony in New York," PEN America, February 5, 2019, https:// pen.org/press-release/sandra-cisneros-achievement-international -literature-nabokov-award/.

129 *at a time when Tucson schools banned Mexican-American studies:* Unsigned editorial, "Books Without Borders," *New York Times,* March 15, 2012, https://www.nytimes.com/2012/03/16/opinion/books-without-borders .html?searchResultPosition=14.

129 *"Bloom where you're planted—and be brave":* Tina Jordan and Elisabeth Egan, "Books You Can Read in a Day," *New York Times,* April 22, 2020, https://www.nytimes.com/2020/04/22/books/books-you-can-read-in -a-day.html?searchResultPosition=8, updated May 1, 2020.

129 *"These stories about women struggling":* Campbell, "Keeping It Short."

129 *"Cisneros writes poetry":* Valerie Sayers, "Traveling with Cousin Elvis," *New York Times,* September 29, 2002, https://www.nytimes.com/2002/09/29 /books/traveling-with-cousin-elvis.html.

IF BEALE STREET COULD TALK

131 *"Today, I went to see Fonny":* James Baldwin, *If Beale Street Could Talk* (New York: Vintage International, 2006), 3.

132 *"When two people love each other":* Ibid., 143.

132 *"They been killing our children long enough":* Ibid., 189.

132 *"black, impoverished, gifted, and gay":* "James Baldwin: The Price of the Ticket," *American Masters,* August 14, 1989, https://www.pbs.org/wnet /americanmasters/james-baldwin-film-james-baldwin-the-price-of -the-ticket/2632/.

133 *"What I saw around me that summer":* James Baldwin, "Letter from a Region in My Mind," *New Yorker,* November 9, 1962, https://www

.newyorker.com/magazine/1962/11/17/letter-from-a-region-in-my
-mind.

133 *"I got to Paris with forty dollars"*: James Baldwin, "The Art of Fiction No. 78," interview by Jordan Elgrably, *Paris Review*, no. 91 (Spring 1984), https://theparisreview.org/interviews/2994/the-art-of-fiction-no-78 -james-baldwin.

134 *"You cannot afford to alienate"*: Colm Tóibín, "The Unsparing Confessions of 'Giovanni's Room,'" *New Yorker*, February 26, 2016, https://www.newyorker.com/books/page-turner/the-unsparing-confessions -of-giovannis-room.

134 *"He willed himself into becoming one of the world's most important writers"*: Eddie S. Glaude Jr., "Where to Start with James Baldwin," Department of African American Studies, Princeton University, January 15, 2021, https://aas.princeton.edu/news/where-start-james-baldwin.

135 *"'If Beale Street Could Talk' is a quite moving"*: Joyce Carol Oates, "If Beale Street Could Talk," *New York Times*, May 19, 1974, https://archive.nytimes.com/www.nytimes.com/books/98/03/29/specials /baldwin-beale.html.

136 *"Baldwin . . . made clear that he could work wonders"*: Tóibín, "The Unsparing Confessions of 'Giovanni's Room.'"

IF THIS IS A MAN [SURVIVAL IN AUSCHWITZ]

137 *"I was captured by the Fascist Militia on December 13, 1943"*: Primo Levi, *If This Is a Man*, trans. Stuart Woolf, in *The Complete Works of Primo Levi*, vol. 1 (New York: W. W. Norton, 2015), 9.

138 *"In less than ten minutes all the able-bodied men"*: Ibid., 16.

139 *"The camp was silent"*: Ibid., 154.

141 *though some who knew him have argued his death was an accident*: Diego Gambetta, "Primo Levi's Plunge: A Case Against Suicide," *New York Times*, August 7, 1999, https://www.nytimes.com/1999/08/07/arts/primo -levis-plunge-a-case-against-suicide.html.

141 *"The story of the death camps"*: Levi, *If This Is a Man*, 5.

141 *"The need to tell our story"*: Ibid., 6.

142 *"But only after many months"*: Primo Levi, *The Truce*, trans. Ann Goldstein, in Levi, *The Complete Works of Primo Levi*, 1:397.

142 *"For this articulate survivor"*: Toni Morrison, introduction to Levi, *The Complete Works of Primo Levi*, 1:xii.

JULY'S PEOPLE

143 *"You like to have some cup of tea?"*: Nadine Gordimer, *July's People* (New York: Penguin Books, 1981), 1.

144 *"The vehicle was bought for pleasure"*: Ibid., 6.

145 *She helped edit the "I am prepared to die" speech*: Scott Simon, "In Writing, Nadine Gordimer Explored Why We're All Here," *Simon Says*, July 19, 2014, National Public Radio, https://www.npr.org/2014 /07/19/332634847/in-writing-nadine-gordimer-explored-why-were -all-here.

145 *Mandela was spared*: Glenn Frankel, "When Mandela's, and the World's, Fate Changed at Historic Rivonia trial," *Washington Post*, December 5, 2013, https://www.washingtonpost.com/lifestyle/style /when-mandelas-and-the-worlds-fate-changed-at-historic-rivonia-trial /2013/12/05/22033836-5e10-11e3-be07-006c776266ed_story.html.

145 *"For fifty years, Gordimer has been the Geiger counter"*: Per Wästberg, "Nadine Gordimer and the South African Experience," NobelPrize .org., February 3, 2021, https://www.nobelprize.org/prizes/literature/1991 /gordimer/article/.

146 *"For myself, I have said that nothing factual that I write or say"*: Nadine Gordimer, "Nobel Lecture," NobelPrize.org., December 7, 1991, https:// www.nobelprize.org/prizes/literature/1991/gordimer/lecture/.

146 *Nadine Gordimer died, aged ninety, in Johannesburg*: The Editors of Encyclopaedia Britannica, "Nadine Gordimer: South African Author," *Encyclopaedia Britannica* , updated November 16, 2021, https://www.britannica .com/biography/Nadine-Gordimer.

147 *"In 1979, I wrote a novel, 'Burger's Daughter'"*: Nadine Gordimer, "Nelson Mandela," *New Yorker*, December 8, 2013, https://www.newyorker.com /magazine/2013/12/16/nelson-mandela-2.

THE LATHE OF HEAVEN

149 *"Current-borne, wave-flung, tugged hugely by the whole might of ocean"*: Ursula K. Le Guin, *The Lathe of Heaven* (New York: Scribner, 2008), 1.

151   *As a child, Ursula was immersed in legends and mythology:* Julie Phillips, "The Fantastic Ursula K. Le Guin," *New Yorker*, October 10, 2016, https://www.newyorker.com/magazine/2016/10/17/the-fantastic-ursula-k-le-guin.

152   *"anarchist utopian allegory":* Ursula K. Le Guin, "The Art of Fiction No. 221," interview by John Wray, *Paris Review*, no. 206 (Fall 2013), https://www.theparisreview.org/interviews/6253/the-art-of-fiction-no-221-ursula-k-le-guin.

152   *"I don't think* science fiction *is a very good name for it":* Ibid.

152   *"excluded from literature for so long":* Gerald Jonas, "Ursula K. Le Guin, Acclaimed for Her Fantasy Fiction, Is Dead at 88," *New York Times*, January 23, 2018, https://www.nytimes.com/2018/01/23/obituaries/ursula-k-le-guin-acclaimed-for-her-fantasy-fiction-is-dead-at-88.html.

152   *usually reserved for "classics" by dead writers:* David Streitfeld, "Ursula Le Guin Has Earned a Rare Honor. Just Don't Call Her a Sci-Fi Writer," *New York Times*, August 28, 2016, https://www.nytimes.com/2016/08/29/books/ursula-le-guin-has-earned-a-rare-honor-just-dont-call-her-a-sci-fi-writer.html?_r=0.

152   *"By breaking down the walls of genre":* Phillips, "The Fantastic Ursula K. Le Guin."

152   *public television featured her life, work, and influence:* "Worlds of Ursula K. Le Guin," *American Masters*, August 2, 2019, https://www.pbs.org/wnet/americanmasters/worlds-of-ursula-k-le-guin-about/11575/.

152   *"Ursula was a seer and what she called a Foreteller":* Harold Bloom, "Fellow Writers Remember Ursula K. Le Guin, 1929–2018," Library of America, January 26, 2018, https://www.loa.org/news-and-views/1375-fellow-writers-remember-ursula-k-le-guin-1929-2018#bloom.

153   *"No single work did more to upend the genre's conventions":* Le Guin, "The Art of Fiction."

153   *"I needed to understand my own passionate opposition":* Ursula K. Le Guin, introduction to Ursula K. Le Guin, *The Hainish Novels & Stories*, vol. 1, Tor.Com, August 30, 2017, https://www.tor.com/2017/08/30/introduction-from-ursula-k-le-guin-the-hainish-novels-stories-volume-one/.

154   *"In all her work, Le Guin was always asking":* Margaret Atwood, "Ursula K Le Guin, by Margaret Atwood: 'One of the Literary Greats of the 20th Century,'" *The Guardian*, January 24, 2018, https://www.theguardian.com/books/2018/jan/24/ursula-k-le-guin-margaret-atwood-tribute.

LORD OF THE FLIES

155 *Number 41 on the Modern Library list of 100 Best Novels:* Modern Library, "100 Best Novels," https://www.modernlibrary.com/top-100/100-best -novels/.

155 *"100 Novels That Shaped Our World":* BBC Arts, "Explore the List of 100 Novels That Shaped Our World," British Broadcasting Company, November 5, 2019, https://www.bbc.co.uk/programmes /articles/494P41NCbVYHlY319VwGbxp/explore-the-list-of-100-novels -that-shaped-our-world.

155 Time:*"All-TIME 100 Novels":* Lev Grossman, "All-TIME 100 Novels: *Lord of the Flies," Time,* January 8, 2010, https://entertainment.time .com/2005/10/16/all-time-100-novels/slide/lord-of-the-flies-1955-by -william-golding/.

155 *"The boy with fair hair lowered himself down":* William Golding, *Lord of the Flies* (New York: Penguin Books, 2016), 7.

156 *"'Kill the beast! Cut his throat! Spill his blood!'":* Ibid., 152.

157 *"World War II was the turning point":* Bruce Lambert, "William Golding Is Dead at 81; the Author of 'Lord of the Flies,'" *New York Times,* June 20, 1993, https://www.nytimes.com/1993/06/20/obituaries/william -golding-is-dead-at-81-the-author-of-lord-of-the-flies.html?searchResult Position=2.

157 *with translations in every major language:* "Lord of the Flies," William Golding, undated, https://william-golding.co.uk/books/lord-of-the -flies.

157 *his life had become "unendurable":* John Carey, *William Golding* (New York: Free Press, 2009), 335.

158 *"William Golding's novels and stories are not only somber moralities":* Lars Gyllensten, "Award Ceremony Speech," NobelPrize.org., 1983, https:// www.nobelprize.org/prizes/literature/1983/ceremony-speech/.

159 *"To me,* Lord of the Flies *has always represented":* Stephen King, introduction to William Golding, *Lord of the Flies* (New York: Penguin Books, 2011), xvii.

159 *"Cruelty and lust" writes A. S. Byatt:* A. S. Byatt, introduction to William Golding, *Darkness Visible* (New York: Farrar, Straus and Giroux, 2007), xi.

THE LOST DAUGHTER

161 *"I had been driving for less than an hour when I began to feel ill"*: Elena Ferrante, *The Lost Daughter*, trans. Ann Goldstein (New York: Europa Editions, 2008), 9.

162 *"For the first time in almost twenty-five years"*: Ibid., 10–11.

163 *"She has a classics degree; she has referred to being a mother"*: James Wood, "Women on the Verge," *New Yorker*, January 13, 2013, https://www .newyorker.com/magazine/2013/01/21/women-on-the-verge.

163 *"More than these occasional and fairly trivial"*: Ibid.

165 *"Always, Ferrante's fiction reminds us"*: Merve Emre, "Elena Ferrante's Master Class on Deceit," *Atlantic*, September 2020, https://www.theatlantic.com /magazine/archive/2020/09/elena-ferrante-lying-life-of-adults/614209/.

THE LOVER

167 *"One day, I was already old"*: Marguerite Duras, *The Lover*, trans. Barbara Bray (New York: Pantheon, 1997), 7.

168 *"Bargains, final reductions bought for me"*: Ibid., 11–12.

169 *"Later, Duras said the depiction in 'The Lover' was her actual childhood"*: Rachel Kushner, "'A Man and a Woman, Say What You Like, They're Different': On Marguerite Duras," *New Yorker*, November 10, 2017, https://www.newyorker.com/books/page-turner/a-man-and-a-woman -say-what-you-like-theyre-different-on-marguerite-duras.

169 *After Robert recovered, they ended up in a ménage à trois*: Beverly Fields, "Overstepping Boundaries: A Life of Marguerite Duras," *Chicago Tribune*, March 19, 1995, https://www.chicagotribune.com/news/ct-xpm-1995 -03-19-9503190038-story.html.

170 *"I write about love, yes, but not about tenderness"*: Alan Riding, "Marguerite Duras, 81, Author Who Explored Love and Sex," *New York Times*, March 4, 1996, https://www.nytimes.com/1996/03/04/nyregion/marguerite -duras-81-author-who-explored-love-and-sex.html.

170 *"There wasn't a breath of wind"*: Duras, *The Lover*, 113–114.

171 *"Name a current literary trend"*: Parul Seghal, "Marguerite Duras's 'The Lover,' and Notebooks That Enrich It," *New York Times*, November 21, 2017, https://www.nytimes.com/2017/11/21/books/review-marguerite

-duras-lover-wartime-notebooks-practicalities.html?searchResult
Position=1.

171 *"Duras became a huge star"*: Kushner, "'A Man and a Woman.'"

LUCY

173 *"It was my first day. I had come the night before"*: Jamaica Kincaid, *Lucy*
(New York: Farrar, Straus and Giroux, 2002), 3.

174 *"In photographs of themselves"*: Ibid., 12.

175 *"When I was a child I liked to read"*: Leslie Garis, "Through West
Indian Eyes," *New York Times*, October 7, 1990, https://www.nytimes
.com/1990/10/07/magazine/through-west-indian-eyes.html?page
wanted=all&src=pm.

176 *Jamaica Kincaid is, at this writing, also Professor*: "Jamaica Kinkaid," Department of African and African American Studies, Harvard University,
undated, https://aaas.fas.harvard.edu/people/jamaica-kincaid.

176 *"I Wandered Lonely as a Cloud"*: William Wordsworth, "I Wandered
Lonely as a Cloud," Poetry Foundation, undated, https://www.poetry
foundation.org/poems/45521/i-wandered-lonely-as-a-cloud.

177 *"What a surprise this was to me"*: Kincaid, *Lucy*, 6.

MAUS I: A SURVIVOR'S TALE: MY FATHER BLEEDS HISTORY

179 *"Rego Park, N.Y. c. 1958"*: Art Spiegelman, *Maus I: A Survivor's Tale: My
Father Bleeds History* (New York: Pantheon Books, 1986), 5–6.

181 *"His only response was, 'From this you make a living?'"*: Mel Gussow,
"Dark Nights, Sharp Pens; Art Spiegelman Addresses Children and
His Own Fears," *New York Times*, October 15, 2003, https://www.nytimes
.com/2003/10/15/arts/dark-nights-sharp-pens-art-spiegelman-addresses
-children-and-his-own-fears.html?searchResultPosition=5.

181 *accorded a prestigious front-page review in the* New York Times Book Review:
Lawrence Langer, "A Fable of the Holocaust," *New York Times*, November 3, 1991, https://www.nytimes.com/1991/11/03/books/a-fable-of-the
-holocaust.html.

181 *Spiegelman's art for* Maus *was also given an exhibition at the Museum of
Modern Art*: "Projects 32: Art Spiegelman," MoMA, undated, https://
www.moma.org/calendar/exhibitions/355.

182 *one of the "100 Notable Books of the Year" in 2004*: "100 Notable Books of the Year," *New York Times*, December 5, 2004, https://www.nytimes .com/2004/12/05/books/review/100-notable-books-of-the-year-html.

182 *"Perhaps no Holocaust narrative"*: Langer, "A Fable of the Holocaust."

182 *"No, I thought Auschwitz was in bad taste"*: Dan Kois, "The Making of 'Maus,'" *New York Times*, December 2, 2011, http://www.nytimes .com/2011/12/04/books/review/the-making-of-maus.html.

183 *"In recounting the tales of both the father'"*: Michiko Kakutani, "Books of the Times; Rethinking the Holocaust with a Comic Book," *New York Times*, October 29, 1991, https://www.nytimes.com/1991/10/29/books /books-of-the-times-rethinking-the-holocaust-with-a-comic-book .html?searchResultPosition=7.

183 *"It's hard to explain why these drawings"*: Gussow, "Dark Nights, Sharp Pens."

MIDDLE PASSAGE

185 *"Of all the things that drive men to sea"*: Charles Johnson, *Middle Passage* (New York: Scribner, 2015), 3.

187 *"He paid for my art lessons"*: Christopher Borrelli, "Pioneering Black Cartoonist Started Out in Chicago, Switched Careers and Won a National Book Award—the Many Sides of Charles Johnson," *Chicago Tribune*, July 12, 2021, https://www.chicagotribune.com/entertainment/books /ct-ent-black-cartoonists-chicago-book-charles-johnson-20210711 -ouutntgpqfapfnplqj4iimtbwa-story.html.

187 *"a many-splendored and ennobling weaving-together"*: Annie Gottlieb, "Search for the Good Thing in Hatten County, Georgia," *New York Times*, January 12, 1975, https://www.nytimes.com/1975/01/12/archives /search-for-the-good-thing-in-hatten-county-georgia-faith-and-the .html?searchResultPosition=1.

188 *where Jewish and Black people would never be admitted as members*: Charles Johnson, *The Way of the Writer* (New York: Scribner, 2016), 4.

188 Africans in America: America's Journey Through Slavery: Unsigned, "Introduction," *Africans in America* (1998), https://www.pbs.org/wgbh /aia/introduction.html.

188 *"I have been opposed to being put into boxes my whole life"*: Borrelli, "Pioneering Black Cartoonist."

189 *"combines the physical realities with the internal mysteries"*: Stanley Crouch, introduction to Johnson, *Middle Passage*, vii.

190 *"Mr. Johnson has used his generous storytelling gifts"*: Michiko Kakutani, "The Sorcerer's Apprentice," *New York Times*, February 5, 1986, https:// archive.nytimes.com/www.nytimes.com/books/98/04/05/specials /johnson-apprentice.html.

MRS. DALLOWAY

191 Time: *"All-TIME 100 Novels"*: Lev Grossman, "All-TIME 100 Novels: *Mrs. Dalloway*," *Time*, January 8, 2010, https://entertainment.time .com/2005/10/16/all-time-100-novels/slide/mrs-dalloway-1925-by -virginia-woolf/.

191 *"Mrs. Dalloway said she would buy the flowers herself"*: Virginia Woolf, *Mrs. Dalloway* (New York: Harvest, 1981), 3.

192 *"Virginia Woolf's 'Mrs. Dalloway' is a revolutionary novel"*: Michael Cunningham, "Michael Cunningham on Virginia Woolf's Literary Revolution," *New York Times*, December 23, 2020, https://www.nytimes .com/2020/12/23/books/review/michael-cunningham-on-virginia -woolfs-literary-revolution.html?searchResultPosition=3.

193 *Her diaries would reveal that she was also the victim*: Julia Epstein, "Virginia Woolf and Her Family's Secret Life," *Washington Post*, May 14, 1989, https://www.washingtonpost.com/archive/entertainment /books/1989/05/14/virginia-woolf-and-her-familys-secret-life/be2932af -3db9-4274-bf4a-7ad0f20e9b59/.

194 *"Even if the books have remained the same"*: Italo Calvino, "Why Read the Classics?," *New York Review of Books*, October 9, 1986, https://www .nybooks.com/articles/1986/10/09/why-read-the-classics/.

194 *"Each time, I have found shocks of recognition on the page"*: Jenny Offill, "A Lifetime of Lessons in 'Mrs. Dalloway,'" *New Yorker*, December 29, 2020, https://www.newyorker.com/books/page-turner/a-lifetime-of-lessons -in-mrs-dalloway.

194 *"The War had taught him. It was sublime"*: Woolf, *Mrs. Dalloway*, 86–87.

195 *"The book encompasses, as well, almost infinite shades and degrees"*: Cunningham, "Michael Cunningham on Virginia Woolf's Literary Revolution."

196 *ranked number 15 on the Modern Library list of 100 Best Novels:* Modern Library, "100 Best Novels," https://www.modernlibrary.com/top -100/100-best-novels/.

196 *"He—for there could be no doubt of his sex":* Virginia Woolf, *Orlando* (New York: Harvest, 1956), 13.

196 Orlando *is on the BBC list of "100 Novels That Shaped Our World":* BBC Arts, "Explore the List of 100 Novels That Shaped Our World," British Broadcasting Corporation, November 5, 2019, https://www.bbc.co.uk /programmes/articles/494P41NCbVYHlY319VwGbxp/explore-the-list -of-100-novels-that-shaped-our-world.

THE HOURS

197 *"She hurries from the house":* Michael Cunningham, *The Hours* (New York: Picador USA, 1998), 3.

199 *Cunningham was teaching creative writing at Yale University:* Unsigned, "Michael Cunningham," Yale University, undated, https://english.yale .edu/people/adjunct-professors-and-senior-lecturers-full-part-time -lecturers-creative-writers/michael.

200 *"In* Mrs Dalloway, Woolf *asserts":* Michael Cunningham, "Virginia Woolf, My Mother and Me," *The Guardian,* June 3, 2011, https://www.the guardian.com/books/2011/jun/04/virginia-woolf-the-hours-michael -cunningham.

200 *"She is going to produce a birthday cake":* Cunningham, *The Hours,* 76.

201 *"Grand themes of love, death and loyalty are all played out":* Meg Wolitzer, "Suburban Spawl," *New York Times,* April 16, 1995, https://archive .nytimes.com/www.nytimes.com/books/99/04/11/specials/cunningham -flesh.html.

201 *"Cunningham writes so well":* Jeanette Winterson, "Sibling Rivalry," *New York Times,* October 1, 2010, https://www.nytimes.com/2010/10/03 /books/review/Winterson-t.html?scp=1&sq=sibling%20rivalry &st=cse/.

THE NICKEL BOYS

203 *"Even in death the boys were trouble":* Colson Whitehead, *The Nickel Boys* (New York: Anchor Books, 2020), 1.

204 *When a* Time *magazine cover declares that you are "America's Storyteller"*: Mitchell S. Jackson, "'I Carry It Within Me.' Novelist Colson White-head Reminds Us How America's Racist History Lives On," *Time,* June 27, 2019, https://time.com/5615610/colson-whitehead-the-nickel-boys -interview/.

205 *he dropped "Arch" in favor of "Colson" at age twenty-one:* Ibid.

206 *"The book about the Dozier school seemed relevant":* Alexandra Alter, "Col-son Whitehead's Next Novel Tackles Life Under Jim Crow," *New York Times,* October 1, 2018, https://www.nytimes.com/2018/10/10/books /colson-whitehead-new-novel-will-tackle-life-under-jim-crow.html.

206 *"The strap was three feet long with a wooden handle":* Whitehead, *The Nickel Boys,* 67.

207 *"Whitehead brilliantly reformulates an old-hat genre":* Tom Chiarella, "How It Ends," *Esquire,* September 19, 2011, https://web.archive.org /web/20150130061814/http:/www.esquire.com/fiction/book-review/zone -one-review-1011.

207 *"The result . . . is a potent, almost hallucinatory novel":* Michiko Kakutani, "Review: 'Underground Railroad' Lays Bare Horrors of Slavery and Its Toxic Legacy," August 2, 2016, https://www.nytimes.com/2016/08/03 /books/review-the-underground-railroad-colson-whitehead.html.

NO ONE WRITES TO THE COLONEL

209 *"The colonel took the top off the coffee can":* Gabriel García Márquez, *No One Writes to the Colonel,* trans. J. S. Bernstein, in *Collected Novellas* (New York: HarperPerennial Modern Classics, 1999), 119.

210 *"The colonel saw it dock":* Márquez, *No One Writes to the Colonel,* 128.

210 *"I feel that all my writing has been about the experiences of the time":* Unsigned, "About Gabriel García Márquez," in García Márquez, *Collected Novellas,* 278.

211 *"When you went home at dawn":* Jonathan Kandell, "Gabriel García Márquez, Conjurer of Literary Magic, Dies at 87," *New York Times,* April 17, 2014, https://www.nytimes.com/2014/04/18/books/gabriel-garcia -marquez-literary-pioneer-dies-at-87.html.

211 *"The whole notion that I am an intuitive is a myth":* Gabriel García Márquez, interview by Marlise Simons, *New York Times,* December 5, 1982, https://

archive.nytimes.com/www.nytimes.com/books/97/06/15/reviews
/marquez-talk.html.

212 *"For 18 months, he had holed up in his office"*: Penelope Green, "Mercedes
Barcha, Gabriel García Márquez's Wife and Muse, Dies at 87," *New York
Times*, August 23, 2020, https://www.nytimes.com/2020/08/23/books
/mercedes-barcha-dead.html?searchResultPosition=1.

212 *It would eventually go on to sell more than 50 million copies*: Green, "Mercedes
Barcha, Gabriel García Márquez's Wife and Muse."

212 *"With his stories, Gabriel García Márquez has created a world of his own"*:
The Permanent Secretary, "Gabriel García Márquez, the Nobel Prize
in Literature 1982," NobelPrize.org, undated press release, https://www
.nobelprize.org/prizes/literature/1982/press-release/.

213 *"A tragic sense of life characterizes García Márquez's books"*: Ibid.

214 *"When it gets hot in Macondo, it gets so hot"*: Robert Kiely, "One Hundred
Years of Solitude," *New York Times*, March 8, 1970, https://www.nytimes
.com/1970/03/08/archives/one-hundred-years-of-solitude-memory
-and-prophecy-illusion-and.html?searchResultPosition=3.

214 *"the most popular and perhaps the best writer"*: Unsigned, "About Gabriel
García Márquez," 281.

THE OLD MAN AND THE SEA

215 *"He was an old man who fished alone in a skiff"*: Ernest Hemingway, *The
Old Man and the Sea* (New York: Scribner, 2003), 9.

216 *"Think of the great DiMaggio"*: Ibid., 17.

217 *"Use short sentences. Use short first paragraphs"*: Unsigned, "*Star* Style and
Rules for Writing," KansasCity.Com, June 26, 1999, http://www.kcstar
.com/hemingway/ehstarstyle.shtml.

219 *He was bedridden, drinking heavily*: Mary V. Dearborn, *Ernest Hemingway:
A Biography* (New York: Vintage Books, 2018), 618–619.

219 *"for his mastery of the art of narrative"*: Unsigned, "The Nobel Prize in
Literature 1954," NobelPrize.org, undated, https://www.nobelprize
.org/prizes/literature/1954/summary/.

219 *dismissed* The Old Man and the Sea *as "schoolboy writing"*: James
Poniewozik, "Review: 'Hemingway' Is a Big Two-Hearted Reconsider-
ation," *New York Times*, April 2, 2021, https://www.nytimes.com/2021

/04/02/arts/television/review-hemingway-ken-burns.html?search
ResultPosition=2.

220 *"I went out too far"*: Hemingway, *The Old Man and the Sea*, 120.

220 *"the best short story writer in the English language from Joyce's* Dubliners *until the present"*: Harold Bloom, *The American Canon: Literary Genius from Emerson to Pynchon* (New York: Library of America, 2019), 268.

220 *"There's ugliness in Hemingway"*: Hilton Als, "A New Hemingway Documentary Peeks Behind the Myth," *New Yorker*, April 5, 2021, https://www .newyorker.com/magazine/2021/04/12/a-new-hemingway-documentary -peeks-behind-the-myth.

220 *Number 74 on the Modern Library list of 100 Best Novels:* Modern Library, "100 Best Novels," https://www.modernlibrary.com/top-100/100-best -novels.

221 *"No amount of analysis can convey the quality"*: Unsigned review, "Marital Tragedy," *New York Times*, October 31, 1926, https://archive.nytimes .com/www.nytimes.com/books/99/07/04/specials/hemingway-rises .html.

ON CHESIL BEACH

223 *"They were young, educated, and both virgins"*: Ian McEwan, *On Chesil Beach* (New York: Anchor Books, 2008), 3.

224 *"How this was to be achieved without absurdity"*: Ibid., 8.

224 *"In a modern, forward-looking handbook"*: Ibid., 9.

225 *"a connoisseur of dread, performing the literary equivalent"*: Daniel Zalewski, "The Background Hum," *New Yorker*, February 23, 2009, https://www .newyorker.com/magazine/2009/02/23/the-background-hum.

225 *"We stood at the kitchen counter making toast"*: Ibid.

226 *"When Edward drew Florence"*: McEwan, *On Chesil Beach*, 100–101.

227 *"Although his novels headily explore ideas"*: Zalewski, "The Background Hum."

ONE DAY IN THE LIFE OF IVAN DENISOVICH

229 *"The hammer banged reveille"*: Aleksandr Solzhenitsyn, *One Day in the Life of Ivan Denisovich*, trans. H. T. Willets (New York: Farrar, Straus and Giroux, 2005), 3.

230 *"He heard the orderlies trudging heavily"*: Ibid., 5.

230 *"Shukhov felt pleased with life"*: Ibid., 181.

231 *"Such are the words of Alexander Solzhenitsyn"*: Karl Ragnar Gierow, "Award Ceremony Speech," Nobel Prize.org, December 10, 1970, https://www.nobelprize.org/prizes/literature/1970/ceremony-speech/.

232 *"Many in the West did not know what to make of the man"*: Michael Kaufman, "Solzhenitsyn, 20th-Century Oracle, Dies," *New York Times*, August 4, 2008, https://www.nytimes.com/2008/08/04/arts/04iht-04solzhenitsynB.14974360.html?searchResultPosition=2.

232 *"In the final years of his life"*: Ibid.

233 *"Solzhenitsyn should be remembered for his role as a truth-teller"*: Michael Scammell, "The Writer Who Destroyed an Empire," *New York Times*, December 11, 2018, https://www.nytimes.com/2018/12/11/opinion/solzhenitsyn-soviet-union-putin.html?searchResultPosition=3.

234 *"They compel the human imagination to participate"*: Patricia Blake, "A Diseased Body Politic," *New York Times*, October 27, 1968, https://archive.nytimes.com/www.nytimes.com/books/98/03/01/home/solz-cancer.html.

ORANGES ARE NOT THE ONLY FRUIT

235 *"Like most people I lived"*: Jeanette Winterson, *Oranges Are Not the Only Fruit* (New York: Grove Press, 1985), 1.

236 *"Enemies were: The Devil (in his many forms)"*: Ibid., 1.

236 *"She looked up, and I noticed her eyes"*: Ibid., 82.

236 *Nell Gwyn, who started life in the theater as a scantily-clad "orange girl"*: The Editors of Encyclopaedia Britannica, "Nell Gwyn," *Encyclopaedia Britannica*, undated, https://www.britannica.com/biography/Nell-Gwyn-English-actress.

237 *"I was born in Manchester, England"*: Jeanette Winterson, "Jeanette Winterson," https://www.jeanettewinterson.com/author.

238 *"During the 90s it became commonplace"*: Stuart Jeffries, "Jeanette Winterson: 'I Thought of Suicide,'" *The Guardian*, February 21, 2010, https://www.theguardian.com/books/2010/feb/22/jeanette-winterson-thought-of-suicide.

238 *Following the end of a long-term relationship*: Ibid.

238 *"The memoir's title is the question Ms. Winterson's adoptive mother asked"*: Dwight Garner, "On a Path to Salvation, Jane Austen as a Guide," *New York Times*, March 8, 2012, https://www.nytimes.com/2012/03/09/books /jeanette-wintersons-why-be-happy-when-you-could-be-normal .html?_r=0.

238 *"We had no Wise Men because she didn't believe"*: Winterson, *Oranges Are Not the Only Fruit*, 2.

239 *"Do you stay safe or do you follow your heart"*: Jeanette Winterson, "Jeanette Winterson," https://www.jeanettewinterson.com/book/oranges-are -not-the-only-fruit/.

239 The Passion, *named to the BBC's list of "100 Novels That Shaped Our World"*: BBC Arts, "Explore the List of 100 Novels That Shaped Our World," British Broadcasting Corporation, November 5, 2019, https://www.bbc .co.uk/programmes/articles/494P41NCbVYHlY319VwGbxp/explore -the-list-of-100-novels-that-shaped-our-world.

240 *"This novel is talky, smart, anarchic and quite sexy"*: Dwight Garner, "Jeanette Winterson's Playful New Novel Offers Thoughts on Mad Science and Sexbots," *New York Times*, October 1, 2019, https://www.nytimes .com/2019/10/01/books/review-frankissstein-jeanette-winterson.html ?searchResultPosition=10.

240 *"The purpose of art changes as society changes"*: Jeanette Winterson, interviewer unidentified, *New York Times*, September 26, 2019, https:// www.nytimes.com/2019/09/26/books/review/jeanette-winterson-by -the-book-interview.html?searchResultPosition=1.

PALE HORSE, PALE RIDER

241 *"In sleep she knew she was in her bed"*: Katherine Anne Porter, *Pale Horse, Pale Rider*, in *Pale Horse, Pale Rider: Three Short Novels* (New York: Harcourt Brace Modern Classic, 1967), 141.

244 *She was featured in "Katherine Anne Porter: The Eye of Memory" in the PBS series* American Masters: Unsigned, "About Katherine Anne Porter," September 28, 2002, https://www.pbs.org/wnet/americanmasters/katherine -anne-porter-about-katherine-anne-porter/686/.

245 *"Bells screamed all off key, wrangling together"*: Porter, *Pale Horse, Pale Rider*, 201–202.

246 *Harold Bloom called the novel "an interesting failure"*: Harold Bloom, *The American Canon: Literary Genius from Emerson to Pynchon* (New York: Library of America, 2019), 226.

246 *"There is something a little musty, like old yellowing notes"*: Elizabeth Hardwick, "What She was and What She Felt Like," *New York Times*, November 7, 1982, https://archive.nytimes.com/www.nytimes.com /books/98/07/26/specials/hardwick-porter.html.

A PALE VIEW OF HILLS

247 *"Niki, the name we finally gave my younger daughter"*: Kazuo Ishiguro, *A Pale View of Hills* (New York: Vintage International, 1990), 9.

248 *"The worst days were over by then"*: Ibid., 11.

249 *"I was trying to be the singer-songwriter"*: Kazuo Ishiguro, interview by Terry Gross, *Fresh Air*, National Public Radio, March 17, 2021, https:// www.npr.org/transcripts/978138547.

249 *Ishiguro wrote a master's thesis in creative writing*: Unsigned, "Kazuo Ishiguro: Nobel Literature Prize Is 'a Magnificent Honour,'" British Broadcasting Corporation, October 5, 2017, https://www.bbc.com/news /entertainment-arts-41513246.

250 *"Firstly, we must widen our common literary world"*: Kazuo Ishiguro, "Banquet Speech," NobelPrize.org, December 10, 2017, https://www.nobel prize.org/prizes/literature/2017/ishiguro/speech/.

251 *"Its characters, whose bursts of self-knowledge and honesty"*: Edith Milton, "In a Japan like Limbo," *New York Times*, May 9, 1982, https://www.nytimes.com /1982/05/09/books/in-a-japan-like-limbo.html?searchResultPosition=1.

PASSING

253 *"It was the last letter in Irene Redfield's little pile"*: Nella Larsen, *Passing* (New York: Modern Library, 2019), 3.

254 *"Nearly every State in the union"*: Thadious M. Davis, "Explanatory Notes: Chapter Two, Note 2," in Larsen, *Passing*, 150.

254 *"a strange capacity of transforming warmth and passion"*: Larsen, *Passing*, 5.

255 *While her birth certificate classified her as "colored"*: Carla Kaplan, "A 'Queer Dark Creature,'" in Nella Larsen, *Quicksand* (New York: W. W. Norton, 2020), ix.

255 *she worked as superintendent of nurses:* Bonnie Wertheim, "Overlooked: Nella Larsen," *New York Times,* undated, 2018, https://www.nytimes.com/interactive/2018/obituaries/overlooked-nella-larsen.html.

255 *a wedding widely described as Harlem's social event of the decade:* https://www.google.com/books/edition/Countee_Cullen/WavXDwAAQBAJ?hl=en&gbpv=0.

256 *its first female graduate identified as Black:* Wertheim, "Overlooked: Nella Larsen."

256 *"You will be amused that I who have never tried this":* Nella Larsen letter to Carl Van Vechten, in Allyson Hobbs, *A Chosen Exile* (Cambridge: Harvard University Press, 2014), 175.

256 *"the first African American woman" to receive the honor:* Wertheim, "Overlooked: Nella Larsen."

257 *Larsen never published again:* Kelli A. Larson, "Surviving the Taint of Plagiarism: Nella Larsen's 'Sanctuary' and Sheila Kaye-Smith's 'Mrs. Adis,'" *Journal of Modern Literature* 30, no. 4 (2007): 82–104, muse.jhu.edu/article/222941.

257 *The oversight was corrected in 2018 in the series "Overlooked No More":* Wertheim, "Overlooked: Nella Larsen."

257 *Larsen was among four writers of the Harlem Renaissance honored:* Unsigned, "Honoring Four of Harlem's Historic Voices," U.S. Postal Service, May 20, 2020, https://about.usps.com/newsroom/local-releases/nc/2020/0520-honoring-four-harlem-historic-voices.htm.

258 *"Once one circumvented the law, fooled coworkers":* Hobbs, *A Chosen Exile,* 5.

259 *"an original and hugely insightful writer whose literary talent developed no further":* Richard Bernstein, "Books of the Times: Anguish Behind the Harlem Renaissance," *New York Times,* January 15, 2001, https://www.nytimes.com/2001/01/15/books/books-of-the-times-anguish-behind-the-harlem-renaissance.html.

THE PERFECT NANNY

261 *"The baby is dead":* Leïla Slimani, *The Perfect Nanny,* trans. Sam Taylor (New York: Penguin Books, 2018), 1.

262 *"The winter days seemed endless":* Ibid., 8.

262 *"My nanny is a miracle-worker":* Ibid., 25.

263 *"The Killer-Nanny Novel"*: Lauren Collins, "The Killer-Nanny Novel That Conquered France," *New Yorker*, December 25, 2017, https://www .newyorker.com/magazine/2018/01/01/the-killer-nanny-novel-that -conquered-france.

264 *"Best Books of 2018"*: Unsigned, "The 10 Best Books of 2018," *New York Times*, November 29, 2018, https://www.nytimes.com/2018/11/29/books /review/best-books.html.

264 *"The subject came from the fact that I myself had nannies growing up in Morocco"*: Benoît Morenne, "Leïla Slimani Wins Prix Goncourt, France's Top Literary Award," *New York Times*, November 3, 2016, https://www .nytimes.com/2016/11/04/books/prix-goncourt-leila-slimani.html.

264 *French president Emmanuel Macron appointed Slimani*: Unsigned, "Leïla Slimani," Institut français, updated March 16, 2021, https://www.institut francais.com/en/interview/leila-slimani.

264 *based on interviews with Moroccan women*: Sylvie Kauffmann, "A Toxic Mix: Sex, Religion and Hypocrisy," *New York Times*, November 13, 2017, https:// www.nytimes.com/2017/11/13/opinion/france-sex-islam-hypocrisy.html.

264 *Based on the life of Slimani's maternal grandmother*: Laura Cappelle, "Leïla Slimani Has Written About a Sex Addict and a Murderous Nanny. Next Up: Her Own Family," *New York Times*, August 8, 2021, https://www.nytimes .com/2021/08/08/books/leila-slimani-in-the-country-of-others.html.

264 *"It is hard to think of a more primal sentence"*: Collins, "The Killer-Nanny Novel."

265 *"Actually, when I began to write"*: Leïla Slimani, interviewed in "A Conversation with Leïla Slimani," in "A Penguin Reader's Guide to *Adèle*," in Leïla Slimani, *Adèle* (New York: Penguin Books, 2019), 6–7.

266 *In the first installment of a planned trilogy*: Meena Kandasamy, "Leïla Slimani Tells the Story of Her Interracial Grandparents in Post-WWII Morocco," *New York Times*, August 10, 2021, https://www.nytimes.com/2021/08/10 /books/review/in-the-country-of-others-leila-slimani.html.

A PORTRAIT OF THE ARTIST AS A YOUNG MAN

267 *Number 3 on the Modern Library list of 100 Best Novels*: Modern Library, "100 Best Novels," https://www.modernlibrary.com/top-100/100-best -novels/.

267 *"Once upon a time and a very good time it was"*: James Joyce, *A Portrait of the Artist as a Young Man* (New York: Vintage International, 1993), 3.

268 *"Welcome, O life!"*: Ibid., 244.

269 *"They did not leave a forwarding address"*: Louis Menand, "Silence, Exile, Punning," *New Yorker*, June 25, 2012, https://www.newyorker.com/magazine /2012/07/02/silence-exile-punning.

269 *attacking an Irish politician his father disliked*: Richard Ellman, *James Joyce* (New York: Oxford University Press, 1959), 33.

270 *"When people celebrate Bloomsday"*: Louis Menand, "Silence, Exile, Punning."

270 *he underwent twenty-five operations for a variety of eye ailments*: James Stephen Atherton, "James Joyce: Irish Author," *Encyclopaedia Britannica*, undated, https://www.britannica.com/biography/James-Joyce.

271 *"the swish of the sleeve of the soutane"*: Joyce, *Portrait of the Artist*, 45.

271 *"A girl stood before him in midstream"*: Ibid., 164.

272 *Bloomsday (June 16) is celebrated*: Unsigned, "Bloomsday," James Joyce Centre, undated, https://jamesjoyce.ie/bloomsday/.

272 *"It is a work that . . . compels attention"*: Terence Brown, introduction to James Joyce, *Dubliners* (New York: Penguin Books, 1992), xiv.

THE POSTMAN ALWAYS RINGS TWICE

273 *Number 98 on the Modern Library list of 100 Best Novels*: Modern Library, "100 Best Novels," https://www.modernlibrary.com/top-100/100-best -novels/.

273 *"They threw me off the hay truck about noon"*: James M. Cain, *The Postman Always Rings Twice* (New York: Vintage Crime/Black Lizard, 1992), 3.

274 *"From now on, it would be business between her and me"*: Ibid., 7.

274 *"Rip me! Rip me!"*: Ibid., 46.

274 *"it was sensational enough to help earn the book an obscenity trial"*: John Leonard, "James M. Cain, 85, the Author of 'The Postman Always Rings Twice,'" *New York Times*, October 29, 1977, https://www.nytimes .com/1977/10/29/archives/james-m-cain-85-the-author-of-postman -always-rings-twice-novelist.html.

274 *"It was like being in church"*: Cain, *The Postman Always Rings Twice*, 17.

275 *"She was right, but she could have kept her flap shut"*: Leonard, "James M. Cain, 85."

275 *He would eventually work under three legendary editors:* Ibid.

275 *"and writing the four novels on which his reputation rests":* Ibid.

276 *"There's more violence in 'Hamlet' than in all my books":* Ibid.

276 *"I make no conscious effort to be tough":* James M. Cain, quoted on back jacket of *The Postman Always Rings Twice.*

THE PRIME OF MISS JEAN BRODIE

279 *Number 76 on the Modern Library list of 100 Best Novels:* "100 Best Novels," https://www.modernlibrary.com/top-100/100-best-novels/.

279 Time: *"All-TIME 100 Novels":* Richard Lacayo, "All-TIME 100 Novels: How We Picked the List," *Time,* January 6, 2010, https://entertainment.time .com/2005/10/16/all-time-100-novels/slide/how-we-picked-the-list/.

279 *"The boys, as they talked to the girls":* Muriel Spark, *The Prime of Miss Jean Brodie* (New York: HarperPerennial Modern Classics, 2018), 1.

280 *"Give me a girl at an impressionable age":* Ibid., 119.

280 *where one of her teachers would become the model:* Helen T. Verongos and Alan Cowell, "Muriel Spark, Novelist Who Wrote 'The Prime of Miss Jean Brodie,' Dies at 88," *New York Times,* April 16, 2006, https://www .nytimes.com/2006/04/16/world/16spark.html?pagewanted=all.

280 *"I was attracted to a man who brought me bunches":* Jenny Turner, "Dame Muriel Spark," *The Guardian,* April 17, 2006, https://www.theguardian .com/news/2006/apr/17/guardianobituaries.booksobituaries.

281 *"He became a borderline case":* Verongos and Cowell, "Muriel Spark, Novelist Who Wrote 'The Prime of Miss Jean Brodie.'"

281 *"The words she had once manipulated":* Ibid.

283 *"The archly, tartly narrated adventures of these young girls":* Lev Grossman, "All-TIME 100 Novels: The Prime of Miss Jean Brodie," *Time,* January 8, 2010, https://entertainment.time.com/2005/10/16/all-time-100-novels /slide/the-prime-of-miss-jean-brodie-1961-by-muriel-spark/.

283 *"I always think of* The Girls of Slender Means*":* Alan Taylor, interview by Cal Flyn, "The Best Books by Muriel Spark," Five Books, undated, https://fivebooks.com/best-books/muriel-spark-alan-taylor/.

284 *"Muriel Spark is the first writer":* George Stade, "The Abbess of Crewe," *New York Times,* October 20, 1974, https://archive.nytimes.com/www .nytimes.com/books/97/05/11/reviews/spark-morality.html.

THE RED BADGE OF COURAGE

285 *"The cold passed reluctantly from the earth"*: Stephen Crane, *The Red Badge of Courage* (New York: Bantam Classics, 2004), 1.

286 *"It had suddenly appeared to him that perhaps"*: Ibid., 8.

286 *"Henry, don't think of anything 'cept what's right"*: Ibid., 5.

289 *"the first great 'modern' novel of war"*: Alfred Kazin, introduction to Crane, *The Red Badge of Courage*, vii.

289 *"He proves that any authentic war novel"*: Herbert Mitgang, "Books of the Times: Making Real a War He Never Fought," *New York Times*, August 18, 1998, https://www.nytimes.com/1998/08/18/books/books -of-the-times-stephen-crane-making-real-a-war-he-never-fought.html ?searchResultPosition=8.

RITA HAYWORTH AND SHAWSHANK REDEMPTION

291 *"There's a guy like me"*: Stephen King, *Rita Hayworth and Shawshank Redemption* (New York: Scribner, 2020), 1.

292 *"In all my years at Shawshank"*: Ibid., 4–5.

293 *"Not yet"*: Stephen King, "Frequently Asked Questions," StephenKing .com, undated, https://stephenking.com/faq/.

293 *"They asked me if I could pay cash"*: Stephen King, "The Art of Fiction No. 189," interview by Nathaniel Rich and Christopher Lehman-Haupt, *Paris Review*, no. 178 (Fall 2006), https://www.theparisreview.org/interviews /5653/the-art-of-fiction-no-189-stephen-king.

294 *"So where is the tragedy"*: Ibid.

294 *but his publisher balked at the risk of saturating the market*: King, "Frequently Asked Questions."

295 *"So whether you talk about ghosts or vampires"*: King, "The Art of Fiction No. 189."

THE SAILOR WHO FELL FROM GRACE WITH THE SEA

297 *"'Sleep well, dear'"*: Yukio Mishima, *The Sailor Who Fell from Grace with the Sea*, trans. John Nathan (New York: Vintage International, 1994), 3.

298 *"Certain he had watched a tangle of thread"*: Ibid., 13.

300 *"A sickly, scholarly schoolboy"*: Philip Shabecoff, "A Man Torn Between Two Worlds," *New York Times*, November 26, 1970, https://www.nytimes .com/1970/11/26/archives/mishima-a-man-torn-between-two-worlds -the-writer-of-the-following-a.html?searchResultPosition=39.

301 *"Fusako was wearing a black-lace kimono"*: Mishima, *Sailor Who Fell from Grace*, 42.

302 *"Mishima is far superior to me"*: Philip Shabecoff, "Everyone in Japan Has Heard of Him," *New York Times*, August 2, 1970, https://archive.nytimes .com/www.nytimes.com/books/98/10/25/specials/mishima-mag.html.

THE STRANGER

303 *"Maman died today"*: Albert Camus, *The Stranger*, trans. Matthew Ward (New York: Vintage International, 1989), 3.

304 *"She was right"*: Ibid., 17.

304 *"It occurred to me that anyway"*: Ibid., 24.

306 *"for his important literary production"*: Unsigned, "The Nobel Prize in Literature 1957," NobelPrize.org, undated, https://www.nobelprize .org/prizes/literature/1957/summary/.

306 *"By the same token, the writer's role"*: Albert Camus, "Banquet Speech," December 10, 1957, https://www.nobelprize.org/prizes/literature/1957 /camus/speech/.

306 *"the exemplary existentialist novel"*: Claire Messud, "A New 'L'Étranger,'" *New York Review of Books*, June 5, 2014, https://www.nybooks.com /articles/2014/06/05/camus-new-letranger/.

306 *"Nothing, nothing mattered, and I knew why"*: Camus, *The Stranger*, 121.

306 *"Camus admitted using an 'American method'"*: Herbert Mitgang, "Classic French Novel is 'Americanized,'" *New York Times*, April 18, 1988, https://www.nytimes.com/1988/04/18/books/classic-french-novel-is -americanized.html.

307 *"Judging whether life is or is not worth living"*: Albert Camus, *The Myth of Sisyphus*, trans. Justin O'Brien (New York: Vintage International, 2018), 3.

308 *"The plague is, of course, the virus of Fascism"*: Jill Lepore, "What Our Contagion Fables Are Really About," *New Yorker*, March 23, 2020, https:// www.newyorker.com/magazine/2020/03/30/what-our-contagion-fables -are-really-about?intcid=inline_amp.

SULA

309 *"In that place, where they tore the nightshade"*: Toni Morrison, *Sula* (New York: Vintage International, 2004), 3.

310 *"So when they met, first in those chocolate halls"*: Ibid., 52.

310 *"Young Chloe grew up in a house suffused with"*: Margalit Fox, "Toni Morrison, Towering Novelist of the Black Experience, Dies at 88," *New York Times*, August 6, 2019, https://www.nytimes.com/2019/08/06/books /toni-morrison-dead.html.

311 *"characterized by visionary force and poetic import"*: Unsigned, "Toni Morrison Facts," NobelPrize.org, undated, 1993, https://www.nobelprize .org/prizes/literature/1993/morrison/facts/.

312 *Toni Morrison died of pneumonia*: Fox, "Toni Morrison, Towering Novelist of the Black Experience."

312 *"Her flirting was sweet, low and guileless"*: Morrison, *Sula*, 42.

312 *"Outlaw women are fascinating"*: Toni Morrison, foreword to *Sula*, xvi–xvii.

313 Beloved *was selected*: "What Is the Best Work of American Fiction of the Last 25 Years?," *New York Times*, May 21, 2006, https://archive.nytimes .com/www.nytimes.com/ref/books/fiction-25-years.html.

313 *"With remarkable speed, 'Beloved' has"*: A. O. Scott, "In Search of the Best," *New York Times*, May 21, 2006, https://www.nytimes.com/2006/05/21 /books/review/scott-essay.html.

SURFACING

315 *"I can't believe I'm on this road again"*: Margaret Atwood, *Surfacing* (New York: Anchor Books, 1998), 3.

316 *"But then I realized it wasn't the men"*: Ibid., 155.

316 *Margaret Atwood has written more than fifty books of poetry*: "Margaret Atwood: Biography," undated, https://margaretatwood.ca/biography/.

317 *"I grew up in and out of the bush"*: Margaret Atwood, interview by Joyce Carol Oates, *New York Times*, May 21, 1978, https://archive.nytimes .com/www.nytimes.com/books/97/09/21/reviews/oates-poet.html.

318 *"Atwood's best novels"*: Jia Tolentino, "Margaret Atwood Expands the World of 'The Handmaid's Tale,'" *New Yorker*, September 5, 2019,

https://www.newyorker.com/magazine/2019/09/16/margaret-atwood
-expands-the-world-of-the-handmaids-tale.

318 *"Madame sold khaki-colored penny candies"*: Atwood, *Surfacing*, 23.

319 *on the BBC list of "100 Novels That Shaped Our World"*: "100 Novels That
Shaped Our World," BBC Arts, "Explore the List of 100 Novels That
Shaped Our World," British Broadcasting Corporation, November
5, 2019, https://www.bbc.co.uk/programmes/articles/494P41NCb
VYHlY319VwGbxp/explore-the-list-of-100-novels-that-shaped-our
-world.

THEIR EYES WERE WATCHING GOD

321 "100 Novels That Shaped Our World": BBC Arts, "Explore the List
of 100 Novels That Shaped Our World," British Broadcasting Corporation, November 5, 2019, https://www.bbc.co.uk/programmes
/articles/494P41NCbVYHlY319VwGbxp/explore-the-list-of-100-novels
-that-shaped-our-world.

321 *"Ships at a distance"*: Zora Neale Hurston, *Their Eyes Were Watching God*
(New York: HarperPerennial Modern Classics, 2013), 1.

322 *"a cityfied, stylish dressed man with his hat set an angle that didn't belong in
these parts"*: Ibid., 27.

322 *"She looked him over and got little thrills"*: Ibid., 96.

322 *"Tea Cake wasn't strange"*: Ibid., 99.

324 *"Although the case was eventually thrown out"*: Claudia Roth Pierpont, "A
Society of One," *New Yorker*, February 9, 1997, https://www.newyorker
.com/magazine/1997/02/17/a-society-of-one.

324 *"Hurston herself was refreshingly free"*: Harold Bloom, *The American Canon:
Literary Genius from Emerson to Pynchon* (New York: Library of America,
2019), 234.

325 *"In* Their Eyes Were Watching God, *Hurston ransacked the language"*:
Valerie Boyd, "About the Book: A Protofeminist Postcard from Haiti,"
in Hurston, *Their Eyes Were Watching God*, 12–13.

326 *"offering a people their own language freshly caught on paper and raised to the
heights of poetry"*: Pierpont, "A Society of One."

THINGS FALL APART

327 *"100 Novels That Shaped Our World"*: BBC Arts, "Explore the List of 100 Novels That Shaped Our World," British Broadcasting Corporation, November 5, 2019, https://www.bbc.co.uk/programmes/articles/494P41NCbVYHlY319VwGbxp/explore-the-list-of-100-novels-that-shaped-our-world.

327 Time: *"All-TIME 100 Novels"*: Richard Lacayo, "All-*TIME* 100 Novels: *Things Fall Apart,*" *Time*, January 11, 2010, https://entertainment.time.com/2005/10/16/all-time-100-novels/slide/things-fall-apart-1959-by-chinua-achebe/.

327 *"Okonkwo was well known throughout the nine villages"*: Chinua Achebe, *Things Fall Apart* (New York: Penguin, 2017), 3.

328 *"The white man is very clever"*: Ibid., 177.

329 *"father of modern African literature"*: Associated Press, "Achebe Wins Booker Prize for Fiction," *New York Times*, June 13, 2007, https://www.nytimes.com/2007/06/13/arts/AP-Booker-International.html.

329 *"The best first novel since the war"*: Chinua Achebe, "The Art of Fiction No. 139," interview by Jerome Brooks, *Paris Review*, no. 133 (Winter 1994), https://www.theparisreview.org/interviews/1720/the-art-of-fiction-no-139-chinua-achebe.

329 *"So it was a very small beginning, but it caught fire"*: Ibid.

330 *"It would be like asking how Shakespeare influenced English"*: Jonathan Kandell, "Chinua Achebe, African Literary Titan, Dies at 82," *New York Times*, March 22, 2013, https://www.nytimes.com/2013/03/23/world/africa/chinua-achebe-nigerian-writer-dies-at-82.html?searchResultPosition=2.

330 *with more than 20 million copies sold*: "Things Fall Apart," PenguinRandomHouse.com, undated, https://www.penguinrandomhouse.com/books/565351/things-fall-apart-by-chinua-achebe/9780385474542/.

330 *"The point of my observations should be quite clear by now"*: Chinua Achebe, "An Image of Africa: Racism in Conrad's 'Heart of Darkness,'" *Massachusetts Review* 18 (1977), reprinted in Joseph Conrad, *Heart of Darkness: An Authoritative Text, Background and Sources, Criticism*, ed. Robert Kimbrough, 3rd ed. (London: W. W Norton, 1988), 251–261, http://kirbyk.net/hod/image.of.africa.html.

331 *"For more than 20 years a case of writer's block"*: Kandell, "Chinua Achebe, African Literary Titan."

331 *"It is a work in which 22 years of harsh experience"*: Nadine Gordimer, A Tyranny of Clowns," *New York Times*, February 21, 1988, https://www.nytimes.com/1988/02/21/books/a-tyranny-of-clowns.html?pagewanted=all.

331 *"African literature is incomplete and unthinkable"*: Toni Morrison, in "The African Trilogy," PenguinRandomHouse.com, undated, https://www.penguinrandomhouse.com/books/553284/the-african-trilogy-by-chinua-achebe/9780143131342/.

331 *"Achebe guides us through the intricacies of Igbo culture"*: Lacayo, "All-TIME 100 Novels."

TOKYO UENO STATION

333 *"There's that sound again"*: Yu Miri, *Tokyo Ueno Station*, trans. Morgan Giles (New York: Riverhead Books, 2020), 1.

334 *"The pair gave us a look"*: Ibid., 168–169.

335 *"My father fixed pachinko machines"*: Jonathan Napack, "A Rebel in Japan Clings to Her Freedom," *International Herald Tribune*, April 6, 2002, https://www.nytimes.com/2002/04/06/style/IHT-a-rebel-in-japan-clings-to-her-freedom.html.

335 *"Books were the escape room"*: Motoko Rich, "Her Antenna Is Tuned to the Quietest Voices," *New York Times*, November 27, 2020, https://www.nytimes.com/2020/11/27/books/yu-miri-tokyo-ueno-station.html.

336 *At this writing, she resides there*: Ibid.

337 *"That day the sky was as blue as a strip of cloth"*: Miri, *Tokyo Ueno Station*, 13.

337 *"It is a passionate 'J'accuse'"*: Napack, "A Rebel in Japan."

WAITING FOR THE BARBARIANS

339 *"I have never seen anything like it"*: J. M. Coetzee, *Waiting for the Barbarians* (New York: Penguin Books, 2010), 1.

340 *"First I get lies, you see"*: Ibid., 6.

341 *"J. M. Coetzee's novels are characterised by their"*: Press release, "The Nobel Prize in Literature 2003," NobelPrize.org, October 12, 2003, https://www.nobelprize.org/prizes/literature/2003/press-release/.

342 *"100 Novels That Shaped Our World"*: BBC Arts, "Explore the List of 100 Novels That Shaped Our World," British Broadcasting Corporation, November 5, 2019, https://www.bbc.co.uk/programmes /articles/494P41NCbVYHlY319VwGbxp/explore-the-list-of-100-novels -that-shaped-our-world.

WE HAVE ALWAYS LIVED IN THE CASTLE

343 *"My name is Mary Katherine Blackwood"*: Shirley Jackson, *We Have Always Lived in the Castle* (New York: Penguin Books, 2006), 1.

344 *"the most mail the magazine had ever received"*: Ruth Franklin, "'The Lottery' Letters," *New Yorker*, June 25, 2013, https://www.newyorker.com /books/page-turner/the-lottery-letters.

345 *Jackson's mother told her she was the product of a failed abortion:* Charles McGrath, "The Case for Shirley Jackson," *New York Times*, September 30, 2016, https://www.nytimes.com/2016/10/02/books/review/shirley -jackson-ruth-franklin.html?searchResultPosition=1.

346 *"Reading her work today":* Heather Havrilesky, "Haunted Womanhood," *Atlantic*, October 2016, https://www.theatlantic.com/magazine /archive/2016/10/the-possessed/497513/.

347 *"'The Lottery' came out in the June 26, 1948, issue":* Judy Oppenheimer, *Private Demons: The Life of Shirley Jackson*, excerpted in "The Haunting of Shirley Jackson," *New York Times*, July 3, 1988, https://www .nytimes.com/1988/07/03/books/the-haunting-of-shirley-jackson.html ?searchResultPosition=2.

WIDE SARGASSO SEA

349 *Number 94 on the Modern Library list of 100 Best Novels:* Modern Library, "100 Best Novels," https://www.modernlibrary.com/top-100/100-best -novels/.

349 *BBC: "100 Novels That Shaped Our World"*: BBC Arts, "Explore the List of 100 Novels That Shaped Our World," British Broadcasting Corporation, November 5, 2019, https://www.bbc.co.uk/programmes /articles/494P49NCbVyH1Y319VwGbxp/explore-the-list-of-100-novels -that-shaped-our-world.

349 Time: *All-Time 100 Novels:* Richard Lacayo, "All-TIME 100 Novels: *Wide Sargasso Sea*," *Time*, January 11, 2010, https://entertainment.time .com/2005/10/16/all-time-100-novels/slide/wide-sargasso-sea-1966-by -jean-rhys/.

349 *"They say when trouble comes":* Jean Rhys, *Wide Sargasso Sea* (New York: W. W. Norton, 2016), 15.

351 *"the best living English novelist":* A. Alvarez, "The Best Living English Novelist," *New York Times*, March 17, 1974, https://www.nytimes .com/1974/03/17/archives/the-best-living-english-novelist.html.

352 *Vaz Dias advertised for news of her:* Letter of Jean Rhys to Maryvonne Moerman, November 9, 1949, in *Wide Sargasso Sea*, 133, 260.

353 *"It is its own jewel of a novel":* Edwidge Danticat, introduction to Rhys, *Wide Sargasso Sea*, 7–8.

353 *"It is a hallucinatory novel":* Alvarez, "The Best Living English Novelist."

353 *"She shows how power works":* Olivia Laing, "'Every Hour a Glass of Wine'—the Female Writers Who Drank," *The Guardian*, June 13, 2014, https://www.theguardian.com/books/2014/jun/13/alcoholic-female -women-writers-marguerite-duras-jean-rhys.

354 *"The elegant surface and the paranoid content":* Francis Wyndham, intro-duction to Jean Rhys, *Wide Sargasso Sea* (London: Andre Deutsch, 1966).

354 *"peculiarly timeless":* Alvarez, "The Best Living English Novelist."

AFTERWORD

357 *"The writer cannot expect to be excused":* Chinua Achebe, *Hopes and Imped-iments: Selected Essays* (New York: Penguin Books, 1989), 44–45.

359 *"Book readers averaged a two-year longer life span":* Rhea Hirshman, "Book-worms Live Longer," *Yale Alumni Magazine*, November/December 2016, https://yalealumnimagazine.com/articles/4377-bookworms-live-longer.

359 *"My task which I am trying to achieve":* Joseph Conrad, "Conrad's Preface," in *The Nigger of the 'Narcissus'* (New York: Penguin Books, 1989), xlix.

About the Author

Kenneth C. Davis has lived a life in books. A former bookseller, he wrote *Two-Bit Culture: The Paperbacking of America* (1984), a history of the paperback and its profound impact on American culture. He is the *New York Times* bestselling author of *America's Hidden History* and *Don't Know Much About History*, which gave rise to his series of books on a range of subjects including mythology, the Bible, geography, and the Civil War. Davis's work has appeared in the *New York Times*, the *Washington Post*, and *Smithsonian* magazine, among other publications. He lives in Greenwich Village in New York City with his wife, Joann Davis.